Hollywood Goes Oriental

HOLLYWOOD GOES ORIENTAL

CaucAsian Performance in American Film

Karla Rae Fuller

With a Foreword by Tom Gunning

WAYNE STATE UNIVERSITY PRESS   DETROIT

14 13 12 11 10   5 4 3 2 1

Library of Congress Cataloging-in-Publication Data

Fuller, Karla Rae, 1958–
   Hollywood goes Oriental : CaucAsian performance in American film / Karla Rae Fuller ;
with a foreword by Tom Gunning.
       p. cm. — (Contemporary approaches to film and television series)
   Includes filmography.
   Includes bibliographical references and index.
   ISBN 978-0-8143-3467-6 (pbk. : alk. paper)
   1. Asians in motion pictures. 2. Stereotypes (Social psychology) in motion pictures.
3. Ethnicity in motion pictures. 4. Minorities in the motion picture industry—United States.
5. Racism—United States—History—20th century. 6. Motion pictures—United States—
History—20th century. I. Title.
   PN1995.9.A78F75 2010
   791.43'652995—dc22
                              2010006422

Typeset by Alpha Design & Composition
Composed in Dante MT

To my daughter, Kelsie, and my mother, Gladys
No one is free until everyone is free.

CONTENTS

FOREWORD

Constructing the Alien in Hollywood's Classical Era

In 1915 the U.S. Supreme Court in a case brought by the Mutual Film Company against the Sate of Ohio decided that the movies as a commercial business should not enjoy the First Amendment rights granted print media and public speech. Film, the court declared, was a "business, pure and simple, originated and conducted for profit," not a means for conveying information and ideas. Furthermore, film's unique power of visual presentation powerfully affected its audience, especially those the court felt were most susceptible to undue influence: children, women, and recent immigrants, all of whom attended the movies in great numbers. Therefore, the court opined, film had a capability for evil influence and deserved regulation. This ruling, which allowed film censorship at least on the local level, stood until 1952, when the issue was raised again over the banning in New York State of Roberto Rossellini's film *The Miracle,* which had been denounced by the Catholic Church as blasphemous. I open this preface to Karla Fuller's important book with this bit of Hollywood history because the controversy over the influence of the movies (and now, of course, television, the World Wide Web, and the media in general) continues, both for contemporary politicians and film historians. Do the movies influence people in different ways than journalism, the novel, or theater? Is the medium of moving pictures more powerful and, because it is more direct and popular than the printed word, a dangerous influence? Certainly anything as powerful as the movies has a possibility of being dangerous, but the deeper question may still be to what degree do the visual and dramatic representations that make up the movies create stereotypes that we should struggle to overcome more intensely than other media? And to what extent do we, as viewers, not only gather our images of others from the movies but also create our own identities based on the images moving on our various kinds of screens?

There are sociological and even philosophical aspects to this question that are likely to be debated forever. Allowing a freedom of discussion—and, I would add, a free circulation of images—is precisely what the First Amendment professes as essential for a healthy democracy and therefore protects. The task of untangling the effects that the movies exert on us seems less suitable to legislation and congressional debate than to historical investigation and discussion, which is what this book by Karla Rae Fuller offers. Careful and in-depth scholarship such as this book provides, rather than simple ideological reactions, allows us to discover the variety of forces that surround the making of films and the various ways they are received by the press and audiences. While we all may feel that we can pick out an offensive stereotype, learning what functions such images served, how they were created, and the variety of ways they were understood produces the knowledge necessary for transformation. This volume deals not simply with the way Asian characters were portrayed during Hollywood's classic era but also probes the actual techniques of manufacturing these characters, from makeup to performance to narrative roles. Fuller offers us a detailed and incisive look at the way Hollywood figured this particular series of racial and cultural issues in ways that may shock or surprise us but that we most certainly know more about after reading her analysis.

While locating and deconstructing stereotypes remains a necessary task especially in teaching our children to navigate the dangerous shoal of popular media, for a cultural historian simply attacking images as false can create what I feel is a dangerous oversimplification. Stereotypes, when understood as false images, stand opposed to something we can claim as the truth. Perhaps the most important lesson that studying ethnic identity in the movies can teach us is in the constructed nature of all representation. Movies deal in images and rarely reflect directly an unproblematic truth. Thus, Fuller goes straight to the center of the issue of ethnic representation, asking less how Hollywood portrayed an Asian character than how it constructed Asian characters. To stress this process of construction, she focuses very specifically not on the broad field of Asian characters in Hollywood film but on the more specific issue of Asian characters portrayed by Caucasian actors.

Of course, as Fuller acknowledges, there are many extraordinary Asian actors who have worked in Hollywood, including the Japanese Sessue Hayakawa, one of the first stars of the silent era; the legendary Anna May Wong (whose career Fuller discusses in some detail) and other native-born actors of Asian heritage who gave us amazing portrayals; the marvelous newcomer Ahney Her (from *Gran Torino*); and the gamut of recent stars coming to Hollywood from Hong Kong or the Mainland, from Gong Li and Maggie Cheung to Jet Li and Jackie Chan. But a very particular aspect of a culture's conception of ethnic identity becomes revealed when an actor has not only adopted a role but takes on a different heritage. As Fuller's nuanced and close readings of the various Caucasian stars who have taken on Asian role reveals, these effects are varied: from burlesque mockery (Mickey Rooney in *Breakfast at Tiffany's*) to idealized cliché (Luise Rainer in *The Good Earth*). In all these cases the circumstance of visibly constructed identity means that a split is sensed between star and role. One could claim that stars always produce this split to some degree, and I think that is true. (Think of the enormous range of accents Hollywood permits its stars to retain, which Fuller amusingly recounts in her treatment of *Dragon Seed:* from Katharine Hepburn's New England patrician tones to Turhan Bey's Turkish and Akim Tamiroff's Russian accents, all portraying Chinese characters!) But in the case of cross-ethnic portrayal the split of familiar star and unfamiliar ethnic type encounters another gulf between the apparent norm of classical Hollywood actors (and especially stars) as white and an ethnic identity that remains somehow alien (nonwhite). The alien can be used to create a sense of monstrosity and threat (as in Boris Karloff's grotesque portrayal of the sinister Fu Manchu) or a sense of almost ethereal goodness and sacrifice (as in Katharine Hepburn's role in *Dragon Seed*). The Manichaean polarity between innocence and villainy, which always dwells in Hollywood melodrama, in this case not only becomes more intense but is somehow figured through racial identity. As Fuller shows in her especially complex treatment of Frank Capra's neglected masterpiece *The Bitter Tea of General Yen*, this splitting into extremes of lustful monstrousness and noble sacrifice actually becomes visualized in a dreamlike fashion in some Hollywood films and seems to become a problem that the film self-consciously poses itself (even if it is unable to resolve it).

The transformation in ethnic identity that therefore forms at least a subtext in these films can be explored in terms of one of the Hollywood crafts that is most often ignored by film historians: makeup. Fuller shows how part of the attraction of the practice of casting Caucasian actors as Asians lay precisely in its almost magical transformation of a familiar face into a different racial mold. Thus, fans were treated to behind-the-scenes explication of how Edward G. Robinson could become a Tong gangster (*Hatchet Man*) or Myrna Loy a half-caste femme fatale (*Thirteen Women*). Lurking behind these demonstrations of movie magic is a double-edged lesson. On the one hand, it protects the Caucasian audience from a direct contact with the ethnic Other (mediating the plight of the Chinese peasant through actors whom the audience knows can wipe the makeup off at the end of the day so that they look like a normal white person). On the other hand, if this seems to reassure a white audience that their identity is the acceptable one, the norm, it also sows the suspicion that perhaps all ethnic identity is less a matter of physical and biological fate than a matter of appearance, flexible and protean. One wonders if perhaps the popularity of the Oriental detective, almost always played by Caucasian actors, to which Fuller devotes a lively and insightful chapter, partly comes from the acknowledged relation between detective characters and the art of disguise. Charlie Chan, Mr. Wong, and Mr. Moto are all Oriental sleuths, but does the audiences also see their character makeup as part of an ultimate disguise behind which reassuring familiar white actors dwell? Is this another hidden aspect (explicit usually only with Peter Lorre's Mr. Moto) of the metatext of the Oriental detective Fuller describes?

Thus, Fuller in her fascinating exploration of a nearly unknown B film *First Yank into Tokyo* uncovers that nightmare of every racist: that race is in one sense only skin deep and that the traits on which identity and superiority are founded can be altered. One certainly can't say that this in itself represents a progressive political position but rather that it reveals that the fantasies at the heart of Hollywood's (and America's?) founding myths may be more ambivalent than either racists or politically correct critics might maintain. Racism springs from anxieties about one's superiority. And even when we recognize abhorrent clichés in classical Hollywood films, we learn something about the nature of their ideology; their nightmare quality reveals the anxieties rather than confident claims of superiority.

Fuller's unique approach asks, as I said, how did Hollywood construct an Oriental character starting from a non-Oriental actor? This emphasis not simply on the meaning of these images but on the process of their construction allows us to deconstruct them, to take them apart into their component parts, many of which are contradictory. Traditionally, the promise of America as a nonracist society was expressed by the image of the melting pot (whose rendering of all diversity into a homogenous soup hardly seems attractive today). Studying classical Hollywood film (and as Fuller's attention to Oriental caricatures in wartime cartoons shows, this is not limited to feature films but appears in the whole film program from cartoons to newsreels) shows not only the way racist assumptions, fear, and fantasies operated in this cinema but also how Hollywood engaged some of these categories in complex ways, expressing attraction to the alien as well as aversion.

Hollywood most fundamentally celebrates not so much an American identity as Hollywood itself as a creator of identities, from its manufacture of stars to its creation of styles (clothes and makeup) that make some bit of Hollywood glamour available to everyone, for a small price. Buried deep within the Hollywood myth is the utopian belief that everyone can become anyone, which as Fuller shows takes an Orientalist form in one of Hollywood's most elaborate fantasies of escaping and refashioning one's identity in a distant otherworldly place, the Shangri-La of Capra's *Lost Horizons*. It has always struck me as significant that one of the earliest films made in the United States about ethnic identity was a Biograph film from 1903 titled *Levi and Cohen, the Irish Comedians*. This brief knockabout farce makes fun of the fact that ethnic comedians, the comic core of the vaudeville stage, rarely belonged to the group they parodied (not only were there Jewish Irishmen, but there were also white clowns in blackface, white performers in yellowface, and dialect comedians of nearly every nationality except their own). Of course, the ultimate irony of this masquerade presentation of race lies in figures such as the great Bert Williams, a black man performing in blackface displaying his own ethnicity as a masquerade.

Can race be recognized as a role, a style one puts on and off? One thinks of the Asian cab driver played by Mark Hayashi in Wayne Wang's

Chan Is Missing (1982), whom one of the character even observes seems to model himself on Richard Pryor, or the wonderful cultural mash-up of Kung Fu and Blaxploitation in Michael Schultz's *The Last Dragon* (1985). However, as Fuller's account moves into the twilight of Hollywood's naive assumption that Caucasian stars can play anyone because being white is to be universally human, the pain of racial difference becomes more tangible and painful. The option of transformation may not be offered to everyone. In *Sayonara* (1957) and *A Girl Named Tamiko* (1962), ethnic prejudice no longer simply provides motives for melodramatic action but instead creates disturbing barriers for romance. The different tone of these films of ethnic masquerade in the 1950s and early 1960s shows the impact of the contemporary American dilemma of racial equality often seeping in as a subtext. Although Fuller mainly focuses on Asians played by Caucasians, her treatment of Oriental roles taken on by the black actress Juanita Hall shows that the practice could be extended to other racial groups.

The issue of reception in film history—how audiences lived through the movies they saw and made their own sense of them—remains both a powerful area for research and one whose predictability we should never take for granted. People remake movies in their memories and even as they watch them. But if individual viewers retain some freedom in the face of the screen, the address that the filmmakers intended may be more predictable. Perhaps the most subtle lesson we learn from Fuller's treatment of these CaucAsian performances is the basic assumption by Hollywood filmmakers during the classical era that the audience of their films was white. This is more than an issue of demographics. The norm established in these films—the spectator positions, whether the viewer was in fact black, red, or yellow—is white, a position as conventional as the use of these inadequate color terms for ethnic groups. Fuller as a critic does not forget her own uncomfortable position in that audience. She poignantly describes her memory when, as a young African American girl, she watched Juanita Hall in *South Pacific* and realized that beneath ethic accent and makeup she recognized a black actress and that her own identity was somehow an issue in this masquerade. We must hesitate before assigning too utopian a possibility to Hollywood's carnivalesque portrayal of ethnicity and bear in mind that as an art of appearance, Hollywood films still address us profoundly. But rather than simply either carrying an ideological message or expressing our deepest desires, the movies remain a contested terrain where fantasies and reality struggle and where crippling fears may get both enacted and deconstructed.

TOM GUNNING

ACKNOWLEDGMENTS

From the conception of this project well over a decade ago, I frequently envisioned the task of acknowledging the people who helped shape this book. Now that the time is here, I am humbled by the attempt to put words to paper that match the depth of my thanks and gratitude.

First, I would like to thank Wayne State University Press, especially Annie Martin, acquisitions editor, who believed in the project even when it seemed as if it would not ever happen.

My thanks also to advisors for the doctoral dissertation on which this book was based: Tom Gunning, Chuck Kleinhans, and Margaret Drewal all encouraged me to seek publication.

A special thanks to Judith M. Wright, law librarian, D'Angelo Law Library, University of Chicago, for delivering to my mother's house books that I desperately needed to complete my research.

The encouragement, support, and inspiration of good friends and mentors, Julie Sandor, Beretta Smith-Shomade, and Gary B. Walls are much appreciated.

Frank Wu read an early draft of this work and also provided advice at key points in the process of publication despite an incredibly busy schedule. I sincerely thank him for his excellent suggestions and steadfast support. You are my hero.

Of course, my family—especially Tara Lamourt, Gladys Fuller, Nancy McDaniel, and Ivan Lamourt—sustained me with unwavering commitment throughout the many disappointments and triumphs in this project's long journey to publication. I simply could not have brought this book to fruition without them.

Introduction

East Meets West

Performing the Oriental

The audience is watching a highly artificial enactment of what a non-Oriental has made into a symbol for the whole Orient. . . . The things to look at are style, figures of speech, setting, narrative devices, historical and social circumstances, *not* the correctness of the representation nor its fidelity to some great original.

—Edward W. Said, *Orientalism*

The most well known Oriental figures on the Hollywood screen were almost always non-Asian actors made up to look Asian. From the film industry's earliest days, African Americans, Latinos, Native Americans, and Asians have been impersonated by performers of other ethnic groups. Notably, the Asian depictions have produced well-known iconic figures still familiar to the present day such as Fu Manchu or Charlie Chan. Still, distinctions between portrayals of Asian roles by Caucasian actors and by Asian actors are frequently collapsed by scholars, critics, and viewers in order to create a generalized Asian typology.

Implicit in the practice of Asian impersonation by Caucasian actors in Hollywood is the assumption that the Caucasian face provides the physically normative standard onto which an ethnic inscription can take place. The Oriental performance by the non-Asian actor is of particular usefulness to film scholars focusing on ethnic representation because it keenly exposes the artificial foundations in Hollywood's depiction of race. Through the act of physical embodiment the Caucasian actor displays patently artificial and theatrical features and also offers a site for the projection of displaced desires and fears. Like any masquerade its artificiality is apparent, and yet this performance practice operates with a high degree of complexity, promoting certain qualities while effacing others.

Edward Said states in the opening quote that the West has created "highly artificial" enactments of an Orient but notably asserts that a more useful approach in any critique of these fabrications lies in their deconstruction rather than their denunciation. Taking Said's analysis further, author Robert Young suggests that the practice of Orientalism provides a vital function in the construction of a Western identity:

> Orientalism did not just misrepresent the Orient, but also articulated an internal dislocation within Western culture, a culture which consistently fantasizes itself as constituting some kind of integral totality, at the same time as endlessly deploring its own impending dissolution. . . . The Orient, we might say, operates as both poison and cure.[1]

The Orient as a Western construct has meant Asia, the Far East, the Middle East, Arabia, China, Japan, and India, among other nations, depending on the historical moment or the nation conceiving it.[2] Hollywood's Oriental exists as an ethnic classification (though loosely based on Asian culture) that supersedes national or racial identity and thus allows for shifts, transformations, and reconfigurations over time due to its flexible boundaries. It is precisely this versatile capacity to re-create and reformulate that makes "Oriental" the term of choice for this study (as opposed to Asian, or Japanese, Chinese, etc.), for it reminds us of the fictional origins and status of Hollywood's Asian characterizations.[3]

This examination of cinematic Oriental archetypes in selected films from the 1930s to the 1960s will attempt to reveal a systematized approach in the depiction of race working within the classical Hollywood studio era.[4] Utilizing a range of Hollywood products such as animated images, B films, and blockbusters, this work primarily focuses on representations by Caucasian actors and yet also includes examples of performances by non-Caucasian actors as well. However, rather than propose a strictly formulaic system of representation, this study instead offers a schema of performance styles by tracing specific cosmetic devices, physical gestures, dramatic cues, and narrative conventions. Baring the device of the Oriental masquerade in this way establishes the concept of racial difference as far more than biologically based. Rather, it considers this device as a complicated textual construct (as opposed to an inert or static stereotype) that functions with classical consistencies and redundancies.

The controversy surrounding the 1991 Broadway production of *Miss Saigon* provided additional inspiration for this topic of study.[5] In brief, the debate focused on the casting of British actor Jonathan Pryce in the role of a Eurasian character—"The Engineer"—that he originated in the play's London production. The central conflict involved the rarely openly challenged performance practice of a Caucasian actor depicting an Asian role when other thespians of Asian ethnic origin were also available to play the part. Even though Pryce went on to play the role on Broadway and win a Tony award as well, the furor surrounding his tenure in the production addressed the issue of race as constructed through individual performing bodies.

Miss Saigon is not only noted as a watershed event in the Asian American community but also attracted significant attention in the broader theatrical and performing arts community. Nearly two decades old, the controversy surrounding the casting as well as the generally retrograde nature of the representation of the Vietnamese in the big-budgeted musical play still retains its power to ignite passionate debate among racial and ethnic activists. It has also inspired numerous essays published in the areas of Asian American studies, cinema and media studies, popular culture, theater history, and performance studies (both in art and life), among many other fields. What accounts for the enduring interest in (and, by extension, the references to) this notorious affair in so many different contexts? While this book is not able to speak individually to each of the areas previously mentioned, the issues raised in the *Miss Saigon* episode that relate most directly to the approach and analysis in this book include (but are not limited to) links between master Orientalist texts such as *Madame Butterfly* and its attendant interpretations of real-life events such as the Vietnam War, the resurrection of the racial impersonation of Asian roles by Caucasian actors as an acceptable institutionally endorsed and commercially supported practice, and the often fluid though persistent relationship between artistic practices and the larger sociopolitical experience of Asian Americans.[6]

According to Marina Heung in her essay "The Family Romance of Orientalism," the story of Miss Saigon was inspired by a photograph of a Vietnamese mother stoically leaving her obviously Ameriasian daughter at an airport to go to live with her American father, whom the girl has never met. These sketchy details were all that were given in relation to the photograph; however, the two French authors of *Miss Saigon*, Claude-Michel Schonberg and his collaborator librettist Alain Boublil according to the musical's playbill notes, interpreted the photograph as a story of a sacrificial mother along the lines of the *Madame Butterfly* narrative: "With 'a heartbreaking photograph and a potential connection with a famous opera to start from,' Schonberg and Boublil began writing Miss Saigon as a contemporary musical, reframing the story of Madame Butterfly against the backdrop of Vietnam in 1975, when the U.S. military evacuated Saigon on the eve of the Communist takeover." Perhaps it is not surprising that *Madame Butterfly* provides the foundation for *Miss Saigon*, as Puccini's well-known opera offers an example of a generalized cultural narrative of the West that constructs the Orient as feminized and sexually submissive, "space that is ripe for conquest and rule."[7]

This controversy also raised questions about the existence of racial groups in the American imagination. Who positions whom as the knower and others as the known? Why is it not acceptable for Chinese to play Chinese? If this is a transgression, what is being transgressed? The implication is that there is safety in casting white actors to construct and embody an Oriental countenance, a fabricated social identity perhaps considered endangered if enacted by real Asian actors. In the case of *Miss Saigon* it was precisely this "notion that real Asian actors ought to have a chance to play Asian characters" that incensed the larger Asian American community.[8]

In the London production it was decided that the Welsh-born Pryce, who possessed decidedly Western features, would not be believable in the role of the engineer/pimp originally conceived as Vietnamese. Thus, the role in the libretto shifted to that of a Eurasian. Additionally, traditional eye prosthetics were applied to "create an epicanthic 'slant' to Pryce's Caucasian eyes."[9] However, the prospect of continuing Pryce's racial impersonation in the New York stage production caused an unprecedented furor of protest:

> In Britain, the use of eye prosthetics and yellowface makeup to "Asianize" white actors attracted little attention. But on the American stage and screen such practices were equated with racial mockery and had fallen into disuse since the days of the civil rights movement. In the way that African Americans rejected blackface, the use of yellowface in a major theater production in 1990 touched a raw nerve.[10]

To add insult to injury, the producer Cameron Mackintosh, under pressure from Asian American activists and actors, reportedly "looked under every rock" for a suitable Asian or Asian American for the part but claimed to have failed.[11] Subsequently, Actor's Equity refused to issue the card that Pryce needed to work in the United States. This initial decision clearly acknowledged and supported the basis of the Asian American actors' protest, that Asian and Eurasian roles should be cast with Asian Americans since historically both groups were portrayed by white actors. Ultimately, Mackintosh announced that he would not bring *Miss Saigon* to Broadway without Pryce. In response, the union rescinded its stance given the potentially huge loss of revenue as well as a significant number of jobs for the theater world.[12]

This episode not only reflects disturbing issues of artistic content and insidious racial (and historical) representation but also reveals the dynamic interplay between creative expression and the impact of racism for Asian Americans. The response to the activism that this controversial play inspired reveals the often hidden animosity toward a supposedly model minority group. The relatively recent label of "model minority" violently collides with the dogged recirculation of all-too-familiar Asian stereotypes. And in the well-publicized instances when this clash occurs, societal and institutional power relations are often held up for intense scrutiny in disconcerting ways. For much of the majority population, this fact alone constitutes urgent justification for reinstating the status quo.

The creation of identity as a central issue with its modes of representation in performance often provides the most visible source of evidence of important societal power structures and relationships. The fact that many prominent Asian roles were portrayed by non-Asian actors foregrounds Said's assertion that "the Oriental is contained and represented by dominating frameworks."[13] The "dominating frameworks" is the West and in this study obviously includes Hollywood. However, in this work the nature of the constructed Oriental identity by (and through) Caucasian actors provides the point of departure and thus seeks to combine issues of ethnicity and performance through embodiment in addition to representation. We incorporate the elaborate makeup practices and distinct performance styles that helped construct the identity of Hollywood's Oriental. This broadened approach may move us to consider the larger issue of racial difference as performance in mainstream media.

The term "yellowface" is commonly used as a classification for any performance of an Asian role by a non-Asian actor. If we are to compare this type of performance to blackface (from which the term "yellowface" derives), yellowface can most effectively describe a broadly sketched Oriental performance that typically emphasizes physicality. Indeed, it often becomes the principle focus. This caricatured figure functions as a device to cope with both the avoidance and acknowledgment of a strong threat.

Emerging during the early nineteenth century, blackface flourished as a performance mode to address the fears of whites as well as to reassure them of their supreme authority and control. In this way, a racialized clown figure mitigates pervasive societal fears by comedically attempting to contain a threat to the social and racial hierarchy. Typically, issues of cultural influence and interracial sexuality provide the standard fodder for the racial lampoon. Eric Lott's treatment of blackface in *Love and Theft: Blackface Minstrelsy and the American Working Class* is worth considering in this context. Lott outlines in particular the ambiguity that blackface minstrelsy sets up between derision and envy or, in other words, the desire to appropriate some aspect of the race imitated at the same time that it derides:

> The very form of blackface acts—an investiture in black bodies—seems a manifestation of the particular desire to try on the accents of "blackness" and demonstrates the permeability of the color line. . . . It was cross-racial desire that coupled a nearly insupportable fascination and a self-protective derision with respect to black people and their cultural practices, and that made blackface minstrelsy less a sign of absolute white power and control than of panic, anxiety, terror, and pleasure.[14]

Likewise, Mary Ann Doane's book on female masquerade, *Femme Fatales: Feminism, Film Theory, and Psychoanalysis,* is relevant for its focus on femininity itself as a cultural construction that can, as a mask, be worn or removed. When combined with yellowface, it results in both the "hyperbolization of the accoutrements of femininity" and the hyperbolization of the Oriental guise.[15]

The antecedents of cinematic yellowface parallel the blackface minstrel and vaudeville shows of the nineteenth and early twentieth centuries in significant ways. Asian American scholar Keith Aoki notes how "white minstrel show actors portrayed the Chinese as effeminate and waif-like, deferentially bowing and scraping but secretly scheming the white race's downfall, simultaneously comedic and menacing."[16] Not only did minstrel and magical acts traveling around the United States include yellowface performances in order to add extra elements of mystery and exoticism to their shows, but earlier Asian groups were also politically satirized especially negatively in relation to the Chinese Exclusion Acts of the nineteenth century.

In her landmark work *Yellowface: Creating the Chinese in American Popular Music and Performance, 1850s–1920s,* Krystyn Moon focuses on the representation of Chinese Americans on the stage and in popular song from the late 1800s to the early 1900s. Her specific focus on the Chinese American experience does not at all limit the value of this work in relation to other Asian American populations; rather, it provides an accessible template for the racist representations for many

Asian racial groups immigrating to the United States in the nineteenth and early twentieth centuries.

From the 1850s forward, contact with Chinese immigrants significantly impacted the Chinese on the stage and in music. Californians were the first to direct their anxieties about Chinese immigration through music. With the support of Bret Harte's creation of the poem "Heathen Chinee," in 1870 anti-Chinese songs emerged in theaters and from singers throughout the country. These songs almost always focused on notions of inferiority and issues of assimilation or perpetual "foreignness."[17] Performers contributed to the representation of the Chinese immigrant on the stage through the use of yellowface—"a combination of dialect, costuming, and make-up similar to blackface . . . to give a more total characterization than previously had been seen." Additionally, these Chinese impersonators often claimed that their performances were authentic to audiences mostly unfamiliar with the Chinese community. The 1870s and 1880s brought a proliferation of songs about and impersonations of Chinese immigrants throughout the United States. These performances asserted notions of difference so strongly that the Chinese were characterized as completely unable to assimilate and as a racial and cultural threat that needed to be restricted from entering the country: "Conceptions of their deviance and inferiority left little room for their acceptance into American society and culture. Instead, they were seen as innately foreign, which was legitimated through the passage of anti-Chinese legislation starting in the 1850s and culminated in 1882 with the Chinese Exclusion Act."[18]

By the latter part of the nineteenth century, the performance practice of white actors in yellowface increased and was codified into visual stereotypes that persist even today. Performers began to rely on certain types of costumes, wigs, props, and sets to create Chinese characters on the stage. Even the makeup was applied to complete the presumption of realism or authenticity.[19]

> The most important aspect were the eyes, the defining factor in making up a Chinese face. Eyes were to be outlined in Indian ink, with the bottom line extending out beyond the eye to create a slanting effect. Early twentieth-century makeup techniques were much more intricate and

complex in order to create "authentic" representations. . . . Drawing a
line about three-fourths of an inch beyond the eye and adding a high-
lighter on the lid were techniques used to slant the eye. In more elaborate characterizations, systems of tape and putty were implemented to
slant the eye, a method used predominantly in the movie industry.[20]

Obviously, the intricacies of both nineteenth- and early twentieth-
century blackface and yellowface traditions are too rich and complex to
go into complete detail here. However, the roots of these performance
practices must be acknowledged as the origins of their cinematic variants. The significance of the term "yellowface" as a creation by anal-
ogy to blackface must also be carefully delineated. For example, the
use of the term "yellowface" began to appear in the 1950s "to describe
the continuation in film of having white actors playing major Asian
and Asian American roles and the grouping together of all makeup
technologies used to make one look 'Asian.'"[21] However, as early as the
1850s, the "conflation of African American and Chinese immigrants
had occurred in political debates about what should be the racial
makeup of states in the Far West" and began to appear consistently in
popular culture at the end of the nineteenth century.[22]

White performers predictably borrowed from both yellowface and
blackface vaudeville traditions to reinforce the perceived joint inferiority of both groups through comic situations and conflict. An even
more surprising (and disturbing) trend by African American performers who included the use of yellowface in their stage performances also
emerged:

African Americans' parodies of Chinese immigrants were related to interracial conflict and awareness of the power of blackface caricatures,
but their intention was somewhat different from that of their white or
Chinese American counterparts. Through Chinese impersonations,
African Americans were able to ally themselves with whites by marking the Chinese as different from the white norm, as they themselves
had been marked. These characterizations, however, focused on both
racial inferiority and the foreignness and inability of the Chinese to
assimilate.[23]

As compelling as these theatrical antecedents to cinematic Asian impersonation by non-Asian actors are, the term "yellowface" has been appropriated in specific relation to film for a myriad of political, cultural, and performative causes and concerns. While enabling a wider variety of voices to employ the term in diverse contexts, this has also resulted in the dilution and imprecision of the origins of this racist performance practice. The danger here is that the original textual, visual, and visceral evidence of yellowface get lost amid the din. This would unwittingly do a disservice to the particular evolution of what has been termed in this study as the Oriental guise. The Oriental performance has earned its own unique trajectory. In fact, many of the variants of this creation can no longer be understood under the rubric "yellowface." Even the term "blackface" has its own limitations as an all-encompassing descriptive designation. The perhaps unique example of Shakespeare's Othello as portrayed on stage and screen by white actors comes to mind as not appropriately suited to the labeling "blackface." Primarily, the label doesn't fit due to the essentially dramatic (and, I would argue, more complex) nature of the role, whereas blackface most often takes comedy and/or caricature as its chief form.

Blackface film performances as a systematic practice essentially ended during the early sound era (the poorly received *Check and Double-check* [1930] cast with the two white radio stars of the *Amos and Andy* series, Freeman F. Gosden and Charles J. Correl, respectively, hastened its demise). Also, while blackface performance in musical sequences by Hollywood stars such as Fred Astaire and Judy Garland continued into the 1940s, no direct parallel exists for the more multilayered and versatile Oriental guise.

Still, yellowface has a central place in the range of non-Asian Oriental cinematic depictions. The delineation of this particular classification of cinematic performance reveals Hollywood's attitudes toward racial difference in a way that other categories of Asian racial representation (i.e., by authentically Asian actors) do not. It moves along a dramatic continuum that, on the one hand, exists to ridicule and, on the other, attempts to demonize. The yellowface mode can be defined as a parody and caricature of race, and while all non-Asian racial impersonations may have some evidence of these elements, they become the major features in this performance style. A character type, by definition, displays a lack of depth relative to more complex portrayals. However, certain stereotypes rely even more on exaggerated manner- isms and physical cues.

As with any topic, there are many different approaches with which to write about ethnic performances in Hollywood films. Many changes have taken place in the writing about ethnic representation in film over the last twenty-odd years. We have moved from image studies that at- tempt to chronicle the evolution of one particular ethnic group's rep- resentation in mainstream/Hollywood cinematic practices to more multifaceted work that encompasses numerous minority groups and classes.[24] The analysis inherent in even the premise of the former pub- lications most often involves the identification of stereotypically nega- tive roles in contrast to more positive ones as vehicles for actors of the particular ethnic group. The assumption underlying this approach is that more positive, diverse, and realistic characters and roles in front of the camera would not only correct historically distorted and inaccurate representations but would also serve to empower and help correct ra- cial and ethnic inequities in the society at large.

Much work exists on the representation of various ethnic groups (along with other subgroups such as gays and lesbians) or work that takes the subject of ethnic representation itself (as opposed to one par- ticular ethnic group) as its unifying theme.[25] Many of these publications tend to not only confront the historical legacy of representations from film's past but also make a prescriptive call for different ethnic images from future filmmakers.[26] Some are authored by independent filmmak- ers who are themselves fighting to create new images of their ethnic group, while others are written by professionals within the dominant Hollywood system. Film critics, popular culture theorists, actors, and political activists, among others, all present discussions on the impact of receiving, creating, and disseminating filmic representation of a given ethnic group from a myriad of perspectives.

However, the exceptional work of Peter X. Feng and Darrell Hama- moto must be noted. The anthology *Countervisions: Asian American Film Criticism,* edited by Darrell Y. Hamamoto and Sandra Liu, cele- brates the analysis of Asian American scholars as well as Asian Ameri- can independent work. *Countervisions* embraces the cross-fertilization of the political, social, cultural, and historical in the consideration of filmic representation. It is a most valuable and dynamic work that offers a more diverse perspective on Asian American media while not sacrificing the depth and breadth of the analyses. Feng's *Identities in Motion: Asian American Film and Video* is a landmark work that reveals the unique challenges and struggles of Asian American film and video makers. He illuminates a neglected history of image making and grapples with the slippery issue of racial and ethnic identity. His subsequent anthology, *Screening Asian Americans,* directly addresses the absence of studies focusing solely on Asian American cinematic representation, a sentiment with which I heartily agree. His primary assertion is that Asian Americans are central to the discourse, depiction, and experience of racism in the United States in spite of the fact that racial conflict is usually framed as a simple binary of black and white. This concern is often referenced in the area of Asian American studies; however, as Feng asserts, it needs to be extended to the cinematic treatment of Asian Americans.

Most often, the work on representation is part of a larger summary of images in the media and popular culture. Though not always focused on the Hollywood film industry, there is value in the assorted approaches in a number of works that attempt to analyze the intricacy of racial representation in the media. Russell Leong's anthology *Moving the Image: Independent Asian Pacific American Media Arts* provides an eclectic collection of ruminations, remembrances, and personal histories by Asian Americans among its creative and critical essays. An illuminating work in both its breadth and depth, this volume has helped to inspire the spirit behind this project and is quoted from several times within these pages. Hamamoto, in his book *Monitored Peril: Asian Americans and the Politics of TV Representation,* addresses the representation of Asian Americans on network television from a sociohistorical perspective. Clearly, there are significant historical, political, and cultural links between the representations in both the mainstream television and film industries. These intersections are often subtle but are nevertheless very important to address.[27]

Matthew Bernstein and Gaylyn Studlar's anthology *Visions of the East: Orientalism in Film,* a collection of essays on Orientalism in American and European cinema, seems clearly inspired by Said's *Orientalism.* Bernstein and Studlar's anthology explores how Western filmmaking has used the cultures of North African and Asia "to stand for some-thing besides themselves."[28] This book represents an exciting direction for Said's concepts utilizing theoretical approaches ranging from cul-tural studies, psychoanalysis, feminism, and genre criticism.[29]

Gina Marchetti's work *Romance and the Yellow Peril: Race, Sex and Discourse Strategies in Hollywood Fiction* represents the first book-length study of Hollywood's treatment of Asia and Asians in the English lan-guage and focuses primarily on "the construction of interracial sex and romance in the Hollywood narrative."[30] Her work explores themes of miscegenation in the context of a broader yellow peril discourse that positions Asia as a threat requiring Western domination and contain-ment. Marchetti's study also places the Hollywood narratives that she discusses within Said's assertion of the West's attempt to exert author-ity over the Orient. Marchetti's analyses primarily highlight narrative patterns operating within each film.

While the present study shares Marchetti's interest in issues of ide-ology, narrative patterns, and themes, it differs significantly particularly in terms of its attention to historical context and, of course, to the racialized embodiment by non-Asian actors. Nearly half of the films Marchetti analyzes—such as *Madame Butterfly* (1915) starring Mary Pickford, *Broken Blossoms* (1919), *The Bitter Tea of General Yen* (1932), *Love Is a Many Splendored Thing* (1955), *Sayonara* (1957), and *My Gei-sha* (1962), some of which are also included in this study—include the practice of racial impersonation operating within the narrative. The present study will look first to the performative aspects of Hollywood's Oriental impersonations as the vehicle and metaphor of Western containment.

Notably, a dissertation from the 1970s by Eugene Franklin Wong offers one of the most comprehensive discussions of Asian representa-tion in Hollywood films. What is most remarkable about this work is his attention to the practice of Orientalizing makeup used in Holly-wood depictions, which he terms "racist cosmetology":[31]

> Racist cosmetology constitutes a special sub-category of makeup. Un-like racial cosmetology which would allow all performers—regardless of race—to simulate all racial groups, the use of racist cosmetology is limited to white performers only . . . concentrating upon . . . the

13

epicanthic fold. . . . Emphasis upon slanted eyes is racially primary in the industry's cosmetic treatment of Asians, with skin color, hair texture, and so on, being largely secondary.[32]

Wong's delineation of makeup techniques reflects an all too rare consideration of the artificial and theatrical construction involved in the racially impersonated cinematic performance in addition to its generally unilateral direction (from white to any nonwhite ethnic group). His section describing the process of "Orientalizing whites" reflects the principal focus of the present study, which seeks to recognize and acknowledge Hollywood's artificiality that, in Wong's words, significantly includes "other affectations, which do not directly come under the heading of cosmetology, . . . stylized body movements, pidgin English, high pitched voice . . . and traditional Asian dress."[33]

Even fewer scholars attempt to delineate the widespread practice of racial impersonation as a discrete area of cinematic performance while attempting to link it to larger social realities. Michael Rogin's book *Blackface, White Noise: Jewish Immigrants in the Hollywood Melting Pot* illustrates an invigorating attempt in this direction. He posits the performance practice of blackface as "a form of racial cross-dressing" that helped facilitate the upward mobility of many white ethnic groups:[34]

> Current writing on gender, race, and popular culture celebrates the subversive character of cross-dressing for allegedly destabilizing fixed identities. Such accounts need to consider history if they are to carry conviction, for far from being the radical practice of marginal groups, cross-dressing defined the most popular, integrative forms of mass culture. Racial masquerade did promote identity exchange, . . . but it moved settlers and ethnics into the melting pot by keeping racial groups out.[35]

The present study will also attempt through its historicization to reveal connections to broader societal perceptions of Asians that change and modify depending on the politics of the moment.

Remarkably, few scholarly works focusing on film acting and performance have been written. Two of the best known are James Naremore's *Acting in the Cinema* and Roberta Pearson's *Eloquent Gestures:*

The Transformation of Performance Style in the Griffith Biograph Films.[36] Early cinema film performance is chronicled by Pearson, who describes the transformation of acting styles during a transitional period in the industry from 1908 to 1913. She suggests that performance styles (though not yet star styles) oscillated between a histrionic style (with origins in stage melodrama of the nineteenth century) and what she calls a verisimilar style (emerging from the contemporary legitimate theater). Using D. W. Griffith's Biograph Company films, Pearson delineates the eventual move away from the histrionic style of codified, predetermined gestures toward a verisimilar style that resembled a less highly stylized offstage human behavior.

Naremore specifically notes that the dominant discourse surrounding movie acting after 1914 stressed natural and transparent behavior. Pearson's book also confirms the predominance of this critical view. Calls for transparency and naturalness in film performance directly parallels what David Bordwell, Janet Staiger, and Kristin Thompson, *The Classical Hollywood Cinema: Film Style and Mode of Production to 1960*, characterize as the movement toward an invisible or effaced narrative style that predominated during the classical Hollywood era. However, Naremore attempts to read against the grain of this conception through his selection of stars (such as Marlene Dietrich, Jimmy Cagney, Katharine Hepburn, Cary Grant, and Marlon Brando) with highly idiosyncratic acting styles. In his analysis of Cary Grant's performance in the film *North By Northwest* (1958), Naremore takes great care to delineate what Grant took great pains to construct: the illusion of a natural personality. Not natural in the sense of possibly meeting someone like him but natural in the sense of convincingly performing a hybrid characterization, which incorporates familiar and proven qualities of his star image, with a role already tailor-made to complement the given image.

Both Pearson's and Naremore's studies do intersect in interesting ways with some of the arguments in the present study. Pearson's work traces a set of codified and predetermined gestures that shift and eventually transform over time. The present study, like Pearson's project, will attempt to trace a set of performance styles—including a codified set of gestures—that shift and reconfigure over the course of several decades. Naremore deconstructs the illusion of transparent or natural film performance in his chapter on Cary Grant, while the present study will deconstruct the plainly artificial Oriental guise. However, although the Oriental performance by non-Asian actors might be highly theatrical and codified, the argument could be made that this performance practice also negotiates the overarching influence toward the invisible or effaced style of the classical Hollywood era. Specifically, despite the often highly idiosyncratic performance style of the Oriental guise, some attempt is customarily made to naturalize this characterization within the narrative. In this way, a level of ambivalence emerges through the analysis of the constructed nature of the Oriental impersonation.

The area of performance studies, though often discussed primarily in relation to the theater, has also proved useful for the present study. For example, Richard Schechner's seminal work in the field of performance theory includes in the category "performance activities" play, games, sport, and ritual.[37] However, in the theatrical setting Schechner suggests an intriguing type of dynamic between audience and performer or "double relationship to the object of performance that its audiences must carry out": "Richard Schechner has memorably expressed this . . . in terms of a double negativity. Within a play frame a performer is not herself (because of the operations of illusion), but she is also not herself (because of the operations of reality). Performer and audience alike operate in a world of double consciousness."[38]

This concept of performance potentially provides a basis for a deeper analysis of the racially impersonated screen performance. What are the performers striving to do on screen; are they simply trying to fool the audience? How conscious are they of their audience? What is the significance of these performances being foregrounded in the narratives over time? We will consider how the performances in this study both individually and collectively created a self-conscious set of parameters that took into account the industry need to perpetuate the star system and, more significantly, racist ideological views.

Marvin Carlson, in *Performance: A Critical Introduction,* discusses issues of identity (particularly in the performance of race and gender) as an important area of interest in the field of performance studies and also more problematically in performance art. In his chapter "Performance and Identity," he describes the predicament of two white female performance artists of the 1970s and 1980s. The artist Suzanne Lacy notably included a Chinese woman in one of her pieces, for which she was criticized by Chinese feminists. Likewise, Eleanor Antin developed a number of alternative personae that included a black ballerina, Eleanora Antinova, but began to be denounced. Antin viewed and commented on the nature of her performances as "alternate versions of herself, and they are created primarily to explore that self, not to comment upon social circumstances."[39]

These two examples of more recent avant-garde performances that insistently utilize racial impersonation unproblematically points to the need to address issues of power and domination inherent in such a practice. Where do we draw the line between an exploration of a single authorial voice and the presentation of an authoritative voice when taking on the guise of a different racial group? Cultural theorist and performance artist Coco Fusco reminds us in *The Bodies That Were Not Ours and Other Writings,* through her references to the exploitation of black bodies from the Middle Passage through the twentieth century, that a body can be inhabited but not owned. She also implicates the role of the media in the continual misappropriation of black bodies:

> Mass entertainment in the United States has depended heavily on the commercial exploitation of black bodies since its inception, beginning in the period of minstrelsy through to the Golden Age of Hollywood and beyond. The sensitivity to the implications of performing blackness for white audiences did not arise from willfulness but rather as a defense against the real existence of abuse of white power that was continuously underscored by degrading, often involuntary performative scenarios.[40]

Fusco's comments can be extended to raise the question of what significance performing the Oriental has for white audiences absent from the Asian body entirely. Here we move beyond the exclusive chronicling of negative stereotypes and degrading narratives to the relationship between this seemingly expedient performance practice and the contorted theatrical efforts that went into the impersonations.

Josephine Lee's excellent study *Performing Asian America: Race and Ethnicity on the Contemporary Stage* draws attention to the racial impersonations that have plagued the theatrical history of Asian American performance and representation. She specifically points out the existence of theatrical makeup guides that provide instruction for the white stage actor to play the "Oriental," "Mongolian types," or "the Chinaman."[41] These guides contain special details instructing actors on how to apply makeup or sometimes even a mask in addition to long fingernails, full-body coloring, and the half-bald, half queued hairstyle. The illustrations accompanying these descriptions often presented caricatures or photographs of white actors in yellowface rather than of Asians themselves. Even contemporary makeup books present distorted views of the Oriental body through their directions and illustrations.

The complete possession of the Oriental body by non-Asian actors reflects an important facet in the history of systematic cinematic racial subjugation and exclusion. The period from the 1930s through the 1960s is significant for examining the evolution and diminution of the practice of cinematic racial impersonation. This was the predominant industry-wide practice in Hollywood during these years of great social change and upheaval. During this era Hollywood reigned supreme, shaping impressions through its fictional characterizations. Still, the question remains as to why racially specific archetypes become saddled with cultural authenticity.

Theoretically, a racial impersonation should be able to be put on or taken off at will, and yet it does not work this way. These depictions contain a larger social component. As we will see through the historicization of these images, they bleed into the social fabric, shaping generalized perceptions as well as the self-image (and sometime destinies) of Asian Americans. Just note the revealing title of a well-known volume of contemporary Asian American fiction, *Charlie Chan Is Dead*. The introduction positions Warner Oland's Charlie Chan as "our most famous fake 'Asian' pop icon—known for his obsequious manner, fractured English, and dainty walk."[42] Clearly, the influence of Oland's racially impersonated performance survives to this day as an image to be conquered and slain. And yet, the artificial elements of Oland's performance as Chan are specifically noted with contempt by the writer. By focusing on the embodiment of the Oriental guise by Caucasian actors, the racialized performance becomes easier to deconstruct and expose. The portrayals tend to be less subtle and more affected.

The final selection of films covered in the present study was based on those that reflected a wide variety of Hollywood product, B films/ programmers, blockbusters, animation, and prestige films from major and minor studios. In addition, the films thought to be most revealing often contain a self-reflexive element in their performances. This study seeks not only to trace the performance practice of Caucasian actors playing Asian roles but also to engage with the idea of how masquerade operates as an explicit element within the narrative structure. The examination of how characters in a given narrative negotiate different parts within a singular role, whether occurring in brief moments or sustained throughout a narrative, raises a host of interesting issues to consider. With the idea and concept of performance and masquerade foregrounded within individual narratives, issues such as the playing of different roles (whether out of duty or preference), utilizing culturally specific behavior, and the consequences of adopting another identity (i.e., mistaken identity) are played out in ways that suggest broader societal effects and ramifications. These examples provide an opportunity for considering the notion of performing a racial role in the broader social order outside the fictional world of the motion picture as a strategy for survival against racism.

For example, the film *The Son-Daughter* (1932) was selected over an adaptation of *Madame Butterfly* (1932) starring Caucasian actress Sylvia Sidney as Cio-Cio San. While Sidney's performance of the archetypal sacrificial Oriental maiden arouses some interest, the issue of performance for Helen Hayes's lesser-known Chinese maiden Lien Wha in *The Son-Daughter* provides the central resource and recourse for her character in the narrative. Similarly, *Behind the Rising Sun* (1943) featuring the performance of Tom Neal as Taro, a Japanese national educated in the United States who returns to Japan to become a fascist zealot, was excluded in favor of *First Yank into Tokyo* (1945) in which Neal portrays a patriotic American officer who volunteers to become Japanese through plastic surgery in order complete an undercover government mission.

Confining the selection of films to the sound period was done to create a more unique and continuous trajectory from the beginning to the end of the performance practice in the early 1960s. By beginning in the sound era, elements of speech and dialogue could be traced along with purely visual cues. Still, the portrayal of Asians begins with the silent period. The following notable examples from comedy, drama, and documentary demonstrate the ubiquity of the Oriental guise even during the earliest emergence of the motion picture form. Indeed, one of cinema's first attempts at film comedy was the brief twenty-second piece *Chinese Laundry Scene* (Edison, 1894). In this filmed scene, an Italian comedy team portrays "the Chinaman Hop Lee" and the Irish policeman who pursues him: "These two heavily stereotyped figures are played by the Italian comedy duo Robetta and Doreto, who condensed one of their vaudeville routines then being produced at Tony Pastor's in New York City for the occasion. Here, as was true in much vaudeville comedy, ethnic stereotypes abound."[43] During this period before projected motion pictures (*Chinese Laundry Scene* no doubt provided product for Thomas Edison's kinetoscope, a large peep show device), the yellowface tradition of non-Asian actors portraying Asian roles inherited from vaudeville and minstrel shows was introduced through this newest media novelty.

After Edison's groundbreaking motion picture projection program at Koster and Bial's theater two years later in 1896, a Philadelphia competitor, Siegmund (Sigmund) Lubin, offered a one-shot reenactment of the Boxer Uprising in China such as *Chinese Massacring Christians* (Lubin, 1900), using exclusively non-Asian actors to represent the Chinese.[44] Also during this period before the advent of feature-length films, actualities or short newsreels provided for domestic audiences exotic locales of the Far East such as Biograph's *Street Scene, Tokio [Tokyo], Japan,* and *Chien-Man Gate, Pekin [Beijing].*[45]

The exoticism of the Orient provided a major influence in the American film industry, particularly from the mid-1910s through the 1920s. Evident in both "the design and ornamentation of the American movie palaces" as well as in films themselves, a popular Orientalism reigned during these years:[46]

> Starting in 1922, the favored style, at least in the movie capital, was what we might now call Middle-Eastern. . . . The discovery that year of King Tut's Egyptian tomb apparently stimulated a move toward Orientalism—in this Middle Eastern sense. . . . Subsequently, starting in 1926, theaters in the Chinese style were built in Mattapan, Seattle,

and Chicago, in a style described by architects as "the Orient as it came to us through the merchants of Venice." In 1928, this Chinese trend culminated in the construction of Sid Grauman's still famous (indeed iconic) Chinese Theater in Los Angeles, described as deriving its "inspiration from the Chinese period of Chippendale."[47]

Clearly, much of the Orientalism of the period openly acknowledged its Western-mediated foundations. Films such as *The Cheat* (1915), starring Japanese actor Sessue Hayakawa (1890–1973), and *Broken Blossoms* (1919), directed by D. W. Griffith and featuring non-Asian actor Richard Barthelmess as the Chinese lead, both silent film classics, reflected an aesthetic manifestation of this trend in their settings, costume designs, and innovative lighting.

Significantly, this period in silent films produced two successful Asian stars, Sessue Hayakawa and Chinese American actress Anna May Wong (1905–61). Clearly the rare exceptions to the customary practice of casting Caucasian stars in leading Oriental roles, Hayakawa and Wong both carved out distinguished careers in leading and substantial supporting roles.

Hayakawa, particularly during the silent era, enjoyed a screen career that included portrayals of a "variety of ethnic and racial types: Japanese, Chinese, Mexican, Asian Indian, and Arab."[48] However, it was the commercial and critical acclaim for his performance as an archvillain in the film *The Cheat* (in which he brands his white female costar [Fannie Ward] with an iron in the narrative to ensure her loyalty) that paradoxically turned him into a matinee idol. This was instrumental in his hiring at Famous Players-Lasky (later Paramount) for a number of very productive years.

The popularity of Hayakawa is quite unique given that there were some well-known nonwhite actors during the silent period, but many were relegated to solely supporting roles to white leading characters. And, of course, when major characters were specified as Asian, they were most often cast with white actors who performed the Oriental guise. Nonetheless, Hayakawa's astonishing rise to stardom raises the issues of the nature of his unique appeal for the American public and the reasons for its relatively short duration and its ultimate decline. The promotion and marketing of a star in the industry can offer the most explicit articulation of a star's unique appeal for the moviegoing public:

> Hayakawa's stardom occupied an extraordinarily unique space in the racial and cultural map of early Hollywood. A Paramount Pictures ad in film trade journals in June 1917 noted that "Sessue Hayakawa has brought to the American motion picture the mysterious, the magic and mystic of Japan. No foreign-born actor of a generation has won so many admirers as this brilliant young Japanese, whose interpretations of the problems of the Oriental in Occidental lands has given him a unique place in the motion picture firmament." Hayakawa was one of the first and most unusual stars of silent cinema.[49]

Hayakawa's star personality appears to have combined a unique civility and culture with a latent danger and brutality. His film career flourished during this time but ended in the United States exclusively by the early 1920s:

> After working at Lasky for three years, Hayakawa established his own production company, Haworth Pictures, in 1918. . . . In early 1922, Hayakawa suddenly left Hollywood for a film and stage career that would take him to Europe, Japan, and, at the end of the decade, back to Hollywood. Until his death in 1973, he would shuttle between three continents, teaching and performing on stage, in films, and on television, exploiting in various ways the stereotypes that he helped to forge in the 1910s and 1920s in American films.[50]

What is even more remarkable about Hayakawa's precedent-setting career in Hollywood as an Asian American is the fact that he is virtually ignored in film history as well as star studies. When Hayakawa is discussed, it is usually almost exclusively as a screen villain despite the fact that he had varied roles both prior to and subsequent to his performance in his most well known character, Tori, in *The Cheat*.[51] Furthermore, the fact that he reached such a rare level of success whereby he could form and run his own production company makes his omission from the narrative of Hollywood history even more egregious.

Perhaps part of the explanation for Hayakawa's systematic exclusion involves the often contradictory nature of his so-called success. Even after establishing Haworth, Hayakawa's artistic choices attempted to negotiate the expectations of himself as an artist, Japanese communities in the United States (and eventually Japan, across the Pacific), and American mainstream spectators. These competing forces complicate a tidy trajectory of the American Dream narrative of "model immigrant makes good":

> No matter how stereotypical, or authentic, the Japaneseness Hayakawa represented in his films made at Haworth was chosen strategically by Hayakawa himself. It was role-playing of an imagined self for others and left a certain degree of authority to Hayakawa over his star image and his portrayal of his nationality. In other words, when he had an opportunity to obtain authority over his star image for the first time, Hayakawa needed to "mimic" the stereotypical Japanese image in American popular discourse.[52]

The decline of Hayakawa's career was swift and decisive. While his year of greatest popularity is thought to have been 1919, by 1922 in the aftermath of World War I the social and political climate had shifted to a virulent anti-Japanese stance. After the peak of his career and in opposition to his high-profile persona as an unofficial Japanese ambassador, he rarely played Japanese roles or appeared in plots that featured Japan in any way.[53] This anti-Japanese shift has been attributed to Japan's increasingly imperialistic activities after World War I that the media covered in more and more detail. Fox Films, for example, released a news film series called "Face to Face with Japan" that would assert "the peril of Japanese expansion" effecting American interests around the world and promise to reveal "the secrets of Japan's Army and Navy" during this period.[54] Ultimately, Hayakawa's career in America had a gap of at least seven years, from the mid-1920s to the transitional sound era of the early 1930s, after which he would return to Europe and the stage. Following World War II, Hayakawa returned to Hollywood as a supporting actor and was nominated for an an Academy Award for his performance as the villainous Colonel Saito in *The Bridge on the River Kwai* (1957).

Hayakawa's career as a star in the United States is commonly thought to have resolutely ended with the coming of sound in Hollywood pictures.[55] His comeback was thought to be his first sound film, a Fu Manchu thriller titled *Daughter of the Dragon* (1931) that has been restored by the UCLA Film and Television Archives. The film costars Warner Oland as Fu Manchu and Anna May Wong as his evil daughter Ling Moy. Hayakawa stars as Chinese detective Ah Kee working with Scotland Yard. However, a review of the film in *Variety* portends the abrupt (if temporary) hiatus of the silent star's career in talkies until after the war: "Anna May Wong and other Orientals will find the going tough in talkers, because they can't synchronize action with the white man's tongue . . . the white actors impersonating Orientals seemed more the Chinese type than did the two principal Oriental players."[56]

This quote not only denigrates its two leading Asian / Asian American actors but also voices precisely the kind of racist dynamic at work that privileged the non-Asian actors and the Oriental guise created by Hollywood. Although Hayakawa's dialogue is heavily accented in the film, Chinese American Wong's is not in the least. And certainly there is no mention of Orientalized actor Oland's dialogue as being particularly hard to understand.

Fortunately, Wong's film career did not immediately end as a result of the less than enthusiastic notices for *Daughter of the Dragon*. Wong, born and raised in Los Angeles, burst on the Hollywood scene during the silent era playing a Mongol slave in the Douglas Fairbanks vehicle, *The Thief of Baghdad* (1924). Wong often costarred with white stars of the day who were known for adopting the Oriental guise in their roles, such as Lon Chaney in *Mr. Wu* (1927) and Warner Oland in *Old San Francisco* (1927). Initially, Wong was restricted to roles that mimicked the self-sacrificing Cio-Cio San of *Madame Butterfly* fame in films such as *Toll of the Sea* (1922). But she is better known for having introduced the most potent incarnation of the dragon lady stereotype to the cinema as in *Daughter of the Dragon*. The "dragon lady" moniker has had a long history in Western verbiage and has endured as a gendered stereotype even in contemporary popular culture. The irony of this stubborn label is that the vast majority of Asian women immigrants to this country were by far in the absolute opposite position of this type. Rather than heartless victimizers, they were victims of widespread exploitation:

Empress Tsu-hsi ruled China from 1898 to 1908 from the Dragon Throne. The *New York Times* described her as "the wicked witch of the East, a reptilian dragon lady who had arranged the poisoning, strangling, beheading, or forced suicide of anyone who had ever challenged her autocratic rule." Decades later, scholars such as Sterling Seagrave attempted to balance this self-servingly racist caricature. . . . But the shadow of the Dragon Lady—with her cruel, perverse, and inhuman ways—continued to darken encounters between Asian women and the West they flocked to for refuge.[57]

Wong utilized the role of the dragon lady and others to extend her popularity internationally and went on to make films in Germany and Great Britain. In fact, her first sound picture appearance occurs in a British film. (Of course, her first Hollywood sound film was *Daughter of the Dragon*.) Wong proved herself to be so much more than a star of silent films with her widely reputed verbal ability that facilitated her transition from silent to sound pictures. The actress's multilingual achievements are frequently cited in the context of her high international profile and cinematic successes throughout the 1920s and 1930s and even more notably allowed her to expand and extend her film career beyond the less linguistically adaptable counterpart Sessue Hayakawa: "In addition to speaking American English, she engaged a tutor to polish her Oxford English accent, learned and dubbed her films in German and French, and added Mandarin Chinese to Cantonese, the language her family spoke at home."[58]

One of the highlights of Wong's exemplary career is her appearance alongside Marlene Dietrich in Josef von Sternberg's *Shanghai Express* (1932). Indeed Wong, with her commanding performance, was thought by many to have nearly overshadowed her German costar Dietrich in this film. Notably, a great disappointment in Wong's career was losing the leading role of O-lan in *The Good Earth* (1937) to Austrian-born actress Luise Rainer. The controversy around the ultimate casting of the white actors in this film is nearly always referenced as a key element in Wong's Hollywood career decline, although the details of the casting process resist this simplistic rationalization. Though a recognizable star of international stature, Wong was turned down by producer Irving Thalberg and MGM for the role of the "faithful and diligent wife" O-lan opposite non-Asian actor Paul Muni, who would play the male Chinese lead, Wang Lung.[59] There have been a number of reasons posed for this, certainly racism against Asian American actors in leading roles, but also rarely mentioned is the limitation of choices for Wong as she aged as a female performer. The main character of O-lan "epitomized [Pearl S.] Buck's perception of the Chinese woman as self-abnegating and servile"; however, despite these stereotypical features Wong actively sought out a prominent role in this rare big-budgeted film adaptation of a Pulitzer Prize–winning novel set in China.[60]

As was standard casting procedure by the major studios during the classical Hollywood period, Muni, a white star, was initially set to star as the male lead, Wang Lung. In this scenario alone Wong would be immediately excluded, as the production code mandated no miscegenation between white and most nonwhite stars. Officially, the code specifically names the forbidden miscegenation as between African Americans and whites; however, this unofficially extended to most other visually discernible nonwhite races and ethnicities. Indeed, the trade paper *Variety* claimed that "various censorship angles" would be exploited if "anything approaching miscegenation" were to exist by casting an Asian in such a prominent role.[61] Wong astutely (and often) recognized a key distinction between her own racial difference and the white actors who impersonated Asians as a major determinant in the roles that she could be cast for:

> Discussing her desire to portray the Asian wife of an Englishman in *Java Head*, she explained, "I know I will never play it. The captain, you see, marries the woman. . . . But no film lovers can ever marry me. If they got an American actress to slant her eyes and eyebrows and wear a stiff black wig and dress in Chinese culture, it would be allright. But me? I am really Chinese. So I must always die in the movies, so that the white girl with the yellow hair may get the man." . . . [Her] presence in a film as a publicly and visibly Chinese American actor . . . served as a reminder that markers of Oriental exotica might adorn a non-Asian actor's body but not ultimately affect his or her innate identity or character.[62]

So why the uproar specifically about *The Good Earth* with its predictable casting of non-Asian actors in all the leading roles that Wong certainly understood despite her vehement public protests? And what of the tendency to identify Wong's exclusion as the primary symbol of Hollywood's misuse of her career? According to MGM production notes on the film, producer Irving Thalberg's assistant, Albert Lewin, expressed "disappointment" in Wong's "looks" during her screen tests. He explicitly states his professional evaluation of Wong's inappropriateness for the role of Lotus (the twenty-year-old mistress of lead Wang Lung, not the leading role of wife O-Lan):

> "Does not seem beautiful enough to make Wang's (the lead male character) infatuation convincing; however, deserves consideration." In a second test four days later, Lewin again reported his concerns about Anna May's beauty. In his reports on tests for Mary Wong, Keye Luke, and other Chinese actors Lewin consistently argued that, despite their ethnicity, they did not fit his conception of what Chinese people looked like. Therefore, Lewin recommended that they be used primarily as "atmosphere" and not as principal actors.[63]

One could potentially substitute the word "youth" for his concerns about her so-called beauty. Wong was thirty years old at the time of the screen test, certainly not old but clearly too old for the role of the twenty-year-old Lotus (actually the fifth billed role in the film). His evaluation of Wong seems separate (though equally reprehensible) from the blatant racism involved in his evaluation of other Asian actors mentioned in the casting notes. Her deficiency seems to be identified with her typecasting as a star, primarily (at least in sound pictures) that of an enigmatic exotic beauty rather than a seasoned actress with years of experience who could play a range of female roles.

Despite the fact of being a qualified, well-known, and racially appropriate star, Wong was never seriously considered for the role of O-lan, which she felt she was born to play. In the end, she was again challenging not only those creative personnel involved in this particular film but also the widespread and embedded racism in the Hollywood industry that sustained a system of portraying Asia and Asians without leading Asian actors. Rainer's awarding of the Best Actress Oscar for the role presents a triumph that reveals a sense of racial superiority; in other words, it takes a white person to portray a real Asian. It also contains a double irony: the failure of the white populace to recognize the original racism in the casting choice and the racism in the lack of awareness of it. As stated earlier, throughout Wong's career this type of treatment was well known to her. For example, Wong did a screen test for MGM in 1932 for *The Son-Daughter* (a film analyzed in the next chapter) only to reportedly be considered "too Chinese to play Chinese."[64] Helen Hayes eventually was cast, and the film was poorly received. It was even banned by the Chinese government as "demeaning to its people."[65]

To add insult to injury in the narrative of Wong's career at this time was her sojourn to China after the painful aftermath of *The Good Earth* casting debacle. Expecting a positive welcome in the land of her ancestors, she was instead criticized by the Chinese for taking what they deemed degrading roles in American films. Wong found herself on the defensive, explaining that when an actress is starting out she must take on roles that she would not necessarily choose for herself to get established in the film industry. Strikingly, Swedish actor Warner Oland, traveling in China around the same time, was greeted with warmth and praise by the Chinese press and government officials, the same cadre that harshly criticized Wong's film performances. While Wong was demonized and castigated particularly for her role in *Shanghai Express* (which was banned in China), Oland—who appeared as a despicable Eurasian warlord in the film—received only acclaim as an actor, pointedly overlooking this unsavory role along with other parts such as his portrayal of the diabolical Fu Manchu.[66]

Wong continued to make films in supporting roles throughout the late 1930s and only sporadically during the 1940s. She hosted a television series in 1951 and was scheduled to play a small role in the Chinese American-centered musical *Flower Drum Song* (1961) but was unable to take up the role due to illness; she died of a heart attack in 1961. The careers of Sessue Hayakawa and Anna May Wong are important to note in that they show that racial impersonation of Asians was not the only option for Hollywood. Yet it was the option almost always chosen. Indeed, at the time when blackface was most visible (e.g., in the part-talkie hit *The Jazz Singer* [1927]), its systematic use would come to an end fairly rapidly. Still, the Oriental guise persisted, even edging out genuine Asian stars. Why the double standard? Even prominent Asian figures behind the scenes such as Academy Award-winning cinematographer James Wong Howe (while experiencing individual success and its concomitant racism) failed to impact the routine use of non-Asian actors or "adhesive taped" performers, as Howe termed "Caucasian actors sporting slanted eyes to play Asian characters" in prominent roles.[67]

Clearly, much more could be said about the careers of Sessue Hayakawa and Anna May Wong. To further define the focus and theme of this study, it is important to contrast the Oriental guise with other possibilities. However, the goal of this study is not to encompass all of Asian representation in Hollywood, only a significant performance practice that necessarily intersects with a number of related histories.

In analyzing the films during the period of this study, I include the important element of critical reception in the discussions of the selected films. Detailed looks into contemporaneous reviews and publicity all reflect how films affected the public's perceptions. These sources give a sense of what the meanings were. Archival studio-generated documents also provided an often illuminating look into the conception of key characterizations and narratives. Reviewing these documents in several cases allowed me to trace the often complex production process from the conception of an idea to script development and, finally, to promotion as well as provided critical support for some of the readings of the films.

The use of close formal analyses of the films is employed as a basis for the discussions. Images, themes, and narratives all necessarily influence the interpretation of the Oriental performances that are the main focus of this study. The methodology herein naturally reflects a demonstrated interest in the field of representation as well as representational practices. But unlike traditional cultural studies discourses that privilege issues of power and their functions within representations, my approach stresses a logic of embodiment rather than of representation. Though not emphatically, the postcolonial theory of Homi Bhabha also relates to this line of argument as well, particularly in relation to issues of cultural hybridity.[68] What is the lure that inspires the construction of a cultural hybrid such as the Orientalized Caucasian actor? The dynamic of attraction-revulsion that occurs within these characterizations as well as in response to them emerges as an important element in these discussions.

Chapter 1 examines some of the contradictory elements in the construction of basic Oriental archetypes (such as Fu Manchu) and specifically addresses issues of how Hollywood's Oriental relates to dreams, nightmares, fantasy, and the unconscious. The focus of chapter 1 also considers how race, sexuality, and human agency function in Oriental-identified individual bodies (characters) as well as their operation within the depiction of a larger sociopolitical body designated as the Orient. Chapter 2 focuses on the most well known Oriental archetype: the detective. We will discuss how this seemingly benign figure deftly balances darker elements from traditional archetypes with more heroic qualities. In addition, we will consider how this figure is constructed to reassure and appeal to a mass audience. Chapter 3 focuses on the strategies of constructing the Japanese Oriental as enemy, outsider, and Other during World War II. Specifically, this is evidenced through a strategy that distinguishes between the "good" Chinese and the "inhuman" Japanese. Chapter 4 traces a shift back to a seemingly more benign, erotic, and often comedic Oriental after the War. In this chapter the performances run the gamut from extreme caricature to more complex and inclusive characterizations.

Again, this examination of the construction of the Oriental guise seeks to expose the complex dynamic involved in racialized characterizations. A discussion of these performances as simply good or bad, right or wrong, misses the opportunity to discuss the details and nuances operating within these portrayals. This type of interrogation hopefully might lead to a deeper understanding of the performative element operating within Hollywood's narrative structures and perhaps might also provide indications as to how the issue of racial difference is perceived and negotiated in society-at-large.

A *Photoplay* article, titled "Loretta Goes Oriental" and featuring the actress Loretta Young, offers images of her in the process of makeup for a part as a Chinese woman in *The Hatchet Man* (1932). Perc Westmore (one of the members of a family of makeup artists who specialized in Oriental guises) is shown applying the feature-altering cosmetics. The artist is described as a skillful professional "who delights in making people what they aren't."[69] At once, the brief article draws detailed attention to the artifice involved in Young's Oriental impersonation while establishing its predominance over an authentic Asian countenance:

> The first step is accomplished by pulling the skin back from Loretta's eyes and pasting it down firmly with spirit gum and fish skin—not adhesive tape. The fish skin is then covered by make-up. Lips are made larger, eyes and nose are lined. The finished job might make you think Loretta was Anna May Wong. And why didn't a real Chinese girl get the part? Well, Loretta is under contract to First National, where "The Hatchet Man" is being made. Her tests were as excellent as the make-up, so they thought you wouldn't know the difference. Loretta has only to worry about the accent.[70]

The mention and dismissal of Chinese American actress Anna May Wong, the acknowledgment of, indeed fascination with, the artifice of Orientalizing makeup and the proud presentation of a finished product suggest the complexity involved in the embodiment of the Oriental guise. The focus is on a dual racial presentation of actor and role rather than a simple stereotype that nevertheless reveals specific attitudes about race and racial identity. Here, going Oriental clearly suggests both a displacement and an adaptation that allow Caucasian stars such as Edward G. Robinson and Loretta Young to delight film audiences with their skills of impersonation through the embodiment of people whom they are not.

This image of the couple of Robinson and Young reflects archetypal qualities commonly found in the Oriental guise. Highly elaborate makeup with an emphasis on altered upper eyelids, ornate costuming (particularly in the headdress on Young), and impassive expressions combine to Orientalize these Caucasian stars. In this instance of racial impersonation, as evidenced through the *Photoplay* article, the actress's makeup and training (i.e., the only element left for her to master is an accent) are acknowledged and recognized. Part of the process in the objectification of racial/cultural groups foregrounds certain qualities while effacing others. One of the elements routinely effaced is the process of training and acculturation required to become a member of any cultural group. The specific qualities ascribed to the objectified group are usually defined as intrinsic and biologically based. The recognition of the actor's skill and effort in the racial impersonation provides an important component that fills a gap, as it were, and presents a performance that may appear more complete than one by an actual Asian actor.

Still, we are left with an unsettling image. The gaze of Robinson looking off to the side appears to reference a codified gesture of shifty eyes that appears in many Oriental characterizations. This gesture imbues the image with a sinister quality. Perhaps this sinister quality can be attributed not only to an archetypal Oriental duplicity but also to the duplicity inherent in the Oriental masquerade. After all, this image presents figures who are overtly pretending that they are who they are not. Indeed, when Hollywood goes Oriental, the Oriental guise becomes a powerful illusion of both fantasy and nightmare.

ONE

Figures of the Imagination
Hollywood's Orient/al

In Hollywood, the face of Asia is cast in shadow and cloaked in darkness. It is often a Caucasian face made up to appear Asian. In the film *The Mask of Fu Manchu* (1932) the face belongs to Boris Karloff as he appears for the first time in the title role. Karloff's facial features are the visual focus in this first shot set in Fu Manchu's scientific laboratory. His figure, dressed in Chinese costume, faces a mirror that reflects a distorted, grotesque, and larger-than-life image of his face. Sounds of crackling electricity from his scientific experiments can be heard over this image.

In the frame Fu Manchu is alone, and yet not alone, when coupled with his disturbing mirror reflection. This image is a monstrous but clearly unreal face. Karloff's reflected image asserts and foregrounds the artificial and theatrical quality of the Fu Manchu character. Here, Fu Manchu functions primarily as a sign of fantasy, an apparent construct of the mind and the imagination. The spectator sees two faces, one simply made up and cast in shadow, but the other, in the mirror, is more expressive, expansive, and monstrous. This character is presented as a Westerner's worst nightmare, and significantly, nightmares are generally assumed to be of the dreamer's own making.

Boris Karloff in *The Mask of Fu Manchu*. (MoMA)

The same year in Universal Pictures' *The Mummy*, Karloff's performance of ancient Egyptian Im-Ho-Tep and his modern alter ego Ardeth Bey created another memorable characterization in the horror genre. Also an Orientalist film, albeit of the Middle East rather than the Far East, *The Mummy* again offers a monstrous Karloff who at key moments gazes straight into the camera with evocative high-contrast lighting. At these times, his makeup (particularly dark eyeliner under the eyes and a wizened skin texture that appears ready to disintegrate as dust) and dark countenance (both literally and figuratively) are isolated from the rest of the action and, indeed, especially the other characters. Though Karloff's initial appearance as Fu Manchu exists as a highly artificial fabrication, he stands as one of the most well known cinematic symbols of the Orient.

This chapter takes as its focus performances from Hollywood films of the 1930s. Elements of makeup, physical demeanor, costuming, and style of speech assemble to create archetypal figures that embody qualities that Western culture both covets and simultaneously seeks to repress. We will specifically examine in this section how cinematic depictions of Orientals and the Orient designed for mass audiences during the 1930s are rendered as products of the Western unconscious mind. Whether portrayed as fantasy figures, nightmarish monstrosities, or inscrutable mystics, these figures of the imagination embody elements both strongly seductive and deeply threatening. The creation of the Orient itself also comes to represent a utopian metaphor for remaking (and often redeeming) one's identity across cultures and time. However, this promise is not without its commensurate dangers and thus offers within its domain, as Robert Young suggests, "both poison and cure."[1]

In the 1930s, Hollywood films were disseminated virtually all over the world. The images at this time had a tremendous impact on how ethnic groups, in particular, were perceived in different parts of the world. Of course, Hollywood's creation of standardized "national types" includes nationalities other than Asian. In the chapter on Asians in the work *Ethnic and Racial Images in American Film and Television,* the authors Allen Woll and Randall Miller describe the rather "fuzzy" designation historically given Asians in Hollywood films. Between Hollywood's vague "geographical boundaries" of Asian characters and the seemingly indiscriminate casting of whites in Asian roles, specific national character types were subsumed under a generalized Oriental character.[2]

Reaction to this Hollywood tradition was not confined to this country. Indeed, Woll and Miller also note a strong international response to a specific and markedly pernicious strain of Asian representation evident in the early years of motion pictures. Specifically, various governments in Asia registered complaints and criticism in response to characters such as the evil Fu Manchu. During the 1930s, Hollywood made some attempt to rectify this tension with the presentation of occasionally more positive images such as Charlie Chan.

However, the play between positive and negative can be seen in the films selected for discussion here. The performances of Boris Karloff in *The Mask of Fu Manchu* (1932) and Nils Asther in *The Bitter Tea of General Yen* (1932) explore both the nightmarish sadism and dreamy romantic fantasy of the Oriental captor and/or lover. *Thirteen Women* (1932), featuring Myrna Loy, and *The Son-Daughter* (1932), starring Helen Hayes, illustrate the archetypal dichotomy between the submissive China doll and the vengeful dragon lady traditionally accorded to female Oriental characters. And finally, *Lost Horizon* (1937) presents the Orient as both utopian haven and hell. These films represent a range of Hollywood product from big-budget prestige pictures to more formulaic B movies and thus reveal the consistency of certain archetypal Oriental features that supersede the production classification of individual films.

Visually constructed as a dark apparition, Karloff's performance in the role of the diabolical fiend Dr. Fu Manchu illustrates how the use of highly theatrical elements in makeup, costuming, and lighting produces an Oriental villain of mythic proportions. However, Fu Manchu's monstrosity stems not only from the distortions of his facial features and garishness of his costumes but also from the imagined threat that his ambitions pose to the Western world order. His link to the actual historical figure of Genghis Khan makes more real the menace of the fictional figure.

Karloff's makeup in the film (eyes taped to appear smaller, long mustache, darkly painted and upwardly sloped eyebrows, heavy eyeliner, and long fingernails) was designed to create a repellent, frightening appearance. Additionally, at key points in the narrative, particularly when the leading British characters are being mortally threatened, Karloff is shot in highly contrasted light and shadow, which further distorts his features. The actor's cheeks appear sunken or fallen, giving him a somewhat emaciated appearance. It is notable that his depiction of the monster in *Frankenstein* (1931) occurred just the year before. In fact, movie posters for *The Mask of Fu Manchu* from the period specifically refer to Karloff as the "Frankenstein of the Orient" as well as the "new Fu Manchu" (he had previously been played by Warner Oland). The British characters describe Dr. Fu Manchu as a cruel "fanatic" who is "insane for power."

Originated in novels of pulp fiction by Sax Rohmer, Fu Manchu is distinguished from contemporaneous African cinematic representation (i.e., the Tarzan series of the 1930s and 1940s) in significant ways that foreground key elements of the so-called yellow menace:

> Just as the brushstrokes of Edgar Rice Burroughs colored the African racial adventure film, Sax Rohmer shaded the outlines of yellow-peril imagery for the Asian variant. In an oeuvre of delirious pulp fiction written from 1913 to 1955, Rohmer went East with a vengeance. His trademark creation was the unkillable Dr. Fu Manchu, mad scientist, master of the occult, and sexual predator. No African equivalent existed for Fu Manchu: a black man might have one or two of the attributes but never all three in combination.[3]

The plot of *The Mask of Fu Manchu* revolves around the race between Fu Manchu and a group of British scientists to recover the remains from the tomb of Genghis Khan, which is located in the Gobi Desert. The prized treasures in the tomb sought by the scientists include a shield, a mask, and a sword. A British scientist asserts the urgency in acquiring the relics before Fu Manchu because in British hands they would simply be "pretty things" on display in a museum. In the hands of the Chinese villain, however, the ancient artifacts would empower his leadership of a newly risen Asia that would then rule the world.

Indeed, toward the end of the film when Fu Manchu finally comes to possess the sword and mask of Genghis Khan, the character's appearance shifts in nightmarish proportions. Wearing both an elaborate Chinese headdress and the golden mask of Khan that covers the top half of his face, Fu Manchu looks nearly unrecognizable, resembling more a ghoul risen from the grave than a human form. As he exults in the power of the mask and sword in front of hordes of cheering Asiatics, the character appears both at his most unreal and most powerful until a lightning bolt from his own electric generator strikes him.

Depicted as twisted combination of high intellect (three doctorates in philosophy, law, and medicine from three Western universities) and evil intentions, the Fu Manchu character is a cultural hybrid in a sense, a product of Western higher learning and Asian cultural elitism. It is as if the combination of his Asian heritage and extensive foreign education in itself produces an evil and alien creation. And yet this individual terror, this mad scientist with a monstrous countenance, is also generalized in terms of a larger Oriental agenda. His character is positioned not just as a sociopathic extremist but also as representative of the latent aspirations of thousands, perhaps millions, of Asians who would follow his lead.

Coverage of the film's preview at the Motion Picture Academy echoed similar sentiments by praising its production values while cautioning against its potentially ill effects. Furthermore, although the comments primarily focus on reception in the domestic market, the reviewer also raises the thorny issue of possible objections by Asians in foreign markets to the "ruthlessly cruel being" embodied by Fu Manchu.[4]

The final scene in the film has the still shaken British survivors of Fu Manchu's capture traveling back to London by boat. Wayland Smith (played by Lewis Stone) insists on throwing the Genghis Khan sword into the sea instead of returning it to the British museum. Smith says that he is "not taking any chances," as he is convinced that "other Fu Manchus" may be tempted to steal the sword and again wreak havoc on the world stage. In the midst of this speculation, the sound of a gong startles all the characters as it reminds them (unpleasantly) of the world and culture of their former captor. However, a diminutive Chinese servant (played by an Asian actor) holds this gong, announcing the beginning of the dinner hour. The servant appears quite simpleminded and has one front tooth prominently missing. His presence prompts Smith to question him in a heavily ironic tone:

SMITH: You aren't by any chance a doctor of philosophy?

The servant shakes his head, giggling.

SMITH: Law?

The servant shakes his head, again giggling.

SMITH: Medicine?

CHINESE SERVANT: I no think so, sir.

SMITH: But are you sure?

CHINESE SERVANT: Oh yes, pretty sure.

SMITH: I congratulate you.

He shakes the servant's hand, and the servant walks away hitting the gong
while announcing "dinner is served."

Sufficiently reassured by the utterances of this uneducated and docile servant, Smith throws the sword overboard. With this gesture the
nightmare of an evil Orient as embodied in the Oriental figures of
Genghis Khan and Fu Manchu is quelled for the moment.

The implication of such a scene can point to a more generalized
perception of the threat that Asian/Asian Americans pose in the U.S.
cultural landscape. Does it take a figure as weak and dull as this Oriental servant to put these Westerners at ease? The following introduction
of the Fu Manchu character from the novel by Sax Rohmer reveals the
answer by what it details about this unqualified yellow peril threat.

> Imagine a person, tall, lean and feline, high-shouldered, with a brow
> like Shakespeare and a face like Satan, a close-shaven skull, and long,
> magnetic eyes of true cat-green. Invest him with all the cruel cunning
> of an entire Eastern race, accumulated in one giant intellect, with all the
> resources, if you will, of a wealthy government which, however, already
> has denied all knowledge of his existence. Imagine that awful being, and
> you have a mental picture of Dr. Fu-Manchu, the yellow peril incarnate
> in one man.[5]

The cunning, the intellect, and the resources of a wealthy government
combine to produce a threat as awesome as Fu Manchu in fiction. Of
course, it would follow that any Asian who lacks these qualities might
offer a reassuring deficiency to the Western imagination. Not always.
Significantly, in this excerpt, Fu Manchu does not stand alone but instead merely stands in for the yellow peril constituted of Asian hordes
waiting to strike the vulnerable civilizations of the West. From the

World War II Japanese American internment for disloyalty (read: potential spies) to more recent allegations of spying by prominent Asian Americans, the central legacy of fictional treachery by the Oriental has undoubtedly influenced broader popular perceptions of many Asians/Asian Americans.

The character of General Yen in *The Bitter Tea of General Yen* could be positioned as a more sympathetic attempt at an Asian film portrayal. Director Frank Capra described the project in his autobiography *The Name above the Title* as a "strangely poetic romance between a Chinese warlord and an American missionary. Representatives of two cultures as far apart as the poles, clash and fall in love."[6] Capra from the outset positions the cultures of China and the United States as diametrically opposed, inherently poised in conflict to clash in his construction of this romantic fantasy. And yet he imbues this Occidental/Oriental romantic encounter with poetic overtones that suggest a dreamlike treatment of the story.

The Bitter Tea of General Yen casts its Oriental hero in dreamlike imagery, most explicitly within the context of an extended dream sequence in the film. However, the character of General Yen inspires more oppositions, contradictions, and open eroticism even within the dream consciousness paradigm. For Capra, *The Bitter Tea of General Yen* was to be "Art with a capital A."[7] The director describes in detail how he carefully constructed the "look" of the character General Yen initially by casting "a not-too-well-known Swedish actor, Nils Asther." Capra goes on to detail the prevailing (and in his opinion unconvincing) makeup process of taping the "outer ends of the eyes back toward the ears" to transform "Caucasian eyes into Oriental ones."[8]

While Capra admits that he did not totally succeed in creating a Chinese Nils Asther, he does claim to have created a compelling otherness on the face and in the body of the actor that ultimately pleased him very much. Though its creators openly acknowledge the artificial nature of the physical construction of this character, they do claim to have constructed an authentic non-Caucasian in this case. But this authenticity is founded upon features that merely oppose Western qualities and values.

Thus, Asther was able to "pass for an awe-inspiring warlord" although his makeup resulted in an admittedly "strange" and "mysterious" figure.[9] Indeed, Hollywood's Oriental in this instance explicitly begins its life in the space of a Western negation—the non-Caucasian—in the shadow of the Western imagination with potentially transgressive implications.

The plot of *The Bitter Tea of General Yen* involves the struggle between American missionary Megan Davis (played by Barbara Stanwyck) and the Chinese warlord General Yen (played by Nils Asther) who kidnaps her on her wedding day and holds her hostage in his palace. Despite Megan's protests for her release, she finds herself strongly attracted to the enigmatic general. Risking her reputation and perhaps her virtue, Megan acts as stalwart defender and protector of Yen's Chinese mistress, believing naively that all human beings are fundamentally trustworthy. When the mistress betrays Yen to enemy soldiers, Megan prepares to bed him as restitution. Appalled by her misunderstanding of his motives, he desires only that she come to him out of love, not duty. Believing him honorable and sensing his isolation as enemy troops close in, Megan—dressed in Chinese costume—goes to Yen of her own accord. At last fulfilled by her emotional surrender, he drinks a lethal poison from a cup of tea. Megan returns to Shanghai by boat profoundly changed by the experience.

It should be noted that *Variety*'s review at the time of the film's release challenges Capra's assumption of creating an authentic or coherent character through General Yen. The reviewer criticizes the diverse elements of the characterization as creating an "otherness" too vague and disparate for movie audiences of the 1930s to understand or perhaps recognize. The writer, who apparently rejects the "otherness" so painstakingly constructed by director Capra, describes General Yen as a "rather questionable human composition of a poet, philosopher and bandit" with vaguely American mannerisms.[10]

Within the plot of the film as well, General Yen is often presented as a construct in the mind of another character, Megan Davis. Our main access to Yen is through Megan as she embodies and expresses the contradictory nature of her attraction to and fear of the powerful Chinese warlord throughout. Nowhere is this clearer than in Megan's dream/fantasy that occurs almost midway through the film. Megan's dream/fantasy about Yen reveals her acute fears, inner moral conflicts, and repressed sexual desires by utilizing the exceedingly malleable figure of Yen to work these issues through. Does he provide for her a convenient repository for potentially disturbing feelings and desires that she wishes to disown? In a sense, her character's psychic journey could be said to parallel those of the film's audience. Could this dream/fantasy sequence also reflect the viewer's process of confronting otherness? How does this sequence force its audience to confront this practice of projection onto an Other ethnicity?

The dream/fantasy sequence begins with the superimposition of a door to Megan's bedroom with the doorknobs being turned from the outside over Megan's sleeping figure in a chair. The door remains locked. An intruder then breaks the door apart with a stick. This intruder is General Yen in grotesque makeup, strongly reminiscent of Fu Manchu. Out of the shadows, he emerges with pointed and elongated ears, buck teeth, and long metal spikes attached to his fingers.

This figure is frightening, ugly, aggressive, and multilayered. This dream image of Fu Manchu's likeness initially effaces the accepted masquerade of General Yen within the narrative by the actor Nils Asther. If the audience has not yet recognized him as General Yen, the next shot will indisputably identify him. The image of General Yen dressed in a Western military uniform is briefly superimposed over the Fu Manchu image. This figure of Yen is represented as static, civilized, and benign. Megan reacts to these contradictory images with distressed confusion.

Abruptly we return back to Asther as a menacing Fu Manchu who approaches Megan. This shot is noticeably out of focus. Perhaps the director chose this blurred visual image of the actor to reflect the distorted quality of Megan's perceptions. The next shot shows Megan recoiling from his point of view surrounded only by seemingly disembodied hands with the long metal spikes. Megan is repelled, yet helpless, as Fu Manchu is shown approaching her bed. He then begins to fondle her shoulders and body as she weakly struggles to resist him.

The image of Megan, surrounded by the advancing long metal-spiked fingers of Fu Manchu, signifies an important component operating in her fear of this figure. Not only is this image fundamentally removed from the more benign General Yen figure, but it also works to isolate and highlight a particular element of the Fu Manchu masquerade. The spiked metal fingernails seem to travel through the space of her bedroom on their own, disconnected from anything else. This shot

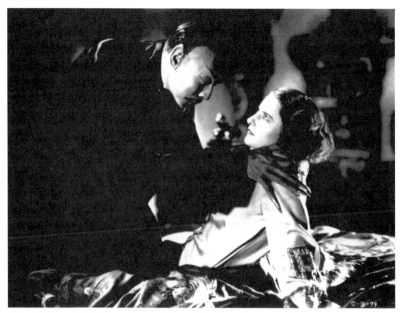

Nils Asther (in Fu Manchu guise) and Barbara Stanwyck in *The Bitter Tea of General Yen*. (MoMA)

captures the dreamlike quality of the sequence as well as injecting a groundless characteristic to the intensely felt fear and dread that Megan experiences up to that moment.

But Fu Manchu's gaze at this point becomes the viewer's gaze as well. Not only does this point of view force the viewer into the position of the monstrous figure, it also horrifies and disorients the same viewer on a deeper level. We see only the fragment of a body here. Edward Lowry and Richard de Cordova discuss in their essay on *White Zombie* (1932), a film made the same year as *General Yen,* how the horror film attempts in the classical model to link the desires embodied in the characters to the desires of the "ideal viewer." In this way, the text attempts to position the viewer by certain conventional techniques. "The production of fear in the viewer depends on the text's success in situating the viewer (in inscribing the viewer position) in a disturbing relationship to the enunciation of desire and the system within which it operates."[11]

Clearly, Fu Manchu's gaze and the viewer's gaze both move to possess Megan sexually with obvious violent undertones manifested and highlighted by the spiked metal fingernails. In this moment the viewer is complicit with the established antagonist Fu Manchu, both intense and discomfiting. The element of desire in this scene moves toward its most extreme expression.

From another side of the room, a jaunty male figure dressed in a Western suit, hat, and eye mask leaps into the action through a set of glass doors. This figure appears as the agent of Megan's rescue in this nightmarish fantasy. Silently, he gestures to her and runs toward the Fu Manchu figure, who immediately begins backing away. This rescuer figure punches and knocks the Fu Manchu figure away from Megan in one blow. Fu Manchu then abruptly disappears as his body hits the wall. Clearly, we are in the world of dreams where figures appear and disappear at will.

The heroic rescuer then throws off his hat and embraces Megan who, though still somewhat confused, tentatively removes his eye mask. Megan's act reveals the face of an ardent and smiling General Yen. She responds fervently and quickly becomes intoxicated by his visage. The background swirls around her to indicate this state as the music swells. And the dream sequence ends with a kiss between them as Megan's solitary and sleeping image in the chair reemerges. This "interracial" kiss, though with a white actor, enacted a daring taboo of miscegenation. Oriental and Caucasian cinematic interracial sexuality remained exceptional despite the fact that miscegenation was officially defined by the Production Code as sexual activity between blacks and whites: "Occidentals playing Oriental in an all-Asian world submerged the erotic tension behind the interracial makeup, but an Occidental cast doing double duty as Asian and American could not disguise the desire for East to meet, and mate, West. In films where white actors romanced white actors in yellowface, the yellow peril was also an erotic possibility."[12]

Charles Wolfe, in his critical survey *Frank Capra: A Guide to References and Resources,* suggests that the dream/fantasy sequence makes plain the subjective nature of Megan's wildly divergent construct of General Yen relative to the more stable construct of Yen within the narrative plot. Her character acts as a surrogate for the audience in her attempt to place Yen in the dual role of demon and hero, although he is neither. And yet the question of who General Yen really is remains difficult to define. Although the term "masquerade" implies a pretense or false appearance, Asther inhabits the General Yen disguise with a sense of complete authority within the plot until we get to Megan's dream sequence. In this sequence, the audience (and Megan) are called upon to distinguish between the actor's role as General Yen masquerade and several other deceptive disguises and masks.

Finally, Megan awakens with a start, she remembers where and who she is, a Caucasian missionary woman held hostage in a foreign country. Distant voices of Chinese soldiers can be heard as she reacts to her dream / fantasy with a mix of guilt and repulsion. General Yen silently enters dressed in a traditional Chinese costume. Here, Yen appears in a third guise after her two dream visions of him. Megan is startled, angry, and immediately guarded again. The dialogue that follows links a potent image from the preceding dream sequence to the suppressed sexual attraction inherent in their waking relationship:

GENERAL YEN: I often envy the common soldier. His wants are so few.

MEGAN: Even a common soldier would have knocked.

GENERAL YEN: I did. I almost broke the door down but you didn't hear me.

This exchange indirectly places General Yen back into Megan's dream / fantasy through the uncanny timing of his words "I almost broke the door down." Indeed, he may have been knocking at the same time Megan was dreaming of him violently breaking through her bedroom door. Here, the line between the dreaming and waking worlds become fuzzy. What are we to make of this thinly veiled reference to Megan's dream sequence?

The sequence itself actually presents a coherent synthesis of Megan's perceptions and feelings about the kind of man General Yen could be. Is he an evil monster of the Fu Manchu variety? Or is he a dashing rescuer who is both a heroic and romantic figure? Still, in this subsequent waking exchange between the two characters, General Yen lapses back into a netherworld of ambiguity. His enigmatic status is quickly reconstituted as it remains at the source of Megan's attraction for him and where he functions most effectively as her psychic Other, the human vessel for her projected unconscious fears and desires.

Nils Asther and Barbara Stanwyck in *The Bitter Tea of General Yen*. (MoMA)

In the last scene of the film, after she has silently but palpably expressed her love for a dying General Yen, Megan returns by boat to Shanghai with Jones (another American as well as Yen's former financial adviser). She appears changed, transformed through the embodiment of her own kind of otherness. Megan appears to adopt an Oriental inscrutability through her silence and stillness and in this way suddenly converts into an enigmatic figure herself. She has loved General Yen, and now her image duplicates his. Megan's "distant gaze" and "faint set smile" replicates Yen's dying countenance. Megan's gaze can be understood as one of possession, though not like a zombie who looks at nothing and sees nothing.[13] Rather, Megan now possesses an inner strength and certainty that seemed only to belong to General Yen. The power of her gaze (even looking out at the sea) attempts to shift the control back to Megan now that General Yen is dead.

Having journeyed through a week-long fantasy in which her repressed sexual desires found an Oriental host, Megan seems to have integrated her formerly disavowed sexual self with deep satisfaction and peace. However, despite her highly charged final encounter with General Yen, Megan's complete silence here imbues any such conclusions with a sense of ambiguity. Significantly, the fate of her husband and their marriage on her return remains uncertain and, most importantly, unaddressed. Perhaps the ambiguity of this ending allows Megan a momentary transgression while holding open the possibility of reintegration into respectable missionary society. And yet, her obvious repose provides a dramatic shift from her introduction into the story as a naive, eager American missionary anxious to preach the gospel and save young orphans.

General Yen's image has been constructed throughout the narrative to serve as Megan's unconscious projection of conflicting desires. Diametrically opposed elements, such as romantic lover versus sexual terror, villainous yellow swine versus gallant rescuer, combine to create the Oriental fantasy of General Yen. Nils Asther performs his Oriental impersonation as a genie would for his master, transforming at will. This key dream sequence clearly demonstrates the essential permutability operating in the Oriental guise.

Feminine Guile

Ambiguity remains a key component in the construction of Hollywood's Oriental archetypes and is frequently used to foster an aura of mystery around a given character. This pattern is quite evident in the film *Thirteen Women* (1932), which features a female Oriental character whose formidable mystical abilities are credited to no source in particular. This ambiguity, in a sense, leads to the assumption that her extrasensory powers are simply by-products of her non-Western racial/cultural origins.

The plot of *Thirteen Women* introduces Ursula Georgi's character as a half-caste (half-Caucasian and half-East Indian) who was brought to the United States from India under the auspices of a missionary. She attends an exclusive finishing school but is ostracized by her classmates. Her revenge comes in the form of mental suggestion that causes the deaths of all but one. Unlike her male counterparts Fu Manchu and General Yen, Ursula Georgi represents and contains the racial bifurcation of Caucasian and non-Caucasian within her body. In *Thirteen Women,* she is alternately portrayed as both victim and victimizer. Her biracial heritage is positioned as the unresolvable conflict of her existence and the singular cause of her emotional pain that has led her to seek vengeance against her former white schoolmates. It provides the driving force behind her actions within the narrative that, almost solely, propels the story forward.

Not only does the narrative situation work out allegorically what the nature of a Caucasian/Oriental split identity can mean, but this also further resonates in the casting of Myrna Loy in the role of Ursula Georgi. How appropriate that Caucasian actress Myrna Loy adopts an Oriental guise to act out a characterization that further divides along Caucasian/Oriental lines. Ursula Georgi's characterization in *Thirteen Women* essentially presents the differences between the Oriental and Caucasian races as irreconcilable. Her racial identification as half-caste attempts to downplay her outcast social status as an Oriental.

Ursula is understood to physically embody both races, and yet actress Myrna Loy is made up with markedly Asian features. Her skin is darkened, and her eyebrows are arched with dark eyeliner applied around the eyes. Interestingly, the facial features of actress Loy are described as lending themselves to an Oriental look that had her virtually specializing in Oriental roles, including the daughter of Boris Karloff in *The Mask of Fu Manchu.* As Ursula Georgi, the way Loy's face is made up reflects a remarkably unambiguous non-Caucasian race. Perhaps any physical ambiguity that would depict Ursula as possibly looking more white would inject a disturbing complexity into the narrative such as the possibility of passing. In that case, Ursula would have an undeniable choice as to which racial group she wanted to be identified with in society.

Ursula's murderous villainy positions her as a threat in the spirit of a Fu Manchu. Yet the nature of her threat draws almost exclusively on suggestion, hypnosis, and trance, all of which symbolize the sphere of the unconscious mind. Ursula's character is represented not only as a vengeful outsider but also as a vengeful outsider who utilizes all that the white Western mind represses. This element is an essential component of many villainous/monstrous Asian cinematic figures who are able to harness the power of an often ambiguous mental mysticism to erode the rationality of vulnerable Caucasian minds. *Thirteen Women* identifies this mental mysticism as astrology.

Ursula's former classmates make themselves vulnerable by requesting individual astrological readings from Swami Yogadachi. They are unaware that Ursula works with him and has made a practice (unbeknownst to Yogadachi) of altering his fundamentally positive readings to ones of murder and suicide. Most often these notes are simply presented as the catalyst for the demise of these women and their loved ones. However, in two instances Ursula personally confronts her victims. Ursula confronts classmate Helen on a train headed from New York to California, the state of her former finishing school.

This sequence of the murder/suicide of Helen has Ursula concealing the intensity of her hatred and jealousy. She casually mentions to Helen how ostracized she felt: "How I used to envy you girls, your parties, your sororities." Helen sadly laments that Ursula is lucky she doesn't belong to their group, which catastrophic horoscopes has suddenly cursed. Ursula again gently mocks Helen's fears, stating, "You straight thinking, oh-so-rational Anglo-Saxons don't believe in such things, do you?" The inherent threat to the "rational" Anglo-Saxon mind by an alien non-Western consciousness is clearly evident in this exchange. Repeatedly, Hollywood's Oriental archetypes are poised to test the strength of Western logical thought, very often within the geographical confines of Asia itself (as in *The Mask of Fu Manchu* and *The Bitter Tea of General Yen*). However, in *Thirteen Women*, Ursula's mental power retains its potency even though her character physically resides in the West.

Irene Dunne and Myrna Loy in *Thirteen Women*. (MoMA)

Ursula says goodnight to Helen and then disappears, but only briefly. Helen's suicidal struggle seemingly begins quite apart from Ursula's mental influence or physical proximity. Earlier, Helen disclosed to Ursula the intense grief she still experiences over the untimely death of her young "blue-eyed" child. Yet moments later, Ursula's menacing figure is revealed to be in the hallway outside her compartment. The editing subsequently cuts back and forth between Helen's solitary fight against suicidal impulses within her compartment and Ursula's trance-like gaze outside her door. Ursula's eyes seem to be rolling up into her head until a shot is heard and we see Helen's body fall dead.

Ursula, on the one hand, could be understood as one of the horror film's generic clichés, that is, "the character possessed with supernatural powers enabling him/her to possess another character."[14] Still, Ursula owns the gaze in this instance along with the power and control that comes with it. Furthermore, the "enunciation of desire," as stated by Lowry and de Cordova, during this period positions the viewer between Ursula's passionate openly desirous gaze and Helen's sexually tinged submission on the other side of the compartment door. This moment provides a veiled reference to the then taboo subject of lesbianism. In *Thirteen Women,* unlike most classical horror films, the virtually all-female cast is pitted against one another. Would this make Ursula's possession of Helen that causes her death more "reactionary" or "progressive," in Robin Wood's terms?[15] The narrative tries to have it both ways, as Ursula's mentor is the evil male astrologer Yogadachi, although Ursula alone carries out the death sentences to her former classmates.

The sequence ends with Ursula closing her eyes in satisfaction at Helen's death. Ursula's face expresses an almost orgasmic emotional intensity at the consummation of this act of revenge. Indeed, the next shot shows the object of Ursula's abject desire. A hand moves into a close-up of Helen's sorority pin unceremoniously ripped from her blouse. Ursula's action explicitly involves her otherness. She is expressly defined by the rejection of her Caucasian schoolmates because of her nonwhiteness. This element directly defines her otherness relative to the women she seeks to destroy. However, Ursula's obsessive harboring of her hateful and humiliated feelings over the years, coupled with the ferocity of her revenge, positions her as a threat in the spirit of a Fu Manchu.

The second time a formerly rejecting schoolmate is personally confronted (just prior to her own preordained death at the film's end), Ursula articulates the discrimination she has suffered at the hands of whites to classmate Laura Stanhope (played by Irene Dunne):

LAURA: What have I done? What has anyone done to make you so inhuman?

URSULA: Do I hear the very human white race asking that question? . . . Do you know what it means to be a half-breed—a half-caste in a world ruled by whites? If you're a male, you're a coolie. If you're a female, you're, well . . . The white half of me cried for the courtesy and protection that women like you get. The only way I could free myself was by becoming white. And it was almost in my hands when you, you and your Kappa society stopped me. . . . I spent six years slaving to get enough money to put me through finishing school. To make the world accept me as white. But you and the others wouldn't let me cross the color line.

Unlike her wholly Asian counterparts Fu Manchu and General Yen, Ursula pushes at the edges of the purely evil Asian stereotype when she explicitly and passionately voices her own subjection to racial discrimination "in a world ruled by whites." And yet, what is left unspoken in this exchange implies even more disturbing elements such as sexual exploitation and prostitution. Significantly, even her verbal protest remains strategically censored. However, the privilege to express outrage at the racial injustice operating within the Western social order may originate from the strength of the Caucasian half of her racial makeup. Nonetheless, Ursula's villainous status ultimately undermines the impact of her potentially disruptive ideological stance.

Still, fidelity to a strict physical standard does not seem to be the only criterion of what being white means in *Thirteen Women*. Ursula enrolls in a finishing school not to alter her physical appearance but rather to adopt a way of being (which remains unstated yet understood within the context of the film) that would allow her acceptance into white society. Ursula's early attempts to reject her nonwhite half at the finishing school seems to be the unspoken price required for entry into white society.

Ursula exhibits a diabolical determination in her revenge on her schoolmates, a monstrous quality indeed. Laura explicitly calls Ursula "inhuman" when face to face with her. And yet Myrna Loy is never made up to look offensive or even costumed in traditional Asian dress. Perhaps this suggests that her mixed-race biology lies at the heart of her bad characteristics. Unlike the character of Fu Manchu, whose distorted physical features and elaborate Chinese costumes clearly work to reinforce a fiendishly alien nature, Ursula's female allure is incorporated as part of her tainted essence. In her occasional encounters with men (Swami Yogadachi and his underling), she expresses a sexuality that has a trancelike effect on them. Even her sexuality is couched less in terms of physical expression than in mind control.

The premise of *Thirteen Women* sets up certain expectations consistent with Oriental archetypes of the villainous variety. In this Oriental figure a latent fiend exists; it has only to be roused by the right circumstances or situation. His or her ability to do harm is facilitated through vague cultural traditions of the Orient at large. The vagueness of these traditions is key, as elements of religion, spiritualism, and psychic tendencies are often ambiguously configured to create an imagined channel for the subjugation of the Western characters. Ursula's mysticism remains resolutely focused on the revenge and destruction of those who wronged her.

Female Oriental archetypes have traditionally utilized elements of either the vengeful dragon lady, emblematic of the character Ursula Georgi or the shy doll-like maidens exemplified by characters such as Madame Butterfly. The dragon lady archetype usually combines a powerful female allure with a serpentine treachery. She embodies a quintessential cunning nature that is often reflected in stark, severe makeup, hair, and costume styles. Yet the starkness of her appearance belies a rapacious appetite for revenge. This version of Oriental femininity as viewed through the prism of Chinese women at the start of the twentieth century has been documented as representing a shift in the broader popular culture from the more pliant and sexually exploitable stock types to an uneasy amalgam of more provocative and incendiary stereotypes:

> In spite of the greater diversity of images of the Chinese in the post-Exclusion era and the emphasis on the sexual availability of Chinese women, it was not until later in the twentieth century that the Dragon Lady character made it into American popular music and performance in the way that China Dolls and Ming Toys had done previously. There were, however, glimmers of this more dangerous image of Chinese

> femininity, particularly in the portrayal of the offspring of interracial
> sex. Chinese female characters, who in the 1910s and 1920s were tied to
> the vamp, evolved into the sensual and maniacal Dragon Lady archetype
> by the early 1930s. For example, . . . Lien Wha from *The Son-Daughter*.[16]

Helen Hayes's performance of the character Lien Wha ("Star Blossom") in *The Son-Daughter* (1932) offers an eccentric attempt to integrate these two seemingly incongruous performance styles. As noted in the previous chapter, Anna May Wong was reported to have been originally slated to appear in the lead role. She was dropped in favor of Hayes, whose casting apparently necessitated the replacement of all other Chinese actors in the cast. Even those actors in bit parts were replaced to avoid comparison between the made-up white actors and authentic Asian performers.[17]

Even at the level of casting, this film epitomized the trenchant nature of the Oriental guise within Hollywood's film industry. The film (especially Hayes's performance) has been considered an aesthetic failure by some; however, the nature of the role and Hayes's attempt (not to mention the vagaries of the casting process) to negotiate a combination of china doll and dragon lady provides an example of the prevailing image of the Asian female: "The filial daughter, good and pure, is also capable of revenge and murder; she can be a dangerous woman. . . . The stereotypes of Chinese (and more broadly Asian) femininity in part marginalized Chinese women as Other and perpetuated stereotypes of the racialized eternal feminine and vamp."[18]

Based on a play by George M. Scarborough and David Belasco, this film takes as its setting the city of San Francisco's Chinatown. *The Son-Daughter* depicts the story of Lien Wha (played by Helen Hayes), an innocent and playful young maiden whose tender relationship with her traditional father, Dr. Dong Tong (played by Lewis Stone), expresses itself through his nickname for her, "Star Blossom." Happy and gay, Lien Wha sets her sights on the shy student Tom Lee (Ramon Navarro), who ardently though timidly pursues her. After she receives her father's permission to marry Tom Lee, Dr. Tong is approached by political sympathizer Sin Kai (played by H. B. Warner) to betroth his daughter to the highest bidder. The money raised would be used to send weapons to their countrymen in China fighting against political oppression.

Helen Hayes and Ramon Navarro in *The Son-Daughter*. (MoMA)

Dr. Tong agrees to this arrangement without his daughter's knowledge. Initially stunned at the news, Lien Wha ultimately obeys her father's wishes and agrees to marry whoever pays the best price. Fen Sha (played by Warner Oland), one of the wealthiest gamblers in Chinatown, offers one hundred thousand dollars for Lien Wha. After she weds Fen Sha, her father is mysteriously killed. Subsequently, Tom Lee dies in his attempt to buy back Lien Wha's betrothal from Fen Sha. Lien Wha eventually learns that Fen Sha has masterminded the death of the two men she held most dear. Feigning complete ignorance, Lien Wha pretends to prepare for their first wedding night together. Sweetly offering to unbraid his queue, she instead strangles him with it. Her loyal servant comes to fetch her, and she is last seen on a boat headed to China.

What begins as a lighthearted tale of romantic love ends in tragedy and murder. However, the most remarkable feature of *The Son-Daughter* lies in the unusual performance style of its star, Helen Hayes.

Her growth from childlike maiden to resolute womanhood during the course of the story requires an unusual range and set of adjustments. When first seen, Hayes reflects the archetypal visual image of an Oriental maid. Her black hair is pulled into a tiny bun with flowers, she has pencil-thin eyebrows, her upper eyelids are cosmetically altered, she wears dark lipstick, and her hand is demurely placed on her face. It is then revealed that she sits for a portrait painted by her father. Her impassive expression and masklike countenance unceremoniously break as she begins wiggling her nose and asks, "Father, may I move one hand? My nose itches." He nods and she quickly rubs her nose, stating if by rote "I am grateful."

With her father, Lien Wha is alternately obedient and disobedient, coy and plucky, as indeed both the freedoms allowed in American culture and the customs required by Chinese tradition demand a constant and comical negotiation. Her initial exchanges with her father are characterized by abrupt changes from an affected Oriental reticence to a high-spirited assertiveness ascribed to her American upbringing. No attempt is made to disguise her cultural switches between Oriental and American modes. Even her father smiles with amusement at his daughter's obvious attempts to indulge his Eastern traditionalism while yielding to her own Western desires.

This film from the beginning possesses a quality of self-reflexivity regarding the idea of individual identity as performance both culturally inflected as well as gendered. By foregrounding the nature of performance itself, the dynamic relationship between and among variables within Hayes's performance, in particular, becomes even more apparent and vivid. As Lien Wha, Hayes is called on to portray alternately a demure maiden/anxious lover, a wily seductress/brave warrior, and ultimately a vengeful murderess all within an Oriental guise. She is even given different names, Star Blossom and "son-daughter," to distinguish her alternative identities. And unlike General Yen, Lien Wha's fantastic transformations all occur within the waking world.

Lien Wha's encounter with Tom Lee, again, begets exaggerated attempts to embody the countenance of a demure Oriental maiden. While Lien Wha's highly theatrical acting style might first be interpreted as evidence of an inferior performance, it eventually reveals itself as a skill that will prove critical in her later consequential need to beguile and delude. Praying to a Buddhist altar, Lien Wha fervently requests that her lover come to her. Once realizing that Tom Lee has overheard her plea, she reacts in a broad double take, brings out a small fan to cover her face, and kneels on the floor, declaring, "Oh, I shall die of immodesty." Her exaggerated performance is matched by Navarro's studied humility as this scene depicts the two lovers' clumsy attempts to interact within the confines of Oriental custom.

The contrast between smaller, more contained physical gestures in the Oriental facade with broadly physicalized burlesques combines for comic effect. Tom asks Lien Wha, "I am unworthy to stand in the sunlight of your presence. Would you condescendingly pardon me?" It then becomes clear that the direction of the performance and dialogue in this sequence borders on parody and caricature. Unlike the other previously discussed (though also highly artificial) Oriental performances that suggest more literal readings, here the exaggerated theatricality tends to create an almost satiric distance. However, this satiric distance appears to gently mock gender relations as mediated through the Oriental guise rather than take as its focus the Oriental guise itself.

Lien Wha's initially naive overtures toward her lover Tom introduces the issue of playacting a female role as an important part of asserting her individual identity. This component of her characterization establishes the art of gender role-playing as part and parcel of charming and attracting a potential suitor. Lien Wha's femininity is overtly depicted as constructed, unlike the underlying Oriental impersonation enacted by its Caucasian star. This sequence ends with a kiss between the lovers, but not before Tom sings a love song to Lien Wha. Ramon Navarro makes no attempt to camouflage his heavy Spanish accent, while Hayes, Stone, and others speak in a more formal manner while retaining their individual inflections.

However, this comedic tone changes dramatically when Lien Wha must marry a man she does not love. When the couple learns of the forced betrothal to the highest bidder, they protest. Lien Wha even challenges her subordinate female status, asserting, "Must she be sent to the temple of unhappiness because she is unfortunate enough not to be born a son?" However, she eventually capitulates, making a self-sacrificing transformation as she embraces the traditional outlook of her culture. She explains to a heartbroken Tom Lee, "Father tried to hide disappointment that I am not a son. I understand. I will take his place. Whatever one does for love of country is right."

In the bidding scene that follows, Lien Wha places herself in the center of a room surrounded by several men, including Fen Sha. Suddenly determined and resolute, the Chinese maiden becomes like steel as her father sits quietly on the margins. She displays a coquettish allure, using a small fan made of feathers. At once demure and insistent, Lien Wha skillfully and explicitly stages a performance of a coy maiden to induce the wealthy men to energetically bid against one another. And yet the scene is punctuated by her dialogue with her father and a determination distinctly out of character with both naïveté and passivity as she insists that they make the bidding go higher. Even Fen Sha expresses admiration for her shrewd "spirit" and guile before he bids the highest price to win her hand.

Lien Wha's performance of an alluring femme fatale in this scene possesses added complexity and dimension, as she ultimately accomplishes an achievement worthy of a son in her father's eyes when he declares her his "son-daughter." This declaration not only acknowledges Lien Wha's female exhibition in front of the bidders as a performance but further characterizes it as malelike. Clearly, the context of her various female performances determines the interpretation it receives. If engaged with Tom Lee, the role is slightly comical but innocent and romantic. However, with the wealthy male Chinese bidders, the role becomes heroic.

However skillful Lien Wha's performance during the bidding appears, her resolve to avenge the murders of her father and lover reflect an even stronger will. Her spirit in this scene seems possessed by grief as Lien Wha, full of sweetness, pretends to anxiously anticipate her wedding night with the traitorous Fen Sha. Clearly, her gesture to unbraid his queue invites an intimacy and trust, and yet we see the maiden's suddenly maniacal expression before she fatally strangles her husband. Though rationalized through grief, this moment changes Lien Wha into a diabolical force of vengeance. A religious coda at a small altar in the room confirms the maiden's deeply agitated state as she screams, both arms uplifted:

"Great Joss, I thank you for the miracle of strength. I ask no pardon for killing this evil man. I pray you remember my kind father and the knife in the heart of my love Prince and friends of China slaughtered."

[She points to the dead body of Fen Sha.]

"Look upon his evil face. Curse him down to the seven low burning hells without mercy. Great Joss! Great Joss! This is my prayer!"

Seemingly possessed by a rabid, feverish vengeance, Lien Wha has to be removed from the room by a servant. Interestingly, her greatest rage positions itself at the site of a religious icon. But rather than inspire a peaceful state, it seems to incite an even more uncontrolled frenzy.

Lien Wha as Star Blossom exudes the archetypal elements of a guileless and demure maiden, while as the son-daughter she displays a calculated intensity that eventually grows to lethal proportions. Utilizing a small though consistent repertoire of deferential affectations such as batting eyes (cosmetically Orientalized), a slightly cocked head, and shy smile peeking from behind a small fan, Hayes renders the character of Lien Wha as evolving from a childlike figure who puts on her doll-like Star Blossom persona to please her traditional father and win over suitor Tom Lee to a woman possessed by grief who will stop at nothing to avenge her loved ones.

Feminist film critic Mary Ann Doane has suggested in her landmark essay "Film and the Masquerade: Theorizing the Female Spectator" that femininity itself is a cultural construction, a mask that can be worn or removed: "a decorative layer which conceals a non-identity."[19] This type of female masquerade expresses itself in an "excess of femininity" that Lien Wha has, in fact, pointedly displayed: "The masquerade doubles representation; it is constituted by a hyperbolization of the accoutrements of femininity."[20] It is also, according to Doane, aligned with the femme fatale that is labeled by men as the incarnate of evil. Indeed, the workings of the female masquerade in *The Son-Daughter* are foregrounded throughout the narrative, culminating in a predictably heinous deed: murder.

Lien Wha exhibits an all-consuming maniacal fury akin to that of the villainess Ursula Georgi. In the end, both characters when wronged resort to violent retribution despite the differing nature of their provocation. Perhaps a latent fiend does exist in the Oriental figure in spite of all indications to the contrary, such as the guileless innocence of Lien Wha. Ursula's extrasensory perception and Lien Wha's climactic confession to the Chinese idol Joss explicitly link their crimes to the realm of the unseen as they wreak a violent justice. Drawing on illusory elements (both performative and spiritual), these female Oriental archetypes exemplify figures of mystery, exoticism, and danger.

The Orient as Utopia

In Hollywood, the Orient has provided a recurrent place for fantasy and adventure, often of epic proportions. In a less threatening mode, the mystery, exoticism, and mysticism of the East proves to be a powerful lure to characters disillusioned with the West. In the film *Lost Horizon* (1937), directed by Frank Capra, an obviously fictional place—Shangri-La—is placed near an actual geographical area of the Orient: Tibet.

Though produced by the same studio and director (Columbia Pictures and Frank Capra), *Lost Horizon* and *The Bitter Tea of General Yen* differ in terms of both their conception and reception. *Lost Horizon,* based on a best-selling novel by James Hilton, enjoyed great success at the box office, even making *Variety*'s list of top-ten grossing films for 1937. Unlike *The Bitter Tea of General Yen, Lost Horizon* was conceived not as an arty pet project of the director but as a project with an already proven track record of widespread appeal.

The plot of *Lost Horizon* involves the main character, Robert Conway (played by Ronald Colman), a British diplomat and widely acknowledged "Man of the East" who, after rescuing ninety white people from the war-torn city of Baskul in China, boards a plane along with his younger brother George (played by John Howard); Lovett (played by Edward Everett Horton), a fussy paleontologist; Barnard (played by Thomas Mitchell), a shady businessman; and Isabel Jewell (played by Gloria Stone), a sickly prostitute. Unbeknownst to the group, a Mongolian pilot forcibly replaces their original British pilot and flies them to the Tibetan mountains (instead of their planned destination in Shanghai). The pilot dies before the plane eventually crashes.

Led by an English-speaking guide named Chang (played by H. B. Warner), a party of Tibetans guides the group through a brutal snowstorm to the beatific and temperate Shangri-La, located in the Valley of the Blue Moon. Despite initial suspicions and anxiety, they settle contentedly into a community from which it is virtually impossible to leave, with one exception: Robert's brother George. He perceives Shangri-La not as a utopia but as a prison and fights to plan an escape.

In the meantime Robert falls in love with Sondra (played by Jane Wyatt), a girl born within this rarefied world, and discovers from the High Lama (played by Sam Jaffe), who runs the community, that he was brought there to inherit his position of authority. Though initially awed by the honor and responsibility, ultimately George persuades Robert to leave. They leave, but along the way George dies. Robert continues on to the outside world but initially cannot remember the year he spent in Shangri-La. Eventually he does, and when he does he vows to return. With superhuman determination and effort, he eludes those who think him mad and faces the ravages of nature in order to return to the land of his dreams.

The fantasy of the Orient created in the film *Lost Horizon* relies on the illusion of an ambiguous and mysterious setting while providing a specifically negotiated path through the Caucasian-enacted performances of Oriental roles. The fantasy comes through the guise of a clash of cultures, but not unlike the other previously discussed Capra film, *The Bitter Tea of General Yen,* the Orient functions principally as a projection of both repressed desires and fears of the West. And while the utopian Shangri-La might narratively dramatize an alternative existence ostensibly free of racial conflict, this film inadvertently exposes a deep ambivalence toward Asian culture through its traditionally archetypal Oriental performances as well as through bizarre and nightmarish renditions of racial difference.

Shangri-La, the place, inspires deeply ambivalent reactions from the newly arrived passengers. Lovett, the paleontologist, whispers the word "magical" when he first glimpses the stately white buildings, meticulously tended gardens, small fountains, and flocks of doves that fly overhead. However, soon after settling into the interior of the palace and dressed in Oriental costume, he begins to express deep suspicion and extreme anxiety (bordering on panic) about his fate in this new place. Significantly, the outside view of Shangri-La appears decidedly more Western than the interiors that exhibit a distinctly Eastern style.

Ronald Coleman (*far left*) and H. B. Warner (*far right*) in *Lost Horizon*. (MoMA)

Indeed, as the group proceeds into the dining room for their first meal of their stay, a small Buddha (indicative of a spiritual realm) with flowers on either side can be seen on the small ledge above the entrance. Accordingly, individual Oriental archetypes presented in this film also embody qualities that inspire contradictory responses of awe, suspicion, gratitude, respect, ridicule, and camaraderie within the psyches of the Western characters.

The character of Chang inhabits a central position within the narrative and functions as an impressive example of an archetypal Oriental film presence. Chang first appears as a rescuer in a fur hat and coat at the site of the plane crash. British actor H. B. Warner, though not aided by elaborate Orientalizing makeup in this role, does wear glasses (perhaps to make his eyes appear smaller). Indeed, his naturally angular facial features along with the weathering of his obviously advanced years only minimally hint at physical racial difference. His countenance and mannerisms are used much more than his physical features to establish his performance as the elderly Chinese wise man.

When Robert Conway first meets Chang, he addresses Chang in a native dialect to which the Chinese guide responds in impeccable English: "I'm from a nearby lamasery. My name is Chang." He bows low and listens patiently to the passengers' various versions of what brought them there. Lovett, the paleontologist, describes their trip as being "at the mercy of a mad pilot," to which Chang responds indulgently and with slight amusement, "Where is your mad pilot?" Chang also reveals through his gentle mocking that the pilot, despite appearances to the contrary (he did brandish a gun with a menacing visage), was in actuality far from mad and, most likely, a helpmeet for the group of rescuers.

As soon as they get to Shangri-La, Chang is the sole voice and presence, which orients them to their new surroundings. And yet, what will become explicit as the narrative progresses is Chang's habit of speaking in a way that obscures more than it clarifies. Even his initial statement to the weary passengers—"Welcome to Shangri-La. You see we are sheltered by mountains on every side. A strange phenomenon for which we are very grateful."—connotes an aura of mystery. In this instance (and throughout), he imparts a fact but imbues it with the specter of something unspoken.

Once ensconced in the palatial quarters of the lamasery, Chang joins the group for an elaborate dinner. But before Chang arrives, Lovett expresses his distrust to Robert, explaining how he doesn't like the place because it's simply "too mysterious." Moments later, Chang arrives wearing a Chinese costume (as do the newly arrived passengers). With hands clasped and soft-spoken politeness, he addresses the group as "my friends" who "shouldn't have waited for me."

Very much like a nurturing shepherd, Chang (almost always seen with his hands clasped) intently listens to the passengers' queries about Shangri-La and answers their questions in a gentle but matter-of-fact manner. His calm demeanor stands in stark contrast to the Western characters, particularly when he tells them that they will be essentially cut off from the outside world indefinitely. Still, when Chang retires to bed, he specifically addresses Robert with a pointed "Goodnight, Mr. Conway," and the diplomat responds politely by rising out of his seat with a "Goodnight, sir." Chang functions here successively as a figure of mistrust, mystery, and, finally, respect. Even Lovett's subsequent grumblings about Chang to Conway—"I do not like that man, he's too vague"—fail to undermine the aura of respect and authority that his character initially establishes.

Chang's status shifts abruptly two weeks after the group arrives in Shangri-La. On the way to dinner, George complains about their lot as virtual prisoners, and Robert attempts to be reassuring. He comments that their stay in Shangri-La is really "not so bad" and is, in fact, "very pleasant." However, when Robert enters the dining room he mocks Chang (who is not present). Robert shuffles in small steps with arms forming ninety-degree angles at his sides and body rocking from side to side. In a forced whisper he intones, "Please, please, do not wait for me. I eat so very little." The group laughs easily at his humor, and the moment quickly passes.

Robert's parody of Chang is revealing in its brevity and clarity. This scene follows several in which Chang and Robert converse about the history, social order, and vision of Shangri-La as they stroll throughout the palace. These conversations appear to intrigue Robert while proving slightly frustrating as well. Chang seems to always be holding some information back. In fact, Robert, at one point, explicitly states to Chang that "for a man who talks a great deal, it's amazing how unenlightening you can be." And despite his reassurances to the contrary that he is quite content with things as they stand, Robert vents more than a little frustration and hostility in his caricatured rendering of Chang.

An element of condescension plainly exists, particularly in Robert's rendition of Chang's walk. Chang's walk incorporates a confident long stride, not the quick stunted shuffle that Robert performs. Director Frank Capra explicitly names a quality of courtly grace that he observed in actor H. B. Warner before casting him in the role of Chang. His dignified manner, in large part, defines his character and makes its derision all the more striking. What might be dismissed as a moment of playacting fun illustrates an attempt to comedically contain the threat that Chang's Oriental authority poses to the group of Westerners. Both seductive and frightening, the Oriental figure inspires containment through the Caucasian performance (however brief), even at the level of plot.

It is not surprising that the next moments and scenes involve angry outbursts and confrontations directed toward Chang from the group of passengers. He immediately diffuses their hot tempers by deferring to the authority of the High Lama. Perplexed, the group thought that Chang "ran the place." However, Chang states that only the High Lama, not Chang, can provide the answers they wish. This shift in authority is significant in that it is eventually revealed that the High Lama is, in fact, a Belgian priest, formerly Father Perrault, who founded Shangri-La. The changing of the guard from Oriental to European effectively, if indirectly, extinguishes the storm of protest from all the group members except George, who remains adamant in his wish to leave.

While embodying different racial identities in the narrative (although they are portrayed by two Caucasian actors), the figures of the High Lama and Chang unexpectedly mirror one another. Dubbed the "number two Lama" by Capra, Chang's role prepares the audience for Robert's visit with the two-hundred-year-old Father Perrault, who also appears as a figure of cultural ambiguity. The heavily made-up Sam Jaffe portrays the High Lama in Tibetan robes under softly diffused lighting. His age is so advanced as to obscure his features as distinctly Occidental or Oriental. His whispered utterances seem only a more exaggerated version of Chang's gently spoken words.

And while espousing an essentially Christian ethos, the High Lama remains a figure who inhabits his position in terms of an Eastern culture. His Tibetan title of High Lama (which virtually replaces his older one of Father Perrault), the Tibetan robes he wears, and his difficult-to-distinguish facial features all work to position his character as a cultural composite of both East and West. Although his palace, furnishings, and books definitely have a Western bias, his vision and appearance suggest a more fundamental influence by the indigenous culture. Clearly, this Oriental fantasy works to construct an Orient that systematically almost eliminates the Oriental figure as demonstrated by the revelation of the Belgian Father Perrault as High Lama. Ultimately, this otherworldly Oriental utopia provides a potent illustration of the Orientalist fantasy to create, enact, and contain the Orient entirely within a Western framework in order to constitute a unified Western morality tale.

The theme in *Lost Horizon* that would seem to transcend cultural divisions of East and West involves the process of aging. One of the benefits of living in Shangri-La, a virtually strife-free environment, results in residents who live to extraordinarily old ages. (They also don't show their age until they become quite elderly.) Yet even this utopian phenomenon takes on a racial and cultural specificity.

In the film version, the issue of physical aging is addressed at key moments in the narrative. Indeed, it provides one of the most powerful climaxes in the film's story. The topic comes up at different points, with the two hundred-year-old High Lama and even Sondra's character, who admits to Robert of being a mere thirty years old. But the plight of Maria (played by Mexican-born actress Margo), being in actuality in her sixties while insisting that she is only twenty, provides the vehicle by which the physical difference produced by advanced age is collapsed with racial difference.

As was stated earlier, the High Lama's age tends to obscure any distinct racial elements in his features. In addition, the elderly Chang's facial features bear little resemblance to a distinctly Oriental racial type. His demeanor and name provide the strongest clues to his racial identity. Curiously, Chang never reveals his age. In a scene leading to the film's central point of crisis, his character is depicted visually and in dialogue as a mysterious and secretive presence. After a leisurely chess game, Robert walks restlessly away from the table. Chang gazes intently at him while smoking a large Oriental pipe. Shot in profile, Chang appears as a highly stylized silhouette. The style of this shot differs from all others of him. The effect is mysterious, mystical, and otherworldly.

Maria, looking for George, then enters and quickly leaves. Chang then tells Robert the story of Maria's actual age. Robert subsequently inquires how old Chang is, only to have him respond with the enigmatic statement of "age is a limit you impose upon yourselves." This is in striking contrast to the High Lama who, despite his position as the most elusive and mystical of figures, permits his age to be revealed early on.

Eventually, Maria helps convince George and then Robert to leave Shangri-La. Chang previously warned that if anyone leaves Shangri-La, they would revert to the physical appearance of their chronological age in the outside world. This is dramatically demonstrated as Maria changes into an old woman on the brutal trek away from the valley through the snowy mountains with Robert and George. Her bizarre change causes George to jump to his death. However, what's most interesting about her change is a point that Leland Poague also notes, namely that while Maria is "depicted as Russian" she "is portrayed in her last moments by an elderly Oriental woman."[21]

What can account for this type of interracial shift within one figure? In *Lost Horizon,* racial divisions are upheld while constantly being renegotiated. These two seemingly contradictory dynamics are central to the depiction of the Oriental in this film as well as in the larger body of Hollywood films. Maria's reversion and demise are rendered in terms of monstrosity. Her character doesn't simply lose her youth but does so with hideous swiftness. And if this process alone wasn't shocking enough, the Oriental guise of racial difference is added to the mix of physical alterity. The collapsing of race and age in this instance is revealing in that it indirectly positions the Oriental countenance as something to be rejected and feared outright.

Overall, in *Lost Horizon* the locale itself provides a malleable repository for both the deep fears and the desires of the Western mind. Immediately after their plane crashes, Robert and George search the cockpit and find the pilot dead and also find a map. The language and terms they use while interpreting the markings on the map subtly suggest a psychological dimension to their physical situation. They describe where they've landed as a place where "civilization ends," as "just a blank on the map" and "unexplored country," and as a site that "nobody ever reached." These phrases not only describe physical proximity but also refer to the realm of dreams and fantasy. The point "where civilization ends" can be translated as a place where Western inhibitions could be cast away. "Unexplored country" can also be understood as unexplored areas of consciousness and desire. A "blank on the map" suggests the mutability of places where dreams dwell, while an area that "nobody ever reached" can be strongly associated with flights of fantasy.

Frank Capra describes the site of Shangri-La as "hidden in the uncharted Himalayas—a thousand miles from nowhere." His description belies the cultural and geographical specificity of Shangri-La within the confines of the Orient. Far from existing as an independent cultural entity, it is significant that Shangri-La adopts the cultural trappings of its neighbors in Tibet. The connection between Shangri-La as a creation of fantasy and its placement on the Asian continent is illustrative of a persistent pattern of cultural containment as Western illusions, desires, and dreams are thrust into an Oriental realm.

Lost Horizon adapts the exoticism of Shangri-La to encompass the strange and seductive dichotomy so clearly embodied by individual Oriental characters such as General Yen and Ursula Georgi in *Thirteen Women.* The utopian Orient incorporates elements of both heaven and hell. The possibility of resurrection and rebirth exists when transported to an otherworldly environment, as Robert's character clearly illustrates. However, the price exacted by this enticing environment in *Lost Horizon* is abduction as hostages. Furthermore, this Shangri-La contains distinctly supernatural aspects, such as its arrested aging phenomena (and its reverse if one leaves) as well as its geographic isolation. Far from being contradictory, these oppositions of the bizarre and the enchanted are fundamental to the archetype.

Whether depicted in more conventional commercial fare or in loftier, more upscale prestige projects, certain conceptions of the Oriental persist. Perhaps the most striking similarity occurs between *The Mask of Fu Manchu,* a modest generic vehicle for Boris Karloff, and *The Bitter Tea of General Yen,* an arty star vehicle for Barbara Stanwyck and its director, Frank Capra. Both utilize the same fiendish Mandarin image (grotesque makeup, long fingernails, and a predatory demeanor) for its Oriental male leads even though the latter film attempts a more complex depiction and social critique on interracial relations.

Thirteen Women presents the Eurasian female figure as both victim and victimizer, a social outcast possessed by a vengeful nature. *The Son-Daughter* depicts a female character who exhibits a wide range of seemingly contradictory Oriental archetypal features (both exceedingly demure and hysterically vindictive), all contained within a single narrative. Actress Helen Hayes's performance enacts a set of traits that reconfigure and reformulate according to the changing contexts in the narrative. This adaptability provides one of the hallmarks of the Oriental guise not only when operating within a narrative but also evident in its evolution in different films over time. Finally, *Lost Horizon* presents the potentially transformative effects of a utopian Orient and yet also reveals an undercurrent of racial antipathy apparent in its pathological treatment of racial difference (when merged with the extremely aged), caricatured role-playing, and nearly total exclusion of Orientals from the fantasy.

Hollywood's Oriental tends to expose deep ambivalences of admiration and danger, desire and repulsion, exoticism and the grotesque, freedom and captivity. These figures create an Other incarnation that functions as a projection of Western fantasies. Releasing transgressive elements of eroticism, aggression, sadism, and magical powers, the Oriental provides a recurrent repository for these repressed wishes. Most importantly, the Caucasian actor who performs the Oriental guise under the mask of makeup, costume, gesture, and speech exposes the artificial constructedness of these characters. The cinematic performances in this chapter involuntarily acknowledge their artificiality, like an unconscious confession.

TWO

Masters of the Macabre
The Oriental Detective

     A black car drives down a dark deserted street. A young Asian woman knocks on a door as she looks around nervously in the shadow of the building's entrance. An Asian manservant answers the door, and the elegantly dressed but desperate young woman asks to speak to Mr. Wong. The servant asks her name, but she refuses, simply stating, "Tell Mr. Wong, someone wants to see him, someone who needs his help." The servant goes to fetch his master, and for the first time in the film we glimpse Mr. Wong, played by Boris Karloff, in a small makeshift scientific laboratory. The lab is well lit, and Karloff appears to be deeply absorbed in his experiments. Unlike his previous screen incarnation as the megalomaniacal Fu Manchu, there is no mirror in this laboratory to magnify his facial features. Rather, the actor in this film wears a shirt, tie, and dark vest and sports dark glasses and dark slick hair.

     This scene occurs in the film *Mr. Wong in Chinatown* (1939), an example from one of three Oriental detective series to be discussed in this chapter. The contrast between the Fu Manchu laboratory and the Wong laboratory would initially seem to be emblematic of a completely dichotomous relationship between Hollywood's Oriental villain and Oriental detective hero. However, the casting of Caucasian actor Boris Karloff as the leading actor in both films and both characters' shared penchants for scientific knowledge and experimentation illustrate how some fundamental similarities can exist between two ostensibly dissimilar cinematic types.

In this chapter, we focus our analysis on the Oriental detective performance. Though commonly positioned as a more normalized figure in relation to the fantastical and often villainous archetypes discussed in chapter 1, the Oriental detective nonetheless negotiates a complex set of traits. A closer analysis of this most popular of Oriental archetypes will consider how both admirable and adverse elements reconfigure to mitigate the threat of even a heroic Asian character.

Like their villainous counterparts, the Oriental detective is performed, as a rule, solely by Caucasian actors. Once again, this performance practice underlies the essential conception of Hollywood's most popular and durable Oriental archetype: the detective. The choice of the term "archetype" rather than the more pejorative term "stereotype" in this chapter attempts to avoid either a strictly positive or rigidly negative connotation. This simplistic dualism limits our attempt to fully appreciate the complex nature of the detective character. Its use refers only to a recurring character who can be traced across several films rather than to a strict Jungian definition.

The casting of particular Caucasian actors and their distinctive visual appearance and physical performances not only significantly influenced the shape and direction of their characters but also the films themselves. This chapter will examine how a succession of Oriental detective characters, specifically the Chinese police detective Charlie Chan, the Japanese secret agent Mr. Moto, and the Chinese private investigator Mr. Wong, were constructed to appeal to a mass audience. These characters and their filmed adaptations reflect the nature of that era's fears and anxieties and the attempt to contain them. There is much we can learn through this analysis about what appears on the surface to be a positive Asian portrayal, especially in relation to patently negative characters such as Fu Manchu.

The Oriental detective exists as a compromise formation in the middle ground between the evil Oriental character of the dark and sinister underworld (as introduced in chapter 1) and a figure who represents the ordinary, commonplace familiarity of the everyday world.

This constant negotiation between these two polarities helped create one of the most acceptable and enduring characters in Hollywood. The Oriental detective archetype is much more than a simple iconic figure. This archetype survives as a cinematic depiction that is simultaneously novel yet deeply conventional. These movie characters served the cultural status quo while appearing to modify it.

This interplay between novelty and conventionality is not, in itself, an innovation; rather, it reflects Hollywood's overall production strategy/dynamic of standardization and differentiation. This strategy not only provided the economic basis for the mass production of motion pictures but also produced an aesthetic framework for film content and its promotion. Similarly, within individual films, specific elements were utilized to encourage a strong measure of stability. This industry practice is particularly relevant to the Oriental detective film series that originated mainly within the highly formulaic (even by broader industry standards) category of B movies.

What is notable about this dynamic between the conventional and the unique, which defines the archetype of the Oriental detective, is that this cinematic character is often positioned as a uniformly positive depiction of an Asian figure. Frequently interpreted as a mere repudiation of villainous Asian screen depictions in the vein of a Fu Manchu, the Oriental detective ostensibly offers a capable, sympathetic hero. The most well known of several actors to play the part of Charlie Chan is the actor Warner Oland. As the Charlie Chan series, in particular, attests, three Caucasian actors (Warner Oland, Sidney Toler, and Roland Winters) were consecutively cast as the durable Oriental detective over the course of the almost twenty-year continuous run of the series. Through the close analysis of distinct elements and patterns within the performances and conventions of this subgenre, this chapter will attempt to reveal how this seemingly benign Oriental archetype is as strictly contained and codified as its more malevolent counterparts. Far from being simply the converse of earlier and patently odious Oriental archetypes as popular opinion would suggest, these detective figures are more complex creations who strongly advance meritorious qualities as well as less admirable ones.

Of course, what must not be overlooked is the paradox of Caucasian actors portraying specifically Asian types. Not only does a Caucasian actor provide a means of identification with a non-Western character, but he also supplies access to an alternative ethnic experience. Through the physical embodiment of an Oriental countenance, the Caucasian actor creates a potent vehicle for a socially transgressive experience (to inhabit the identity of another ethnicity) while, simultaneously, limiting that experience through the recognition of that same actor as also conceivably (if not always definitively) Caucasian.

The Oriental detective possesses elements potentially ominous and sinister, not unlike their explicitly virulent counterparts. However, these qualities are often couched in terms of the character's accomplishments and achievements. Areas such as mental agility, education, scientific knowledge, physical prowess or proficiency in the martial arts, language expertise, and mastery in disguise can be positioned as either threatening or admirable. Recall the intimidation and danger that the highly educated character of Fu Manchu (with three graduate degrees) posed to both the other white characters and the West as an entity.

This archetype embodies a range of customary traits such as a generalized congeniality and a cooperative temperament. A fundamental good humor and good-naturedness along with employment in respectably well-known vocations mitigates the unusual capabilities these characters routinely display that potentially border on the bizarre, weird, and mysterious. Yet any enigmatic traits such as psychic abilities, highly developed powers of observation, and the razor-sharp deductions that dazzle and amaze other characters nevertheless initially provokes some fear and concern by some character in the narrative.

The detective is routinely subjected to insults by certain characters during the course of the narrative. These affronts are sometimes silently tolerated by the character but more often are structured within the narrative as opportunities for the detective to earn the respect of characters, particularly those unfamiliar with his reputation and stature in his vocation. These moments of ridicule are often preceded by an undeniably singular achievement or accomplishment by this archetype. This pattern is explicit and through all three detective series is an illustration of a strategy of containment in the heroic status of this archetype. Patently bigoted views are routinely given voice by supporting characters followed by momentary gratification of their comeuppance by the Oriental detective.

The Detective Character as Metatext

A number of key components common to all three selected series (Charlie Chan, Mr. Moto, and Mr. Wong) effectively establish a metatext of the Oriental detective archetype. This metatext not only transcends narrative singularities within individual film texts but also surpasses dramatic patterns occurring within each of the three film series. Which qualities and traits are fundamental to the creation of this Oriental characterization? What elements are consistently projected and allowed or, conversely, contained, repressed, and displaced within this cinematic model? How do the combination of factors create a distinctly Oriental character?

One of the hallmarks of the Oriental detective archetype is an implicit or explicit affiliation with the national political interests of the United States and/or Europe. In this context, the Western affiliation is rather diffuse but still remains a critical element in the creation of a more heroic Oriental archetype. Rather than acting as a government agent for specifically political ends, the Oriental detective is, without exception, depicted as a loyal servant of any number of chosen institutions of Western authority. Through his adherence to the authority of the West, the detective is fundamentally distinguished from his villainous counterparts, whose actions are motivated by a non-Western–oriented agenda (often both personal and nationalistic). In part this is achieved through the effacement of any traces of fealty to a non-Western country of origin and/or a perceived racial/cultural homeland. Clearly, the detective, when identified as solely non-Western, is interpreted by these other characters to be a figure with the strong potential for treachery and betrayal. However, in these instances, the detective is given the opportunity to demonstrate his fidelity to the West through the naming of a close association with a Western institution, or another Caucasian character intervenes on his behalf. A variety of components help foster the representation of this patriotic profile.

What is often counterposed to or substituted for the detective's non-Western origins is his residency and/or citizenship in the United States, U.S. territory, or some other Westernized locale. The Western residency/citizenship component of this archetype provides an implicit yet uniform cultural context for the detective's formation as an ardent operative of the West. Charlie Chan is from Honolulu, Hawaii (then a U.S. territory), and Mr. Wong resides in San Francisco, California. On the basis of residency and citizenship alone, these two detective characters establish a fundamental affinity for the West as well as being effectively positioned as subject to its authority. When this issue is not dramatized in this way, it is left decidedly vague, a contrary yet not dissimilar effort that also serves to mollify any possible threat of national infidelity within this archetype.

Charlie Chan attains his detective status within the Hawaiian police force. Thus, he acquires his rank through an institutional policing structure/hierarchy. In this way, his status is conferred solely by the West. Also, Chan exclusively works in concert with other Western policing authorities both within the United States and its territories and abroad. Mr. Moto, whose professional status is left very vague, represents somewhat of a departure from Chan's depiction. This is a major change from the written stories where Moto's character is quite explicitly working as an agent on behalf of the Japanese government. As a literary figure, the Japanese detective is perceived as a fair and just individual but is clearly working in his country's national/political interests. However, the film series' initial installment, *Think Fast, Mr. Moto* (1937), depicts Moto as the owner of an import-export business whose involvement in mysteries is strictly a hobby.

In later films, Moto is expressly identified as an active and reputed agent for the "international secret police." Significantly, even in this context, Moto's presumed internationalism routinely translates into a Westernized political context. Either working for and with American and European clients and/or government authorities or working within a Western milieu, the detective remains essentially an operative of Western political agency and authority. Clearly, the cinematic adaptation reverses and effaces the central nationalistic element that provided, in the literary source, the fundamental motivation for much of his character's actions.

The character of Mr. Wong, like Chan, also works in tandem with the U.S. policing structure. Sought out and consulted by the local police as a loyal citizen, Wong operates in the interests of the country's established power structure. Though his professional status as a detective is left somewhat vague, his investigative activities are performed with the sanction of local law enforcement authorities. Loyal to the place where he lives and where he is a citizen, the Oriental detective is never depicted as working in any capacity for non-Western interests. The detective functions as an individual agent unquestionably working in concert with, reporting to, or in association with local police authorities in the United States and abroad.

Each Oriental detective character has particular elements in his profile or background that are utilized in the service of presenting a more culturally homogeneous figure for Western audiences. These elements tend to fall into two general categories: higher education and a lack of association with a larger racial/cultural community. Interestingly, the perceived racial/cultural homeland or country of origin of Charlie Chan, Mr. Moto, and Mr. Wong is based on physical evidence rather than statements of fact. In none of the films do the characters specifically mention a place of birth. The naming of a Western institution of higher learning, however, often serves as a crucial component in the perceived assimilation and nationalistic allegiance of the Oriental detective. Still, the ultimate Oriental screen villain, Fu Manchu, who represents the antithesis of Western assimilation with his patently hostile ambitions for Asian world domination, also earned three doctoral degrees in philosophy (Edinburgh), law (Christ College), and medicine (Harvard). Clearly, indications of a Western educational experience alone may not signal an affinity for and loyalty to the West. Nonetheless, for the Oriental detective archetype, this factor supplements many other similar elements that support a broader Western cultural orientation, particularly as they appear in key dramatic moments.

Mr. Moto is recognized as a Stanford University graduate and fraternity member in the first film of the series, *Think Fast, Mr. Moto* (1937). After these facts are revealed as part of a rather casual conversation over drinks, Moto is embraced as a "brother" by a younger Stanford graduate from the same fraternity. However, moments later this fact is presented in response to another character's suspicion of Moto after he is introduced as being from Japan. This academic association and degree completion do not alone categorically represent acceptance by or cultural assimilation to the West. What distinguishes Moto's portrayal, in this respect, is the addition of the social cachet of membership in a college fraternity. His status as a fraternity brother to another character in the narrative adds a critical social dimension in the assimilation of Western mores. This extra dimension expands the boundaries of his acceptance by, affinity with, and knowledge of the West. He is more intimately enveloped into the cultural fold and made more palatable as an operative for American interests.

In the first installment of the Mr. Wong series, *Mr. Wong, Detective* (1938), Wong refers to his work with an American physicist/scientist character at Oxford University. In the second film of the series, *The Mystery of Mr. Wong* (1939), the detective is reputed to have studied at both Oxford and Heidelberg. Attendance at two European universities here functions as a meaningful vehicle for the cultural legitimization and assimilation of this Oriental detective.

The character of Charlie Chan presents a variant of the Western education/assimilationist trope. Though Charlie Chan is not directly associated with any institution of higher learning, his children are depicted as unmistakable products of American cultural life. The frequent appearance of his very Americanized children is a vital part of this detective's persona. They speak with no trace of a Chinese accent; in fact, their speech is peppered with decidedly American colloquialisms such as "Pop," "swell," and the like. The general demeanor of these offspring explicitly indicates, if indirectly, a U.S.-based education and socialization. Both Chan's Number One Son (played by Keye Luke) and, later in the series, his Number Two Son (played by Victor Sen Yung) not only appear but perform significant supporting roles. This also applies to an offspring who never appears, Chan's oldest daughter Rose who is said to be attending a university on the mainland (United States). Thus, Chan's closest association to Western education comes through the portrayals of his children, with the elder detective as the doting, proud patriarch.

The omission and repression of certain cultural characteristics systematically weakens the link between the detective and the larger community of his kinsmen. This critical connection between the individual character and a broader group is either highly restricted or suppressed altogether, the result of which works to support the depiction of this Oriental archetype as essentially an outsider and an isolated figure. This is particularly evident with Charlie Chan, who appears to function primarily in a world of Americans and Europeans and owes his greatest loyalties personally to them. Mr. Moto, though ultimately classified as an international operative, is also depicted as essentially separate from members of his country of origin, Japan. He too functions within a fundamentally Western cultural context.

Mr. Wong is less cut off from a larger Chinese community, although his encounters and associations with his fellow Chinese are quite specific and pointed. In the film *Mr. Wong in Chinatown* his encounter with the Chinese secret society in San Francisco's Chinatown is rendered far from comfortable or desirable. Mr. Wong interacts somewhat awkwardly with the members of the association, and the small group of Chinese men are portrayed as vaguely criminal, unseemly, and suspicious.

Originally serialized in *Collier's* magazine by author Hugh Wiley beginning in 1935, the exploits of the distinguished private detective Mr. Wong began in 1938 through Monogram Pictures. Monogram, a low-budget studio specializing in B movie production, clearly hoped to duplicate the success of Fox's Chan and Moto series with films based on the Mr. Wong character. The Oriental detective series, with its total of six films, spanned only three years until its demise in 1941. Confined to a minimum of characters and sets, these films are notable for their casting of veteran actor Boris Karloff in the title role of the Chinese detective, James Lee Wong.

While the meager production values of the Wong series might not measure up to its more costly predecessors, these films do offer a lead-ing performance that utilizes a minimum of cues to indicate his inter-pretation of an Oriental detective such as distinctive costuming (e.g., slick black hair, black glasses, three-piece suit, boutonniere, umbrella) and a generally deferential acting style. Lacking narrative elaborations such as disguises, doubles, or caricatured playacting, Karloff's perfor-mance of the Mr. Wong character relies primarily on its association to the actor's previous screen roles, the character's highly codified manner of dress, and his method of interaction with other characters. Due to the film's exceedingly formulaic structure—including the use of two recurring supporting characters, a police detective and a girl reporter—the archetypal qualities of this Chinese detective tend to be more ob-vious and static. Remarkably, after Karloff's tenure this low-budget detective series cast Chinese actor Keye Luke (formerly, Chan's Num-ber One Son) to replace him in the leading role of Chinese detective

Wong in what turned out to be the sixth and final film in the series, *The Phantom of Chinatown* (1941).

The Chan, Moto, and Wong characters are all conceived as exceptional figures in the Western cultural milieu. Indeed, it is precisely the unusual phenomenon of the Oriental character inhabiting an officially sanctioned position of authority in law enforcement that distinguishes this Oriental archetype. Other Oriental agents are not routinely featured; however, when an appearance does occur, these characters are depicted as minor players who are basically inconsequential to the film's narrative plot. *Mr. Moto's Gamble* (1938), originally conceived as a Charlie Chan picture, provides a rare exception to this pattern. The film's cast includes Keye Luke as Lee Chan, eldest son of the Chinese detective Charlie Chan. In the first scene of this film, Lee Chan briefly sends greetings to Moto from his "Pop," Charlie, for whom Moto humbly expresses admiration, and yet Charlie Chan is never mentioned again.

In all three film series, the detectives are sought out as the "only" detective able to solve the case. This is not, in itself, unusual; most leading detective characters are positioned as the inevitable choice for solving the case. However, unlike the Oriental detective archetype, most other cinematic detectives' distinct individual abilities, attributes, and disposition (i.e., those of Sherlock Holmes or Sam Spade) are not depicted as primarily the result of a specific racial or cultural heritage. The closest any of the detectives comes to an Oriental professional colleague occurs in the final Mr. Moto installment, *Mr. Moto's Last Warning* (1939). However, the role (notably performed by an Asian actor) is that of a double who masquerades as Mr. Moto during the opening scenes of the film. It is only after the death of this character early on in the plot that this character is acknowledged as an individual presence and esteemed colleague in his own right. This illustration comes closest to acknowledging that there might be other Oriental detectives or agents out there. Still, the standard pattern in the exclusion of any similar detective figures in the film's narratives implicitly establishes the Oriental detectives not only as exceptional characters but also, more significantly, as generally anomalous figures.

With the exception of Charlie Chan, all the detectives ordinarily function in a familial vacuum. Mr. Moto has no friends like himself. However, in at least one of the films from the series, he is allowed a date with an attractive Asian woman (portrayed by an Asian actress) who also works as an operative. Yet this instance provides a notable exception to the usual narrative model of communal isolation of the Oriental detective archetype. Frequent fraternization with members of one's own race, even in recreational activities, threatens to undermine the established pattern of cultural/racial segregation that defines these characters. Mr. Wong appears to be on the periphery of American/Chinese American social life. In fact, a client who surprises Wong at home one evening in *Mr. Wong, Detective,* finds the detective amusing himself with a scientific experiment. His encounters with other Chinese almost always occur in a professional capacity utilizing a professional distance. Other Chinese are related to primarily as suspects or clients or as communal resources to aid him in his objective in a current case. His home life is not depicted as extravagant, yet he employs a live-in Asian servant, a luxury usually available only to the wealthy elite. Wong appears to be both a member of a more privileged class and an uneasy member of the Chinese cultural minority.

Charlie Chan's character is a notable exception to this pattern. The famous detective often refers to other characters (almost always Caucasian) as friends and colleagues while also frequently mentioning the activities and accomplishments of his children. Yet when Chan's Number One Son or Number Two Son appear in the film narratives, they are positioned strictly as comic relief. Though Chan's children are performed as thoroughly Americanized Chinese, they are depicted as thoroughly inept at detective work. Whether portrayed as characters in the film series or merely displayed as curious figures (one of ten children) in a family photograph, Chan's offspring are presented uniformly as fodder for the amusement of the other characters. Significantly, Chan's wife is rarely seen or referred to in the series, which works to position the detective as an indulgent paternal figure rather than a virile husband. Chan's familial connections with his children, though frequently acknowledged, are not rendered as culturally affirming or providing traditional continuity.

Actor Warner Oland played the role of Charlie Chan for Twentieth Century Fox sixteen times beginning in 1931 until his death in 1938. His successor Sidney Toler played the role twenty-two times for Fox and Monogram, and Roland Winters continued the series after Toler's death in 1947 six times for Monogram until the series ended in 1949. According to William K. Everson in his book *The Detective in Film,* Warner Oland did not originate the role of Charlie Chan in Hollywood but was the fourth and best-known actor to play the role. The detective was first played by George Kuwa in a 1926 ten-chapter serialization, produced by Pathe, of the Charlie Chan book *The House without a Key.* This portrayal was followed in 1928 with a performance by Sojin Kamiyama in *The Chinese Parrot* and then the first sound film portrayal by actor E. L. Park in *Behind That Curtain* (Twentieth Century Fox, 1929). Oland's portrayal began two years later in 1931. Although actors Kuwa and Kamiyama were of Japanese descent, Park was British. Notably, none were Chinese.

Why Hollywood discontinued the portrayal of Chan by Asians is unknown, but this certainly reflects a consistent creative dynamic within the film industry. The move from Asian to Caucasian actors as the players of Orientals in the American imagination—systematically fabricated from within and, most insistently, from without—is quite clear in this instance. It is interesting to note that the two Japanese actors cast as Chan occurred during the silent era before the vocal component of the character's performance had emerged. Additionally, in both of the silent depictions, Chan has a supporting rather than a leading role. By the time of the most complete performative depiction in the sound film *Behind That Curtain,* the invariable Hollywood casting correction had transpired, with the character safely embodied by a British actor.

Overall, for the Oriental detective archetype, friends, family, and broader communal contacts are omitted, significantly minimized, or strictly codified. Because the Oriental detective is rarely associated with a larger racial/cultural community, his cultural rituals appear essentially out of their cultural context. Cultural rites such as the Japanese tea ceremony, prayer at an altar, or ink brush painting are customs that usually would link an individual to a community but here are rendered as activities distinctly separate from any communal practice. Not only do these activities hold the detective character in cultural isolation as solitary activities, but the selection and repetition of similar activities reveal a pattern attributable to Western cultural stereotypes of both the Chinese and Japanese.

Qualities such as close observation, resourcefulness, tenacity, and mastery that the Oriental detective characteristically embodies are commonly ascribed to their non-Western racial and cultural heritage. They are presented as part of a specifically cultural way of being, means of perception, and state of mind. These attributes are also depicted as distinctly lacking in the Western officials who have requested his help to solve a case. Thus, the capabilities of a Chan, Moto, or Wong are placed within the limits of a specialized or dissimilar mystical knowledge, which seems alien to the West. By setting apart certain attributes as racially and culturally defined, the Oriental detective is prevented from direct competition with his Western colleagues. The Western police are inclined to display impatience along with a quickness or hastiness to draw conclusions, whereas the Oriental detective is very slow, methodical, and closely observant, very much a listener and receptor. Armed with his culturally specific traits, this archetype operates more as a strange marvel and less as the superior competitor to his Western counterparts.

The extraordinary capabilities that distinguish the Oriental detective from his Western counterparts ultimately produces either effusive admiration or, at the very least, a grudging respect from the other main characters. Yet the detective's progress during the course of each case tends to be vigorously resisted by at least one character. This explicit resistance is most frequently expressed through the amusement and/or mockery of the detective's manner rather than through openly antagonistic confrontations. Although Charlie Chan also customarily offers his unique sayings in the context of witty and amusing banter, he (along with Mr. Moto and Mr. Wong) also consistently tolerates the bemused reactions or ridicule of other main characters when they suggest and propose a course of action relating to a case. This occurs to a lesser degree with friends and acquaintances already familiar with the distinct manner and process of the Oriental detectives, whereas with other more oblivious characters (who, not insignificantly, are frequently depicted as objects of ridicule in their own right) the response can be laden with barely veiled hostility.

At first glance, a funny dismissal or amusing trivialization of the Oriental detective's knowledge and capabilities by a character who, himself, is considered comical or humorous might be assumed to substantially temper the reception of such remarks. Indeed, the tacit indulgence of the detective as well as other familiar acquaintances would appear to position any potentially unfavorable or offensive responses as patently absurd and humorous. On one level this does occur: the audience and any other characters who know of the detective's flawless crime-solving reputation recognize the foolishness of any figure who doubts his capabilities. However, it is important to also consider why a character of this type exists as an indispensable element in these narratives. These characters articulate some of the most well known clichés and stereotypical beliefs about the Chinese and Japanese with their often careless or disagreeable attitudes. Yet they appear to provide both a mouthpiece for these biases as well as a means to refute them. Whether through a known acquaintance, an antagonistic stranger, or a comic buffoon, the routine inclusion of such a perspective, though always expressed through humor, illustrates the delicate balancing act in the portrayal of a more heroic Oriental archetype.

All three detectives possess distinctive and distinguishable styles of speech. Although Earl Derr Biggers, author of the Charlie Chan novels, insists that Chan's speech patterns verge on "poetry" rather than "pidgin" English, his character has unique speech patterns along with a thick accent.[1] Significantly, the speech styles of all three detectives function as an important character feature. This feature identifies the character as part of a non-Western culture, provides a distinctive (though racially associated) character trait, and also makes these characters particularly vulnerable to mockery and ridicule. The particular modes of speech for these two characters have their origins in the literary renderings of their characters. Mr. Wong's accent in the film series seems derived less from any non-Western source than from the actor portraying this character, Boris Karloff.

Each character possesses a formality in manner most often expressed as politeness and courtesy toward the other main characters. In this way, the Oriental detective is perceived as exhibiting a demeanor that is unusual yet pleasantly nostalgic, as if this level of civility had somehow departed in the Western hustle and bustle of social interactions. The Oriental detective is, without exception, courtly and respectful in most of his social encounters as well as consistently deferential to those around him. This civility displayed in mannerly behavior is but one element of an overall restraint in expressing all emotion in this archetype.

Most often in these films the Western characters are portrayed as highly distressed, usually in response to a murder or a mystery or some sort of tragedy in the plot. Whether demonstrated by the frustration of a police chief who remains baffled by a case or the emotional turmoil of a witness to a murder, these characters display their emotions through raised voices and often hysterical conduct. Enter the Oriental detective, who is enlisted precisely because he is a partially or wholly disinterested party (not unlike other detective heroes) and would naturally exhibit less excitability along with a professional detachment. Still, even when there is more of an emotional investment in the case or the threat of physical danger becomes apparent for the detective, his emotions are always restrained and subdued.

The operation of formality, civility, and restraint so clearly evident in the metatext of this archetype provides an essential component of the archetype and also, significantly, functions as the requisite mode for all social contacts with other Western characters. These attributes take on a different meaning when taken as the condition under which the detective becomes positive. And yet, these same qualities also grant him the authority to police the emotions and/or actions of those less-controlled characters around him. Once again, the workings of seemingly contradictory elements contributes to a fundamental dynamic that both asserts and contains the traits of this archetype.

When do social formality and restraint become social confinement? Each film in all three detective series includes at least one subplot of romantic love, but almost without exception this occurs between two Caucasian characters. Ordinarily, the Oriental detective does not engage or respond to the opposite sex (Caucasian or Asian) in anything but a paternalistic and detached way. However, the detective does with some regularity compliment female characters on their physical beauty, but only with a manner of high-minded gallantry. For instance, Charlie Chan's compliment to a beautiful female Caucasian character in the film *Charlie Chan in Paris* (1936) remains completely consistent with his overall courtly demeanor rather than revealing any intimate admiration.

Mr. Wong shares this disposition with Chan's character. In these interactions both detectives are rarely alone with a female character, hence the lack of intimacy. And in the case of Mr. Wong, the detective often pointedly directs his comments at the woman but offers his remarks to a discourteous Caucasian male character as a gentle scolding. In other words, detectives Chan and Wong quickly assess the sexual dynamics among the characters (utilizing keenly observant faculties) and work to make a match of two often reluctant lovers. This again places them in the position of father figures as opposed to potential rivals.

Of course, Charlie Chan's character is well known as fathering many children. His familial interactions are never characterized as being in the nature of a spouse; his sexuality and virility are defined almost entirely in terms of fatherhood. Mr. Wong is also very observant of the sexual tensions among the other characters in the plot. Yet he is never coupled with anyone in the film narratives. He never refers to any woman in his life (present or past), and there is no mention of children. This dimension of a personal life for his character is not developed or even invoked.

Mr. Moto, on the other hand, is allowed a date in *Think Fast, Mr. Moto,* the initial film in the series, but this date ultimately proves inconsequential to the progress of the plot. Issues of sexuality tend to play the least important role in Mr. Moto's character, who does not usually engage in matchmaking activities (unlike Chan and Wong) but instead concentrates almost totally on his work. However, Moto does display a physical prowess through his martial arts skills, distinctly lacking in Charlie Chan and Mr. Wong. Yet despite this masculine expertise, Mr. Moto still leaves the most asexual impression of all the detective characters. Indeed, another acknowledged area of superior skill—his well-established mastery of disguise—for the Japanese detective may significantly contribute to a generalized impression of a more fluid and mutable physical/sexual identity.

This missing romantic side or sexual identification of the Oriental detective archetype is particularly noteworthy. The typical Hollywood version of the hard-boiled detective is usually characterized as a hat-wearing, cigarette-smoking, booze-drinking tough guy. Additionally, there is invariably the distressed femme fatale who comes along seeking the detective's assistance. By the end of the film, this woman invariably falls for the detective. Not only are women of this sort missing from the Oriental detective series, but when there is a spouse (as in the case of Charlie Chan), they are given little to no reference in individual films.

This most fundamental dichotomy of a Caucasian actor portraying an Asian role provides the essential foundation on which the Oriental detective archetype is constructed. Even in more recent years the role of Charlie Chan has been played exclusively by Caucasian actors, notably, by Peter Sellers in *Murder by Death* (1976) and Peter Ustinov in *Charlie Chan and the Curse of the Dragon Queen* (1981). The roles of Mr. Moto and Mr. Wong were also originated by European actors, Peter Lorre and Boris Karloff, respectively.

Obviously, one reason for this would be to provide a cinematic figure with whom a mostly Caucasian film audience could identify. So, clearly in this instance, the ethnicity of the actor depicting the part would play a decisive role in how a film character might be received by most audiences. But more practically, during the classical Hollywood studio era movies were designed fundamentally as vehicles for the talents of established stars, the vast majority of whom were Caucasian and not made to showcase lesser-known ethnic performers. The Oriental detective is generally presented as an essentially novel character and yet exists only through the standard use of a Caucasian actor in the leading role. Clearly, the employment of a Caucasian leading actor reflects the traditional combination in Hollywood of the conventional and the novel.

The contribution of individual actors to the roles they depict cannot be overemphasized. Warner Oland is considered to have established the definitive portrayal of Charlie Chan on the screen, and certainly both Peter Lorre and Boris Karloff offered their indelible interpretations on the characterizations of detectives Moto and Wong. In this analysis of an actor's influence on a role, teasing out what is characteristic of the character and what is characteristic of the actor is essential for examining this archetype most effectively.

All three actors who primarily shaped the screen adaptations of the Oriental detectives had notable screen roles previous to their respective detective series. Not just any Caucasian actors could be cast in the role of a Hollywood Oriental. Elements such as physical appearance as well as previously sinister screen roles were likely to have substantially influenced the casting of these particular Caucasian actors to play

Oriental detectives. For example, actor Warner Oland's career began in the silent era and included a number of highly visible ethnic screen portrayals as a Jewish patriarch in *The Jazz Singer* (1927) and as a Chinese half-caste in *Shanghai Express* (1932), to name only two. However, just prior to his initial depiction of Charlie Chan, Oland also portrayed the diabolical Fu Manchu character in *The Mysterious Dr. Fu Manchu* (1929), a fact that might appear random or coincidental but actually illustrates a curious consistency among the actors initially cast as Oriental detective heroes.

Oland (along with Lorre) also possesses an exotic name in the sense that it was uncommon in the United States and not obviously Anglo-Saxon. Despite Oland's Swedish cultural roots, the actor's unusual name has contributed to the frequent misperception that he is Chinese.

Also apparent in the casting of Peter Lorre as Mr. Moto was an association with sinister roles and mystery narratives (usually as a murderer or murder suspect). This fact is acknowledged in a 1937 *New York Times* review of *Think Fast, Mr. Moto* that specifically notes the actor's previous work with Alfred Hitchcock in the film *The Man Who Knew Too Much* (Britain, 1934) and with German director Fritz Lang in *M* (Germany, 1930).[2] As an extension of this trend, it is particularly noteworthy that the most recent Mr. Moto installment, *The Return of Mr. Moto* (1965), starred character actor Henry Silva, who has been described as an American actor of Italian and Basque descent and often seen as a sadistic villain.

Perhaps the most illustrative example of the decisive influence that preceding roles can have on an actor's career is the casting of Boris Karloff as Mr. Wong. His portrayal of the villainous Fu Manchu is discussed in chapter 1. And, of course, his indelible depiction of the monster in *Frankenstein* (1931) remains to this day the film performance with which he is most closely associated. Therefore, it is especially striking that Karloff would subsequently be cast as an apparently harmless Oriental detective. Although eyeglasses are not part of Oland's repertoire of props, both Lorre and Karloff in their performances routinely wear eyeglasses. While wearing the glasses, the actors' eyelids don't seem to be cosmetically altered or made-up in any special way. The eyeglasses alone seems to furnish a substitute for the conventional Orientalizing cosmetic makeup (of heavy eyeliner, eyeshadow, and altered eyebrows).

Both Charlie Chan and Mr. Wong sport facial hair of a distinct style: almost always, a mustache that has grown a bit long on the sides and a short goatee. The facial hair of these detectives appears to be a modified version of the prevalent Fu Manchu screen depiction that showcases a very long mustache and goatee. This element of physical similarity underscores the Oriental detective figure as a modification of evil Oriental archetypes rather than providing a simple repudiation or negation of them.

The clothing for these detectives is typically of Western (U.S. / European) style; however, a common set of choices within this classification yields a distinctive appearance applicable to all three Oriental characters. While the fundamental selection of Western clothing for the Oriental detective archetype could be assumed to function solely as an inclusive and reassuring signal to Western film audiences (i.e., a sign of his fundamental affiliation with Western power and authority), the specific type of attire chosen has the added effect of rendering this character as often quite incongruous with his surroundings. Very often the detectives are dressed in three-piece suits, in contrast to other Western characters who are dressed in more traditional two-piece suits. While this could merely indicate a more cultivated sensibility, this schism (supported by the detective's decidedly formal demeanor) works to both individualize and differentiate the appearance of this character through the projection of a studied and markedly affected mode of dress. This basic anachronistic quality is associated with the garments of this character in the original literature that inspired the screen adaptations. It is particularly elaborated in the 1935 publication *Your Turn, Mr. Moto* in which author John P. Marquand focuses on the Japanese detective's dress, scrutinizing the apparently incongruous blend of European and Japanese: "a short dark man with his hair cut after the Prussian fashion—a habit which so many Japanese have adopted—was seated at a table near me, regarding me with curiosity. He was dressed in a cutaway coat and wore tiny patent-leather shoes. . . . He seemed like a Japanese trying to masquerade as a continental European and not succeeding very well."[3]

The clothes may be Western; however, the end result of this foreign-based effort to conform is quite the opposite of acclimation. Rather, it produces a visibly eccentric style that underscores the character's position as an outsider. Of course, the image of a diminutive Japanese man wearing "a cutaway coat" and "patent-leather shoes" is also associated with appearances of Japanese national figures such as the emperor as well as Japanese diplomats in U.S. newsreels at the time. One of the most recognizable features of Charlie Chan's character is his sporting of Panama hats (slightly rounded with an upturned brim). He frequently wears a Panama-styled hat along with his various tailored three-piece suits. Mr. Wong's dress is infused with even more formality. He routinely wears dark hats similar to Chan's and dark pin-striped three-piece suits along with a boutonniere. He also carries an umbrella while in the heart of the city of San Francisco, lending one more affected yet idiosyncratic feature to his accoutrements.

Still, there are times when all three detectives do dress in the traditional costumes of their country (or in at least what Hollywood deems as Chinese or Japanese traditional dress). They are usually at leisure, inside their residences and alone at those moments. The donning of non-Western attire appears to be generally reserved for solitary periods of relaxation and tranquility. This is quite a contrast to the visual incoherence ascribed to these characters when in Western clothes. The confinement of the traditional costumes within these precisely demarcated boundaries creates rare moments of unity and harmony between the Oriental detective and his surroundings. Even if this occurs only when the character is physically isolated from his broader environment, his neighborhood or city, it is a significant convergence of cultural elements within the narrative.

In the role of Mr. Moto, Peter Lorre is frequently seen with the addition of a prosthesis for his upper front teeth. This cosmetic addition substitutes slightly crooked and protruding teeth for the actor's own less prominent set. Reflecting another common Asian stereotype of buck teeth, the addition of this prosthesis is clearly designed to draw attention to this facial feature. Indeed, the combination in the treatment of Moto's eyes with the noticeable protrusion of his front teeth serves to effectively distinguish his character from the more widely known Charlie Chan.

Ordinarily the detective's physical movements are quite deliberate and considered. Usually he works very slowly and methodically, which seems unrelated to advanced age or physical infirmity. Karloff's Mr.

Wong is the most cautious in his movements in comparison to Oland's more active Charlie Chan and particularly in relationship to the periodic expeditiousness of Mr. Moto's martial artistry (almost certainly executed by a stunt double). The overall unhurried pacing of this character's physical actions works to augment the detective's exacting investigative process rather than allude to any inherent physical limitation or restriction. Moto is quite unusual in his recurrent and accelerated displays of martial arts mastery (they actually appear to be shot in fast motion, a convention in Hollywood action sequences of the 1920s and 1930s), and yet they still occur within the larger context of his cautious, self-conscious, and self-effacing demeanor.

The most racially and culturally identifiable component of body language—bowing—is not only executed with the head but also includes the full upper body. The action of bowing is referenced prominently in the novels of Chan and Moto usually as a quaint and culturally based affectation. Ritualized bowing exists as a common element of all three detectives discussed in this chapter, providing a clear marker of cultural deviation and difference. Bowing not only functions as a highly identifiable part of the detective's overall demeanor but also operates as a modest assertion of his own cultural manners securely couched in an explicit gesture of deference.

Each detective character covered in this chapter began as a literary figure. Whether originating in magazine serializations or novels, these characters all had a degree of popular success prior to their screen depictions. Many filmgoers would probably have some familiarity with the fundamental traits of each character as established in the original texts. Accordingly, a brief discussion of key character features from the written texts seems warranted, as they most certainly also provided the initial context for Hollywood's screen adaptations.

It was widely believed that author Earl Derr Biggers's creation of the most popular of Oriental detectives, Charlie Chan, was based on Chang Apana, an actual Chinese police detective living in Honolulu. This speculation Biggers flatly denied, stating unequivocally in a 1931 *New York Times* interview that "Charlie Chan, for better or worse, is entirely fictitious." Apparently, only Apana's then unique existence as a Chinese policeman served as his inspiration for Chan. In this same interview Biggers declares his view that "sinister and wicked Chinese were old stuff in mystery stories" but that a law-abiding and "amiable" Chinese had yet to be created. Ultimately, the author claims that Chan's first appearance as a "Chinese sleuth" was motivated primarily to add "local color" to a mystery story he was in the process of completing.[4]

In the first Charlie Chan novel, *The House without a Key* (1925), the Chinese detective's introduction is noteworthy in what it details about its ethical and amiable hero and also speaks to white racism:

> The third man stepped farther into the room, and Miss Minerva gave a little gasp of astonishment as she looked at him. In those warm islands thin men were the rule, but here was a striking exception. He was very fat indeed, yet he walked with the light dainty step of a woman. His cheeks were as chubby as a baby's, his skin ivory tinted, his black hair close-cropped, his amber eyes slanting. As he passed Miss Minerva he bowed with a courtesy encountered all too rarely in a work-a-day world. . . .
>
> "Charlie Chan," Amos explained. "I'm glad they brought him. He's the best detective on the force."
>
> "But—he's a Chinaman!"[5]

Biggers's first description of the Chinese detective is significant particularly for its curious depiction of Chan's physical attributes. The author introduces a character who is initially portrayed as physically imposing ("very fat indeed") and yet is subsequently rendered remarkably subordinate with the references "he walked with the light and dainty step of a woman," a clearly feminine affectation, and "his cheeks were as chubby as a baby's," an obvious association to infancy. Yet ultimately Chan is celebrated for the anomalous contrivance that he is "the best detective on the force" who, astonishingly, happens to also be a "Chinaman." Chan's intricate description reflects the attempt to feminize and infantilize his character so that his achievements are contextualized in demeaning terms.

Although this first Chan mystery is set in Charlie Chan's native habitat of Honolulu, Hawaii, he is presented often as essentially alien, particularly in terms of his physicality and gestures. Often at points in the story where the other characters actively look to Chan in authority and esteem, Biggers inserts an illustration of the gifted detective's physical peculiarities: "The huge Chinaman knelt, a grotesque figure, by a table. He rose laboriously as they entered." "He held out a pudgy hand." "The slant eyes blinked with pleasure." "Chan's little eyes widened at mention of that." "'What is to be, will be,' he replied in a high, sing-song voice."[6] Again, this is the author's attempt to mitigate the anxiety aroused by Chan's prowess by introducing these feminized and racially differentiated qualities.

"Most clever excellent likeness of rotund Chinese"

The casting of actor Warner Oland (who was stocky and heavyset but certainly not obese) for the film series attempted to modify some of the distinctive physical qualities written in the novel. The actor had been cast as the villainous Oriental Fu Manchu (among other ethnic roles) before his stint as Charlie Chan. Indeed, in a *Newsweek* review of *Charlie Chan at the Circus* (1936), Oland is identified by the writer as "Johan Warner Oland, the Swedish actor who has played oily Oriental villains since 1917."[7] The actor's eyes appear somewhat small and narrow under the application of makeup, which is often the main focus of Orientalizing a non-Asian face. This, it seems, and his large size are the two innate physical requirements that Oland brought to the role.

The above reference to "rotund Chinese" is from the film *Charlie Chan in Paris* (1935) and is a response from the detective to an artist who has just shown him a quickly rendered sketch of his portrait. The camera also reveals the sketch to the audience. It is only a rough charcoal outline, a mere suggestion in a few lines of the character's discernible physical features, but is nevertheless received with delighted enthusiasm by Chan's character. This dramatic moment is emblematic of a larger performative dynamic operating in the depictions of Charlie Chan. Selected elements in performance such as makeup, speech, and gesture are utilized to construct and define the detective's character, just as a few selectively chosen lines in the portrait sketch are presented as an accomplished replication.

Less obvious in the construction of Chan's character is the inclusion of clearly stereotypical enactments by other actors that attempt to cast actor Warner Oland's primary interpretation of the "rotund Chinese" as both natural and unequivocal. In other words, when juxtaposed to an obviously caricatured exhibition, the actor's rendition appears more plausible and credible in comparison.

Produced during the middle of actor Warner Oland's run as the Chinese detective, the film *Charlie Chan in Paris* reveals many of the previously identified tropes that circulate within a seemingly one-dimensional narrative. The plot of the film involves Detective Chan arriving in Paris ostensibly on a vacation, but in fact the detective is on the trail of a forger of bank bonds. In one of the first scenes in the film, Chan disembarks from an airplane only to be accosted outside the airport by a persistent beggar. Chan gives the beggar some coins, intoning the aphorism "Good fortune to give alms when first arrive in city," clearly a characteristic gesture of humility, obeisance, and appeasement. After Chan boards a taxi a large rock is thrown into it, barely missing the detective. A note threatening his life is attached. The detective, with a determined look, decides to continue his stay as he tells the taxi driver to drive on.

The taxi takes him to the apartment of the son of an "old friend." Chan is welcomed warmly by the son, Victor Descartes, who waxes poetic on Chan's previous success solving a case in London. Oland's performance includes his customarily deferential body language most often expressed through bowing (either from the waist when standing or just the head when seated) when either addressed or addressing another character. His voice is evenly modulated so that even given his enigmatic phraseology, Chan's aphorisms sound reassuring to the ear.

However, when Victor's friends arrive at the apartment, the congenial tone shifts temporarily. Max Corday (the artist who eventually sketches Chan's portrait) while entering with the carousing group appears as the most inebriated and giddy. Chan is often distinguished by calm, in contrast to the reckless and high-strung performances by the rest of the cast. After being introduced to Charlie Chan by Victor, Corday quickly takes in Chan's Oriental countenance, shakes his hand, and responds, "Me velly happy know you. Maybe you like havey little dlinky?" The other characters all react with silent expressions of dismay at Corday's words, and yet Chan is left to refute the obviously caricatured display on his own. The detective responds politely, in a carefully modulated tone, "Very happy to make acquaintance of charming gentleman." But Chan doesn't let Corday off with simply a

Warner Oland in *Charlie Chan in Paris.* (MoMA)

shamefaced expression; he follows up with his own imitation of Corday's chop-socky performance: "Me no likey dlinky now, perhaps lata!" Chan smiles, having cowed his detractor, and everyone laughs, relieved. Corday and a young woman proceed to the bar in the apartment, with the woman saying to him laughingly, "Me likey dlinky now!"

This scene contains seemingly contradictory elements of genuine admiration (from Victor) along with a plainly racist exhibition (from Corday) and then a reconciliation couched in humor, and yet these components combine to create an acceptably heroic enactment of Chan's character. Clearly, there are many moments when Chan customarily promotes self-deprecatory remarks used to demonstrate his innate humility and gentle humor. However, this scene is particularly striking in the playing out of dual character types: the ignorant immigrant (which Corday mimics) and the cultured gentleman (which Chan apparently embodies). Not only is the immigrant impersonation performed by Corday, but it is also performed by the detective himself. Chan's typical delivery is immediately followed by his immigrant imitation. The most obvious difference in the performance is in the enunciation of the words used (mainly, the substitution of "l" for "r"). However, Oland also adds another dimension in his delivery, a very curt and aggressive tone. The normally serene Chan almost spits the words out.

Chan's performance within a performance not only displays a split between obvious Oriental caricature and its more pleasing incarnation but also carefully positions Oland's portrayal of the Chinese detective as narratively legitimate and sound. This less obvious function of the pejorative caricatured exhibition attempts to naturalize the primary impersonation by Caucasian actor Warner Oland. In this way, the film audience is presented with a decidedly improper and seemingly proper Oriental portrayal to interpret and assimilate.

Even Chan's Number One Son Lee (played by Keye Luke) functions as a comic counterpoint to Oland's performance style. Initially in this film, Lee appears unexpectedly in his father's hotel room. The elder detective enters the room cautiously, gun drawn, as Lee casually emerges from a bath toweling wet hair with the words, "Hello, Pop! Gosh, it's good to see you!" Lee's energetic demeanor and chatty delivery of his lines bear a striking contrast to Oland's gently laconic mode of expression. Indeed, later in the film after Chan emerges from a murder crime scene, he gently rouses his son, who is asleep in a waiting car. On awakening, Lee abruptly launches into a rapid litany of Chinese with his hands up, clearly in a panic. To this Charlie responds reassuringly, "I know you did not kill anybody." In this scene, Lee's broad performance works to place Charlie's portrayal as the performative reference point around which all other Oriental enactments revolve.

Within this film narrative as well as in other installments in the series, Detective Chan is routinely lionized by some characters and derided by others until they are grudgingly proved to be wrong, usually at the very end of the film. Caricature and humor play a major role in the negotiation of the constantly shifting insider/outsider status that Chan invariably occupies in the narrative. Chan's successive encounters with either the approval or disparagement of other characters are structured within the series' narratives as opportunities for the detective to earn the respect of those unfamiliar with his reputation and stature within his profession. Indeed, in the film *Charlie Chan at the Opera* (1936) one character, Sergeant Kelly (played by William Demarest) provides the single mouthpiece challenging Chan's authority. Similar to the drunk Corday, Kelly's character is initially set up as generally thoughtless and reckless. A kind of inside joke between the characters who are familiar with Charlie Chan's accomplishments and also most likely with the film's audience begins to unfold as the designated troublesome character, in this case an irascible policeman, underestimates the qualities of the esteemed detective.

A *Variety* review of *Charlie Chan's Secret,* produced the same year, acknowledged this narrative thread when it characterized Chan as a "shrewd detective" whose "customary feigned dumbness" is "intelligently maintained" in the service of catching the murderer.[8] Interestingly, an earlier review of *Charlie Chan's Greatest Case* (1933) in the *New York Times* noted a perceived schism between the audience's "respect" for Charlie Chan and the lack thereof among "some of the characters in the film."[9] Despite the seemingly benign function of this narrative strategy, it also can be perceived as a dramatic device used to moderate the superior capabilities and exploits of the Chinese detective vis-à-vis his American and European counterparts in the films.

When Kelly is brought on the case his supervisor, Inspector Regan, admonishes him after he questions the ability of Chan (who is then

Warner Oland and Keye Luke in *Charlie Chan at the Opera*. (MoMA)

out of the office). Regan states that Sergeant Kelly needs to become a "real detective" and "learn some politeness" from the venerable Charlie Chan. This effectively sets up an abiding resentment in Kelly, which is given full rein throughout the film. Comments such as "Is that a laundry ticket?" in response to a piece of evidence presented by Chan and "Egg Foo Yung" (a pseudonym for Chan) and "He's hitting the pipe again" (an obvious reference to the drug opium) are respectively aimed at Chan's competency, race, and morality. Chan's responses to these and other challenges are predictably indulgent, such as his response to the first comment: "Not [laundry] ticket, but all dirty." Ultimately in the final scene of the film after Chan is proven a hero, Kelly gives his grudging approval: "You're like Chop Suey, different, but all right." Kelly's acceptance of Chan with the phrase "Chop Suey" raises the issue of the terms inherent of such approval, such as the idea of Americanization through a cultural melting pot and a reference to a dish not ethnically authentic but rather designed for American consumption.

Even though Kelly (or another selected character) is proven wrong in the end, the routine inclusion of clearly racist references raises the question of their function in the plots of individual films as well as in the series as a whole. The mocking speech by Max Corday ("Velly happy meet you") in *Charlie Chan in Paris* as well as the continual referral in slang to the Chinese detective alternately as laundryman, Chinese dish ("Egg Foo Yung"), and drug user ("hitting the pipe") by Sergeant Kelly in *Charlie Chan at the Opera* perhaps indicates an attempt to acknowledge and then dismiss patently racists attitudes. Or could the function of these dramatic interactions seek the opposite objective: to affirm a racist status quo while only appearing to challenge it? Such an opposition merely reveals the inherently composite nature of Charlie Chan's portrayal, at once superior and inferior, capable yet resented, uniquely sovereign in his own cinematic environment.

Finally, an element of danger and suspicion lurks within the boundaries of Chan's heroic constitution. Although he works tirelessly to outwit the perpetrators of mysteriously murderous criminal deeds, Chan's celebrated familiarity with the seamy side of human behavior often adds a cryptic ambiguity to his otherwise stable and sound incarnation. On the trail of the killer at the end of *Charlie Chan in Paris,* Detective Chan (along with Victor Decartes, the son of an old friend introduced earlier) proceeds through the dank and dark sewers below the City of Lights. Clearly familiar with this sinister setting, Chan is focused and is authoritative with Victor, ordering him to be "Quiet!" and "Follow!" When Victor nervously utters "Creepy place, isn't it?" Chan responds ominously, "Many strange crimes committed in the sewers of Paris." They proceed to the murderer's hideout, and the police arrive and turn to Charlie, of course, to solve the case. However, in the highly charged moment preceding the ending when Charlie speaks so knowingly and intently to Victor from the literal underbelly of Paris, Chan's dramatic presence embodies less a detective and more a harbinger of all things depraved and nefarious.

This is also the case in the film *Charlie Chan's Secret* (1936) in which Charlie simply states, "Chinese people interested in all things psychic." Although Chan as detective shares cinematic iconic space with Basil Rathbone's Sherlock Holmes, Charlie's wisdom and knowledge that he brings to bear on a mysterious case are characterized as more instinctual or cultural than intellectual. "Chinese people interested in all things psychic." One could easily substitute the word "mysterious" for "psychic," apparent in Chan's surroundings and suggested as his essence. Impervious in the face of mystery, Charlie Chan is often shot in the shadows, a figure at home among the sinister elements surrounding him. Even the title suggests that it is Charlie Chan who is keeping a secret as opposed to unmasking one. In this film, Chan is often shot as a lone figure proceeding through underground passageways of the supposedly haunted Colby House (the main setting for a number of murders and murder attempts). And again, in the final climactic scene (a séance) immediately before the murderer is to be revealed, a tight close-up on Oland's furtive glances is rendered more ominously than the subsequent series of short cuts of the main suspects. It is as if Chan's character were displayed ultimately as the principal figure of clandestine misdeeds to the audience.

By the mid-1930s, with Oland as the leading player, the Chan series had achieved a considerable measure of success, particularly in light of its modest budgets and usual casting of contract players in supporting roles. Despite the films' design as programmers (movies occupying the position between upscale A-list studio product and more modest B films), the series consistently attracted major audiences and box office grosses on par with A-list products at this time.[10] Correspondingly, the Charlie Chan character within the narrative of the films at this time appears as more of an accepted insider whose reputation precedes him and/or with whom other characters are often personally familiar prior to the case. This is indicative of a shift originating in the Chan novels.

However, the actor's performance style contributes much to Biggers's initial conception of the Chinese detective. Not only is it the altered eyebrows or idiosyncratic arrangement of facial hair (if Chan's grew out longer, it would copy Fu Manchu's sinister mustache and goatee), it is also an impassive facial expression. Oland's range of facial expressions generally extends from a deferential smile to an expression devoid of a clearly discernible meaning. We read Chan more by what he says and what he does in conjunction with what may be termed his Chinese cultural restraint. Except for Oland's eyes, frequently seen darting from side to side in reaction to another character's more

Warner Oland in *Charlie Chan's Secret*. (MoMA)

emotive speech and body language, Chan is rendered in an acting style that suggests more than it presents.

Response to the Charlie Chan film series (starting with Warner Oland) in the popular press remained fairly positive throughout the decade of the 1930s. Early in the series reviewers credited much to Oland's performance style, which was almost always noted (no matter how briefly) in reviews and articles of the time. A *Variety* film review of the first installment, *Charlie Chan Carries On* (1931), rates Oland's performance as "swell though a bit lethargic" but then attributes that "lethargic" tendency principally to the "the picture pace which lacks some punch." However, it predicted that Chan's "quaint" sayings "will be liked by audiences," not unlike the proverbs found inside fortune cookies.[11]

Despite the fact that a literary market existed for the Charlie Chan mysteries prior to the screen adaptations, Warner Oland, according to most of the popular press, initially made an indelible mark on the role.

Indeed, a reviewer of *Charlie Chan in London* (1934) in *Variety* characterized Oland's portrayal of the Chinese detective as virtually "second nature,"[12] while a *New York Times* review of *Charlie Chan's Chance* (1932) described Oland as the "mainstay" of each picture.[13] However, by the late 1930s, the highly conventionalized Chan series pictures were, themselves, widely considered as a reliable moneymaker in the industry. By this time, even the mainstream press characterized the films as formulaic Hollywood commodities, as illustrated in a 1936 *New York Times* review of *Charlie Chan's Secret* that states that "there is nothing in it (including Warner Oland) to surprise or disappoint the Chan addict, whose name, apparently, is still legion."[14]

It is this industrial and artistic context that ushered in Sidney Toler's initial appearance in the role of Charlie Chan two years hence. After the unexpected death of Warner Oland in 1938, Toler took on the role for the first time in the film *Charlie Chan in Honolulu* (1938). The reviews were not only favorable but also reaffirmed the now firmly encoded set of conventions so commonly anticipated in each film, "beginning with the body on the floor and ending with Charlie saying 'thank you so much' to the snarling killer."[15]

This commentary on the transition from actor Warner Oland to Sidney Toler illustrates the emergence and preeminence of a Charlie Chan formula (both in terms of the films' plots and leading performances by Oland) in relation to the individual contribution of its new leading actor. At this point in the series' evolution the role of Charlie Chan has been so clearly prescribed (i.e., "the round Panama hat," "the oriental mustache," saying "thank you so much") that it can readily accommodate (and perhaps absorb) the dramatic interpretation of another actor.

Throughout the 1930s, the Chan series served as a model that all Oriental detective series would emulate. As argued in this section, a complex configuration of elements produced the familiar formulaic model of the Chan series. This was a model so commercially successful that it spawned not only many more films than the actual Chan stories but also at least two moderately successful challengers. Ultimately, however, none outlasted the perennial Chan.

The press initially positioned the first installment of the Mr. Moto series, *Think Fast, Mr. Moto* (1937) (also produced by Twentieth Century

Fox), as an extension of the then powerhouse Chan series. Like Chan, the Mr. Moto character was based on a literary model originally serialized in print, in this case the *Saturday Evening Post*. Mr. Moto's Japanese operative shares a number of traits with his Chinese counterpart: a sound capability to bring wrongdoers to justice and a cultured, polite demeanor along with a distinctly bizarre physical presence. Mr. Moto's film incarnation, even in recent years, is frequently characterized simply as "a whimsically obsequious, lisping Japanese" as well as a "bowing and foot shuffling little detective," but like Charlie Chan his character, as originally conceived in print, embodied exceptional qualities both remarkable and strikingly peculiar.[16]

In the first story in the series, *Your Turn, Mr. Moto* (1935), author John P. Marquand renders his extraordinary title character in terms alternately distinguished and anomalous. Initially described as "a suave scion of the Japanese nobility" and "a most accomplished gentlemen," the Japanese detective is subsequently depicted as a visibly queer figure. Marquand's description of the agent's dress is rendered with extraordinary detail: "Mr. Moto came alone, without a suspicious glance. He was dressed for the evening, carefully, in what is known as a dinner coat in America, and what the French call a smoking, an inoffensive man bowing, smiling, and holding an opera hat. . . . There was a row of pearls on his pleated shirt front; a handkerchief was sticking neatly from his pocket; his small feet glittered in their patent-leather pumps."[17]

Mr. Moto's dress is constantly scrutinized throughout the novel quite apart from the "most capable" reasoning and judgment he consistently displays; "his clothing was more incongruous—a tweed golf suit and a brown tweed cap. I knew enough not to laugh because Mr. Moto was serious." This emphasis on the quality of Moto's dress diverts attention away from his influential position in the plot machinations of the mystery. Marquand inverts Moto's rational, reasonable, and sensible qualities during the course of his investigative duties through the Japanese detective's preposterously "careful" and "conscientious" attempts to adopt a European style.[18]

Thank you, Mr. Moto (1936), published the next year, is most notable for the author's shift in emphasis from the detective's clothes to his bodily attributes. Gold fillings in Moto's front teeth are detailed for the first time, an odd addition to an already unusual characterization. In this story Mr. Moto, once again, is lauded for knowing "exactly what to do" as part of the secret service, but also emphasized are Mr. Moto's "delicate" features, his hands, and "his dark eyes," which possess "a birdlike intensity." In this instance, his qualities of reliability, authority, and strength are undermined by the inclusion of these feminized and undersized physical traits. Indeed, the author likens Moto's lesser physical characteristics to well-known cultural landmarks of his home country: "He [Moto] had never seemed so delicate as he did when I stood there looking down at him, a miniature of a man, as small as the gardens and the dwarfed trees of his island."[19]

Hungarian-born Peter Lorre portrayed the Japanese secret agent Kentaro Moto on the screen from 1937 to 1939. The diminutive Lorre managed to create a popular Oriental characterization in the eight films that comprised this series. Hollywood's newly minted adaptation of Mr. Moto for mass consumption includes, most strikingly, the addition of trademark eyeglasses (wire-rimmed as well as black) and the expunging of his clear allegiance to the government of Japan, which is very apparent in the published stories.

In contrast to the generally high-profile presence of Charlie Chan as the assigned detective on a case, Mr. Moto offers a much different impression of generally covert behavior and shadowy deeds. Indeed, the preceding exchange of words is from a confrontation between Mr. Moto and a murder suspect, his shipboard room steward in the initial film of the Mr. Moto series, *Think Fast, Mr. Moto*. The steward is swiftly revealed to be the murderer of one of the Japanese agent's operatives in San Francisco. In this scene Moto states enigmatically "I dislike to be strenuous" before throwing the steward overboard. The next morning, Moto "innocently" inquires about his missing steward, only to hear that he is strangely unaccounted for. To this, Moto "regretfully" states he only wished to give him a tip before disembarking.

While the fact that his steward turned out to be a murderer could easily justify the detective's actions, the concealment of his act reveals a persistent element of duplicity and deceit in this character's profile. Charlie Chan's momentary divergences from the local police authorities also furnish a key component of the detective's singular success as a master of crime solving. However, in this instance Mr. Moto does not reveal his fatal act of revenge against the steward or the reasons for it to

Peter Lorre in *Think Fast, Mr. Moto.* (MoMA)

any authority. Is he working inside or outside a recognized system of justice, or is he working just as a personal avenger? This level of ambiguity does not exist for Detective Chan, although it plainly does for his more elusive Japanese counterpart. This Japanese agent is constructed as a darker, more secretive Oriental detective and as such provides a concurrent mystery to be solved along with the main plot within the narrative.

> SUSPECT: You think you're timid, but I know who you are, Mr. Moto.
>
> MOTO: That is most unfortunate for you.

In *Think Fast, Mr. Moto,* "Who are you, Mr. Moto?" is the question most frequently asked throughout the film. Loosely based on the first novel *Your Turn, Mr. Moto* (1935), this film illustrates how this fundamentally enigmatic character functions as a mysterious presence to be himself unmasked in addition to his obvious role as an individual agent of justice who is evidently committed to the exposure and disclosure of criminal wrongdoing. In this film, Mr. Moto is after a ring of smugglers involved in contraband. These traffickers have used the well-known Hitchings shipping line to facilitate their operation. Moto links up with the naive young heir to the shipping line, Bob Hitchings, who unknowingly carries an important piece of evidence crucial to solving the case on a passenger ship headed to Shanghai, China. What is most evident in this narrative is how Moto's character is depicted as profoundly slippery and shifting, so much so that his very identity and motives remain most ambiguous despite his unceasing pursuit of the criminal smugglers. Not until the end of the film does Moto identify himself as an amateur sleuth. And yet his sober demeanor, his familiarity with a network of operatives, and his calculated acts of vengeance throughout the plot contradict his proclaimed nonprofessional status.

The film begins with actor Peter Lorre dressed as a Persian street peddler in the midst of a Chinese New Year celebration in San Francisco. He wears a fez and sports bushy eyebrows, a scruffy mustache, and a goatee. He does not wear glasses. Notably, Moto also approximates an Arab accent when he speaks. After entering an Oriental curio shop, the peddler tries to sell an expensive jewel but is violently thwarted in his attempt. He subdues his would-be captors with a flurry of expert martial arts throws and narrowly escapes. Having returned to his hotel room, the peddler stands in front of a mirror while methodically removing the fez, bushy eyebrows, and facial hair to reveal a distinctly mild-mannered countenance. He neatly slicks down his black shortly cropped hair, carefully puts on his delicate wire-rim eyeglasses, and smiles satisfactorily. This smile reveals a slightly uneven tooth alignment. He tenderly takes a black cat in his lap and strokes it while calling to make reservations on the Hitchings passenger ship to Shanghai. At last, he identifies himself as Moto in a mild-mannered Japanese accent: "The name is Moto, M-O-T-O," he says, and he smiles again.

Unlike Charlie Chan, one of the hallmarks of Moto's character is his affinity for disguises. Surely he is not the only cinematic detective character to periodically utilize the element of disguise in his work. However, this component is particularly significant in light of the primary level of artifice practiced to transform European actor Peter Lorre into the Japanese Mr. Moto character. In theory, Moto's Arab disguise challenges the dominant Hollywood practice of allowing only Caucasian actors the latitude to portray other racial groups. The scene depicts within the narrative that a Japanese figure can credibly be transformed into another ethnic group. Of course, this is ultimately rendered impotent due to the obvious fact that Lorre is in actuality a European performing the twofold racial impersonation of a Japanese portraying an Arab. This bias is also apparent in the manner in which Moto reveals his disguise. Specifically, he is shown reverting to his Japanese self from the Persian incarnation, not the other way around. In this way, we miss the opportunity to observe how his transformation might have taken place.

The Persian peddler is the only fully elaborated disguise involving a physical transformation acknowledged in the narrative. Subsequently and for the duration of the narrative, Mr. Moto adheres to his customary appearance: wearing eyeglasses, a protruding tooth prosthesis, slick shortly cropped black hair, and often color-coordinated white three-piece suits. Still, even within this apparently normal appearance mode, Mr. Moto's dress generally appears ill-suited to his form. Although Mr. Moto's first encounter on board ship is fraught with conflict, his distinctive appearance also attracts our attention. The diminutive agent enters the hallway in a white double-breasted coat, dark gloves, dark hat, and glasses along with an intensely somber expression.

At the same time commanding and peculiar, Moto's entrance goes unnoticed by a group of young people seen carousing in the stateroom across the hall. Noticing the loud noise, Moto comments to his room steward, "They seem very happy, my neighbors." It is then that the steward, Carson, explains that Bob Hitchings, son of the owner of the shipping line, is one of the revelers. Interestingly, the two actors appear in a number of scenes wearing "identical" white suits; however, Hitchings's suits are carefully tailored to the tall actor's frame, while Moto's appears to always be slightly oversized, dwarfing the already diminutive actor in the presence of this character as well as others.

What follows is a scene in which Moto is unwillingly pulled into the stateroom with Hitchings and friends (who pick him as an unwitting fool) and coerced into enduring their condescending humor. An invariably dazzling martial arts display eventually cows the group and earns the young Hitchings's respect. Indeed, the stunned and subdued Hitchings declares to Mr. Moto, "Well, served us right, we asked for it. Now we're friends. My name is Hitchings, Bob to you." And Moto pleasantly responds, "So pleased, I'm Mr. Moto."

As in the Chan films, use of this scene of initiation in which Moto must decisively dispel the myth of the foolish, weak Oriental is provided here. Clearly, his peculiar attire plays an important part in this. Through the act of putting this young group in their place, the agent proves himself to be an unexpectedly different model of his race worthy of respect and admiration. In this inaugural film, Moto presents a multifaceted characterization that includes an eccentric visual presence; a deferential, innocuous persona; and a darkly surreptitious alter ego. The contrast of these competing dispositions produces a truly enigmatic film performance style.

After Hitchings's cohorts depart, the ship sails, and Moto tends to the tipsy young heir. Moto advises Hitchings to get some sleep and even folds his clothes. However, the secret agent also happens to glimpse an important letter that Hitchings has been entrusted to deliver to Shanghai. Moto smiles satisfactorily while Hitchings innocently remarks, "Mr. Moto, you'd make a swell valet." Moto does not contradict, saying simply "Goodnight, sleep tight" as he smiles. But as Moto starts to leave, Hitchings sleepily asserts from his bed, "I know who you are." At that, Moto turns around with a start, looking intently at the young shipping heir with a mixture of hostility and fear. But Hitchings only dreamily offers, "You're the Japanese sandman." To this Moto speaks to himself, utterly relieved, "Strange people these Americans." He turns out the light and then closes the door.

This brief but telling exchange alternately positions Moto as either humble caretaker or furtive spy. Of course, by contrast, the young Hitchings does appear to be ignorant and foolish yet notably essentially guileless, while Mr. Moto's heroic character is revealed to routinely use intrinsically duplicitous means as he pursues a just end. This dark side of the detective is also manifested visually, particularly in the way Lorre is shot. For example, one evening on ship deck, the steward, Carson, is seen stealthily spying the young Hitchings and his date when suddenly Mr. Moto's low voice is heard. He startles the deceitful character by his unexpected presence but also surely through what he sees when he turns around: a truly mysterious vision of the detective reclining in a deck chair, in near total darkness except for a narrow beam of light across his eyes. In this moment Moto is Hitchings's protector but is also sinisterly rendered as a threat to Carson. Moto delivers his lines in this scene enveloped in darkness.

Mr. Moto presents a set of seemingly contradictory characteristics. The morning after Moto puts Hitchings to bed, the two meet on ship deck. Hitchings is seriously hung over, and Mr. Moto handily prescribes an utterly awful-sounding concoction of ingredients for the young man to drink. Miraculously, it works. Afterward Hitchings asks again who Moto is: the jujitsu expert who controlled his friends or the man who confidently suggests "the greatest hangover cure." Moto identifies himself as an exporter of Oriental goods with magic for a hobby. He takes out a deck of cards and begins some simple card tricks. This leads into Moto's revelation that he is also a Stanford graduate, as is the young Hitchings. They declare themselves brothers and bond for the remainder of the journey.

The pursuit of the real identity of the Japanese detective occupies considerable time in the narrative. Unlike Chan who is usually in constant contact with local authorities as well as plainly identified to a community of suspects, Moto acts basically alone in this film, unbeknownst to friend or foe. When the Japanese detective finally arrives in Shanghai, he consults with the local police ostensibly to locate a missing woman, whom he obviously suspects. Instead, Moto uses an extended network of undercover agents who permit the central work of the case to proceed without direct supervision or official intervention. The pace of the mystery relies solely on the wits of the Japanese detective.

As the film comes to a close, Mr. Moto divulges the machinations of the smuggling ring and reveals another murderer, this time for all to see and the Chinese police to apprehend. Still confused, Bob Hitchings asks for the final time "Who are you? . . . Then you're not a detective?" Suddenly mild-mannered and reticent, Mr. Moto shows his business card as an exporter and humbly responds to the young man, "Oh, only as a hobby." In this final scene, the supposedly real Moto is revealed to be merely an amateur of amazing ability. His demeanor, in this moment, fits the description of meek and mild and a little overwhelmed by all the attention. Moto's professional status shifts markedly over the course of the entire series. Beginning as an admittedly rank amateur and ending as an internationally known agent, Mr. Moto (who began as an operative for the Japanese government in print) in his cinematic incarnation represents a most adaptable film character.

A notable departure occurs in the film *Mr. Moto's Gamble* (1938) in which the detective's official vocation is that of a criminology instructor. Originally intended to be a Charlie Chan vehicle (titled "Charlie Chan at the Ringside") according to a *Time* magazine review, the film casts Chan's Number One Son Lee (played by Keye Luke) as one of Moto's student sleuths.[20] Interestingly, Lee mentions his "Pop" to Moto, who sends warm greetings to "his honorable father." This installment reflects the uneasy introduction of Chanisms that Moto's character is forced to incorporate: a strong connection to a student community and the police authorities as well as a high profile with the usual suspects.

By the release of *Mr. Moto's Last Warning* (1939) in the final year of the series, the Japanese detective's professional standing has progressed to a highly regarded member of the international secret police who inspires awe and fear among the criminals in the narrative. His mastery of disguises is singled out as particularly impressive. In fact, this film begins with a completely different actor posing as Moto. Significantly, the Japanese actor double wears no glasses and no prosthesis of protruding teeth, though he wears a similar white suit and speaks in heavily accented English. It doesn't appear to matter that they look nothing alike, which is rather odd since the double might easily have worn glasses to more closely approximate the appearance of the Japanese detective. They merely substituted Lorre's highly idiosyncratic Mr. Moto (distinctive glasses, teeth, and general demeanor) with a Japanese actor. This plot detail appears to indicate a rather random approach to Orientalizing a character, as if fidelity to an ethnically Japanese actor has no pertinence to Lorre's predominant Oriental enactment. However, a more specific attempt at imitation by the Japanese actor could potentially draw unwanted attention to the degree of artifice used to establish and maintain Lorre's portrayal.

In this example, we have a genuine Asian actor characterized as an impostor of a racially impersonated performance by Lorre. At one point Moto and his double meet, bumping into one another (on purpose). After a brief exchange in Japanese, Moto passes a secret message to the operative. In this moment a plot point in the narrative is

George Sanders (*left*) and Peter Lorre (*center*) in *Mr. Moto's Last Warning.* (MoMA)

satisfied, but also an Asian actor playing a role comes face to face with his Hollywood alter ego, the Oriental. The former is a mild-mannered and refined figure, while the latter is an oddly configured grouping of highly theatrical qualities.

This paradigm of actual Asian actors appearing in secondary, supporting, or extra roles with Orientalized white actors in leading roles occurs repeatedly in the films of the classic Hollywood period. It happens in virtually all the films discussed in this study but not in quite the direct doubling effect as in this Mr. Moto vehicle. We are confronted here with a disturbing suspension of disbelief whereby a more genuine performance by Asian actors is killed off (as is the double early in the Moto narrative) in favor of its racist Hollywood-inspired counterpart.

Reaction in the press to the first Moto film, *Think Fast, Mr. Moto*, includes commentary on actor Peter Lorre's previous film work with directors Alfred Hitchcock and Fritz Lang. Reviews specifically consider how Lorre's individual performance style might influence his interpretation of Mr. Moto. The *New York Times* review describes Lorre's previous efforts as a favorable element for the new series:

> Mr. Lorre has not been particularly well used since he left the guidance of Mr. Hitchcock for the gold of Hollywood. In the Hitchcock melodramas he was a specialist in exquisite villainy, a service-with-a-smile scoundrel. Before that, for Fritz Lang in Berlin, he dabbled deftly in psychoses.
>
> Mr. Lorre is certainly the man for Mr. Marquand's Mr. Moto; maybe Mr. Lorre and Alfred Hitchcock can get together on the next Moto assignment.[21]

However, *Variety* saw Lorre's depiction of Moto as a welcome departure from his earlier patently perverse screen incarnations. The reviewer suggests that although an "air of mystery surrounds his activities," Moto is "developed humanly."[22]

What is particularly striking about these reviews is how Lorre remains so closely tied to his portrayals of psychotic scoundrels and grim villainy. And while these dark elements are seen to be more or less appropriate to the Mr. Moto mystery series, clearly this film vehicle is perceived as transitional for the actor, either as an opportunity to exploit his sinister performances in a different venue or as a chance to moderate these same tendencies in order to broaden his overall appeal. According to Ted Sennett, author of *Masters of Menace: Greenstreet and Lorre*, the actor was well aware of his typecasting and apparently welcomed the change that the character of Mr. Moto offered, stating that "instead of committing murders, I'll be solving them."[23]

The Moto series received generally good reviews even into its final year. Indeed, *Mr. Moto's Last Warning,* released in January 1939, was deemed by *Variety* as "one of the better 'Moto' pictures,"[24] as was *Mr. Moto in Danger Island,* released only two months later.[25] What was eventually dubbed "the phenomenon of Mr. Moto" in a *New York Times* review of *Mysterious Mr. Moto of Devil's Island* in 1938 referred not only to the leading actor's cinematic performance but also the series' commercial success.[26] Throughout its run, the series was acknowledged as having "won wide popularity" and accordingly providing a healthy profit for author John P. Marquand as well as for Fox and Lorre.[27] What ended the evidently popular and successful series remains uncertain. Brian Taves, in his essay "The B Film: Hollywood's Other Half," suggests that the series was perceived as "too positive to continue in light of Japanese aggression in Asia at that time."[28] William K. Everson, in his book *The Detective in Film,* implies that the series was dropped "because the war situation made acceptance of a Japanese hero dubious" but also indicates that Lorre's own ambitions as an actor to seek out different parts might have played a significant role in ending the series.[29] Of course, what we do know from the films of World War II is that after the attack on Pearl Harbor, Hollywood's depictions of the Japanese suddenly became resolutely adversarial.

Apart from the Chan and Moto series produced by Twentieth Century Fox, Monogram Pictures, a member of the so-called Poverty Row group of low-budget film production companies, began the Mr. Wong series starring Boris Karloff. The series was established to take advantage of the popularity of the two Oriental detective series from Fox. The third film in the series, *Mr. Wong in Chinatown* (1939), is the first vehicle to incorporate all the qualities that this series would come to be known for. The second installment, *The Mystery of Mr. Wong* (1939), establishes the Chinese detective as a brilliant scholar (having graduated from both Heidelberg University and Oxford University) as well as being "one of the five foremost living authorities on ancient art and literature in the Orient." This picture introduces the female reporter Bobby Logan (played by Marjorie Reynolds) as a sometime love interest for Wong's contact in the San Francisco police department, Inspector Street (played by Grant Withers).

The plot of *Mr. Wong in Chinatown* begins with the mysterious murder of a Chinese princess and ends with the arrest of an American bank president. In the Mr. Wong series the presence of Boris Karloff alone guarantees an association with the darkly sinister underworld of murder mysteries. In nearly every scene, the actor is seen dressed meticulously in a dark three-piece suit and tie with a carnation bouton-niere, slick black hair wig, dark glasses (similar to Moto's), and a black umbrella, evidently a paragon of legitimacy and cultivation. And yet Karloff's well-known voice and visage tend to subsume any distinctive physical features of the Chinese detective.

What does effectively modulate Karloff's dark persona is Wong's position as a reactor rather than a precipitator of narrative action. Be-cause the character of Wong is so often relegated to the sidelines of the action until the end of each film, Karloff's interpretation of the Chi-nese detective remains relatively tame. Even though local authorities routinely bring Charlie Chan into a case after the fact, he immediately begins to strongly influence the direction of the case. This places the depiction of Mr. Wong in the uneasy middle ground between the in-dulgent reassurance of Chan and the vaguely sinister quality of Moto.

Inspector Street, reporter Bobby Logan, and Mr. Wong all share as-pects of the investigation into the princess's murder in the film. Earlier in the story, Bobby comes in to see Street with information on the case that she wants to exchange for a tip from him. As they snipe at each other Mr. Wong stands, looking on with amusement and then concern. Finally, he intercedes politely, asking Bobby "Won't you please help us?" To this Bobby relents, smiling at Wong, and then says pointedly to Street, "For a gentleman, yes." Wong, with his gentle manner, breaks the deadlock between Logan and Street, who both, he subsequently observes, actually possess feelings of affection for one another. The combative relationship between Logan and Street provides the primary dramatic counterpoint to the film's murder mystery plotline.

A key scene that illustrates Wong's kindly style of dramatic inter-vention occurs when Wong and Street visit the apartment where the now-deceased princess stayed during her visit. As the two look around the apartment Street constantly chatters, speculating on the facts in the

Boris Karloff in *Mr. Wong in Chinatown*. (MoMA)

case, while Wong slowly and silently moves around the room, looking carefully for small details. Eventually a frightened Chinese woman emerges from the shadows of another room. Street brusquely questions her but gets nothing but enigmatic responses until Wong intervenes. He gently asks her questions even as Street interjects with his noisy queries. Subsequently a Chinese dwarf enters the apartment, to the surprise of everyone. According to the maid, he knew the princess but is "dumb"; evidently he can hear but cannot speak. Also, the maid cannot communicate with the dwarf due to his unfamiliar Chinese dialect. Therefore, Street attempts a pantomime to question whether the dwarf saw anyone come into the apartment. When the dwarf does not respond, Street expresses impatience and begins to make another attempt, but Wong quietly moves the inspector aside and more deliberately pantomimes the exact same gestures. The dwarf responds enthusiastically and gives the men an important clue.

What is particularly interesting in this scene is the nature of this repetition of Wong's kinder, gentler approach with Street's display of blunt and impatient behavior. And yet, to merely attribute the response of the Chinese characters in the scene to Wong's individual demeanor would completely ignore the issue of race. A cultural bond between the dwarf and the maid is acknowledged even as she articulates her lack of understanding of his dialect. The princess's maid and the dwarf (notably, the dwarf is played by a Caucasian dressed in Oriental garb) instinctively respond to the Chinese detective. Still, Wong in this scene is not allowed an explicit cultural bonding with his fellow Chinese. He offers no words, only gestures, and these only after Street originated them. However, Mr. Wong's detective when compared to Chan or Moto displays the most explicit and consistent ties to his fellow Chinese.

Indeed, in a subsequent scene Wong goes to visit several members of the Chinese community in Chinatown, although it remains unclear whether the Chinese detective also makes his residence in the Chinese enclave or rather in some other part of San Francisco. Looking for some clue to break this case, which has come to involve the purchase of military planes headed for China, Wong goes to see a group of Chinese community leaders. He enters what appears to be a curio shop on a nondescript Chinatown street, but once in the modest shop the detective is led into a back room where several Chinese men sit around a table. He respectfully bows to all as he enters, and the man at the head of the table asks if he comes on "personal business" or "in an official capacity." To this Wong answers that he is there "on behalf of the police." Wong provides a sharp contrast with the group of men dressed in traditional costume, and yet the leader tells the detective that he will have "the resources of the tong" at his command. At once, we know definitely that these men are members of the tong, a secret society in the U.S. Chinese community customarily associated with criminal activity. Wong approaches them to inquire about a possible Chinese connection to the smuggled airplanes while clearly implicating himself in their activity through his familiarity with the group.

This series, more so than the others, incorporates a larger Asian community perspective in its plots. This film not only has a Chinese princess as its primary murder victim but also implicates another identified Chinese operative (spoken about although he never appears) in the smuggling of planes as well as the acknowledged influence of the tong. Of course, whether Wong's esteemed reputation and status become tainted through his association to the secret society or whether the tong appears more legitimate by its cooperation with Wong is a cause for speculation. Even with the inclusion of these Chinese elements, the ultimate culpability is always attributed to a Caucasian character.

The release of the first Mr. Wong film, *Mr. Wong Detective* (1938), was greeted in a *Variety* review not so much with enthusiasm for wide popularity but rather with cautious optimism for a modestly profitable series run. Of course, the casting of Karloff is also acknowledged in the *New York Times* review of the film as particularly appropriate for a role involving the pursuit and outwitting of criminal minds. The actor's past screen roles (described as containing "a few little homicidal tricks") are seamlessly linked to the list of qualities attributed to his current character.[30] However, while Karloff went over well in the role (his minimal makeup is even mentioned as a plus), the film is criticized for "lagging story buildup and action" as well as for "standard to skimpy" production values.[31] Later series installments were rated only "fair-minus" by the *New York Times,* although Karloff's depiction is consistently singled out as being at least "a few millimeters better."[32]

After Karloff's fifth and final appearance as Mr. Wong in the film *Doomed to Die* (1940), Monogram reworked the entire concept of the series with the next installment, titled *The Phantom of Chinatown* (1940). The film stars Keye Luke, sets a precedent by casting the only Chinese American actor to date to portray a Chinese detective in a screen role, and was promoted as the beginning of a new series, headed by Luke. A 1940 feature article titled "Keye Luke Sleuths on His Own" in the *Hollywood Citizen News* reported that the actor was signed to a deal for four pictures a year. The film itself breaks almost every convention in the Oriental detective series, first and foremost with its casting of Luke "as the cinema's one and only genuine Oriental detective."[33]

Luke plays a younger James Lee Wong, now a college student, who stumbles onto the mysterious death of a former professor. The only makeup applied is eyebrow pencil used to fill out the thin mustache that the actor was requested to grow for the part. Luke's performance is completely free of Oriental affectation adopted by his European predecessor, as he is depicted as an Americanized Chinese. Only supporting character Inspector Street (played by Grant Withers) is held over from the Karloff cast and dispenses his role with the usual impatient energy. Interestingly, author Eugene Wong states that *The Phantom of Chinatown* was never released by the studio.[34] According to Wong, the studio feared rejection by film audiences to a Chinese American actor playing the Chinese detective.

Although the film is not listed among the annual releases in the *Film Daily Yearbook,* there exist a daily *Variety* review of a preview screening dated November 15, 1940; a *Hollywood Reporter* review from the same date; and a weekly *Variety* review dated January 1, 1941. The latter reports on a dual-week release at a New York theater during the week of December 28, 1940. While the preview review from the *Hollywood Reporter* was favorable, the *Daily Variety* was not, citing that the film "will suffer from comparison with its predecessors" and specifically identifying the change in the leading character as a "demotion . . . to the role of stooge," which "does not augur well for the future of the series."[35] It appears from this review that the main complaint is that Wong's character was not allowed to maintain his heroic stature with Luke in the role as opposed to overstepping his boundaries as a heroic figure. However, even without conclusive evidence, the film was most likely not considered a commercial success. Indeed, nothing of its type was attempted again for decades.

The real mystery in this in many ways landmark film lies in its fate after production. While clearly political strife escalated in the Pacific, it is possible to speculate that the ethnic authenticity inherent in such an unusual casting decision (Chinese actor as Chinese character) at that time threatened to undermine the chief tenet of this archetype's foundation and popularity: a white actor posing as an Oriental figure.

Despite its symbolic currency, the Oriental detective series/archetype has not customarily been the object for serious critical inquiry. The Chan, Moto, and Wong films are commonly regarded as only entertainment, exceedingly formulaic vehicles with no intrinsic qualities worthy of serious consideration. However, like traditional genre films, these series maintain their appeal precisely through their explicit conventionality, predictability, and repetition. But as this chapter has attempted to argue, the Oriental detective offers a host of divergent elements that produces a most singular and memorable screen character. Strangely conversant with the criminal mind yet equally at home among the cultivated, rich, and powerful, the Oriental detectives Chan, Moto, and Wong function as popular evocations of cinematic fantasy.

As previously discussed, the detective tends to exhibit a general restraint in demeanor. Facial expressions tend to break down into two main categories: (1) impassive, inscrutable facial expressions in reaction to highly emotional situations, highly charged characters, or potential physical threats to the detective himself and (2) the capitulating and deferential smile. The facial cast of the detective tending toward the impassive suggests both an unflappable levelheadedness in the character and the cliché of a generalized Oriental inscrutability. This split between heroic and traditionally cryptic qualities provides another illustration of the central dichotomy operating within this archetype. And the broad polite smile (often accompanied by a bowing of the head) with prominently displayed teeth portrays the detective figure as amiable, amusing, and also shrewd. He routinely appears to capitulate when we know that he will pursue his own hunches in the case.

These carefully constructed and highly codified characters also manage to retain considerable iconic mileage. This seems particularly curious in light of the Caucasian actors who portrayed them. This phenomenon raises the question of how an archetype for a character becomes an archetype for a race. Indeed, the 1960s added the label "model minority" initially to Chinese Americans and then extended it to all Asian Americans. Essentially the model minority thesis in an article appearing in *U.S. News and World Report* in December 1966 compared the "hundreds of billions spent to uplift Negroes and other minorities" to the nation's then estimated 300,000 Chinese-Americans who are "moving ahead on their own—with no help from anyone else."[36]

The strategically vital characters of Fu Manchu and Charlie Chan in particular can easily inhabit positions as representations of the yellow peril and model minority, respectively. But as we have seen in the close analysis of Chan and his ilk, even within the Oriental detective character a split between the acceptable and the potentially objectionable is apparent. However, the yellow peril and model minority paradigms exist not as polar opposites; instead, they "form a circular relationship that moves in either direction":[37]

Fu Manchu/dragon lady and Charlie Chan/lotus blossom, like their dual genders, were the offspring of a miscegenational union: the interbreeding of Asian and European culture, making them doubly dangerous. Both Fu Manchu and Charlie Chan were steeped in Orientalism but learned from the West, and they challenged and threatened white supremacy, and galvanized and attested to the superiority of Europe. They operated from within the white homeland, within the colonial enclaves of Chinatowns and Hawaii, and hated and envied the West. In the end, Fu Manchu and Charlie Chan, yellow peril and model minority, personified the cunning, sensuality, and mysticism of a feminine Asia (the body) and the intellect, logic, and science of a masculine Europe (the mind).[38]

This uneasy continuum between yellow peril and model minority in the guise of Oriental villain and hero becomes increasingly evident during the war years, when signature elements of the heroic Oriental detectives are inverted and vilified. A review of *Mr. Wong in Chinatown* in 1939 (signed only B. R. C., perhaps authored by noted *New York Times* arts critic Bosley Crowther) portends the chilling shift in attitude toward the screen Oriental during World War II:

The cinema has its own Far Eastern problem these days, viz., a largesse of fictional detectives. It is true that the marvelous Mr. Moto has recently been discontinued by his sponsors, because of some alleged anti-Japanese feeling among the customers. But the changeless Mr. Chan is still functioning from time to time, and, at the moment, the wonderful Mr. Wong is operating . . . in a pleasant little murder mystery. . . . Since consular protests and State Department representations would probably be in vain, only two courses lie open to us: we must either accept the situation gracefully, or put teeth in the quota system.

The are no statistics on the subject, of course, but there must be hundreds of good American sleuths out of jobs or on relief because of pictures like "Mr. Wong in Chinatown." . . . This subtle discrediting of the West, this constant insistence on the superior finesse of the yellow races in the presence of homicide, is something which every red-blooded American should resent.[39]

In this chapter, some of the less explicit (and often contradictory) complexities operating within the heroic Oriental detective archetype have been addressed. Chapter 3 turns to the shift in Hollywood's representation of the Oriental brought on by the advent of the Pacific War. We will not only consider how familiar Oriental detective archetypes (such as Charlie Chan and Mr. Moto) become contested symbols for the ally and enemy but will also discuss other often elaborate strategies employed to construct a wartime Japanese enemy in Hollywood films.

THREE

Creatures of Evil
The Wartime Enemy

Lights come up. Vincent portraying a "Jap soldier." Lighting creates the mood of an old 40s black and white movie. Thick Coke-bottle glasses, holding a gun. Acts in an exaggerated, stereotypic—almost cartoonish manner. Sergeant Moto pretends to be falling asleep while guarding American prisoners. The snake-like lids of his slanty eyes drooping into a feigned slumber. Suddenly Moto's eyes spitting hate and bile, flash open, catching the American prisoners in the midst of their escape plans.

—Philip Kan Gotanda, *Yankee Dawg You Die*

The preceding excerpt, which opens the play *Yankee Dawg You Die* by Philip Kan Gotanda, addresses the legacy of wartime films and their impact on the lives of contemporary Asian Americans such as the leading character actor Vincent Chang, who portrays the "Jap soldier." This description captures some of the basic features of Hollywood's wartime Japanese enemy. The "thick Coke-bottle glasses," "cartoonish manner," reference to "Moto," and "slanty eyes" all speak to the conventions exhibited in the films of this period.

According to Edward Said, a strategic formation is a process by which groups and types of text collectively acquire referential power among themselves as well as create and influence a larger social reality. In chapter 2, we discussed the complexity and adaptability of the Oriental detective archetype, how each individual series came to be associated with one another and eventually to emerge as a remarkably unified metatext. Not only did these characters "acquire referential power among themselves," but they also took on new life during the war that clearly engaged "a larger social reality."[1]

Chapter 1 examined Hollywood's depiction of the Orient as the creation of and refuge for Western imaginary reveries, while chapter 2 explored the deep tensions and ambivalences negotiated within the depiction of the popular Oriental detective hero. Although these earlier Caucasian impersonations have their origins within Hollywood's studio system of mass production, Caucasian portrayals of Orientals during the war took on very specific meanings unique to the period that directly drew from and expanded on established cinematic archetypes. This chapter focuses on the remarkable adaptability of this performance practice, which can mean entirely different things at different historical moments.

Although the racial impersonation of Asians by Caucasian actors remained the predominant performance practice during World War II, after the attack on Pearl Harbor the construction of a Japanese enemy in Hollywood films was perceived by government authorities as critical to the war effort. The structure of this Oriental adversary was neither entirely simplistic nor fixed, as the figure of the Japanese enemy shifted and adjusted over the course of the war years (1941–45). This chapter will address how wartime terms and concepts confirm, contradict, or otherwise modify Hollywood's Oriental archetypes through the performances of Caucasian actors.

The films analyzed in this chapter were chosen as emblematic of distinct strategies utilized in the demonization of the wartime Japanese enemy. They provide potent illustrations of how popular Oriental detectives of the 1930s (specifically, Mr. Moto and Charlie Chan) transformed from good guys to bad guys during the war. The selected cartoons from this period reflect this transformation in full effect. Indeed, animation and caricature allow for the combination of wildly hetero-geneous elements into a homogeneous enemy.

The animated depictions exist as something drawn rather than ex-isting as a performance that utilizes the human body. Still, the animated and live-action stereotypical qualities are pulled from the same pool of elements. Sheng-Mei Ma's book *The Deathly Embrace: Orientalism and Asian American Identity* addresses this very issue, targeting the racist rep-resentation of Siamese cats in two of Disney's classic animated feature films from the postwar period:

> Although demeaning racial vignettes are scattered throughout Disney productions, two feature length animations stand out in the depictions of Siamese cats in what are purportedly Asian images. A bucktoothed Siamese cat in *The Aristocats* (1967) performs a "chopsticks" song in "Ev'rybody Wants to Be A Cat." . . . By the same token, *Lady and the Tramp* (1955) features two wily, bucktoothed, cross- and slit-eyed Sia-mese cats disrupting the life of the canine protagonist, the "lady" of the title. . . . The most biting burlesque comes through the lyrics, sung in the affected, high-pitched pidgin. The two cats repeat, in awkward, un-grammatical sentences, that they are Siamese whether or not it pleases others. . . . The logic is frightening because, after all, pidgin English and such physical features are believed to be those of a certain group of humans. These alleged racial markers are transposed from humans to cats, not the other way around. Disney cats may then be regarded as projections of the Western perception of Asians.[2]

There is also cross-referencing from the live-action to the ani-mated shorts: in other words, shared iconography. There is a clear relationship between the two media even though they do not exist on the same ontological level. The animated image can render key elements of artifice and constructedness where the visual shorthand used is most apparent. In this way, the cartoon can explode what the human form can only contain to follow the caricature to its most extreme manifestations.

The construction of Japanese characters as duplicitous, treacher-ous, and evil also results from a strategic positioning as moral opposites to our then-good Chinese allies. Finally, the practices of physical embodiment by Caucasians are analyzed specifically in view of its deployment during the wartime period, primarily as an explicit tool of racial conquest and triumph.

Collectively, the films discussed in this chapter illustrate the mutability of established Oriental archetypes as well as exemplify important shifts in their wartime evolution from more benign prewar types. Both Oriental hero and fiend take on new meaning during this time, as positive portrayals are categorically reversed in the animated shorts *Japoteurs* (1942) and *Bugs Bunny Nips the Nips* (1944). In the epic feature film *Dragon Seed* (1944) we have the appearance of an important wartime strategy to differentiate Asian national identities with the purpose of creating sharp divisions between our Chinese ally and Japanese enemy. And the exploration of racial difference through a single human body depicts the concept of racial alteration as the ultimate fantasy with nightmarish consequences in *First Yank into Tokyo* (1945).

"Orientals don't make good actors"

The preceding quote comes from a *Variety* column announcing the casting of the film *Blood on the Sun* (1945) starring James Cagney and Sylvia Sidney. The notice attempts to rationalize, once again, the portrayal of key Asian roles by white actors:

> Caucasian actors will impersonate Japs in the William Cagney production, "Blood on the Sun," although there are plenty of Oriental thesps who might pass for Nips. Idea is that Orientals don't make good actors, and plenty of good acting is required in the picture, which stars James Cagney as an American newspaperman in Japan. Chief supporting role is that of Hideki Tojo, former Jap premier, to be played by Robert Armstrong, who will be made up by Joseph Norin, an authority on Oriental makeup.[3]

Produced near the end of the war, this film attempts to dramatize the origins of Japanese aggression through a focus on a secret plan for world domination. The central conflict in the film is predictably confined between Cagney's reporter character and Japanese military operatives. Caucasian actress Sylvia Sidney was cast to portray Cagney's Eurasian (British Chinese) love interest, while substantial supporting roles went to Caucasian actors as well.

This article goes on to claim that "Caucasian actors will impersonate Japs" due to the "idea" that "Oriental" actors are inherently lacking in talent.[4] Since this idea about the deficient abilities of Asian actors is not attributed in the article to either a specific person or entity, we are left to assume that this is the ubiquitous assumption of the Hollywood film community. Although Chinese actor Richard Loo and Korean actor Philip Ahn specialized in playing sinister Japanese antagonists in many wartime Hollywood films, the vast majority of these roles were still portrayed by white actors.

While this statement appears at a specific historical moment when the United States is still at war with Japan (clearly indicated by the use of the racial epithets "Japs" and "Nips"), the sentiments apparent in the statement "Orientals don't make good actors" merely adds a contemporaneous dimension to a traditional cinematic casting/performance practice. Still, despite the preeminent position that this performance practice came to occupy in Hollywood's representation of Asians, the portrayal of Orientals by Caucasian players becomes a key element during the war years.

The Oriental Detective as Wartime Foe

"Me No Moto"

There are thousands of Japanese aliens in southern California but Sol Wurtzel can't find one of them to play a heavy role in the forthcoming "Secret Agent of Japan" at 20th-Fox.

American-born actors of Nipponese descent are side-stepping the idea and Chinese players won't even discuss it.[5]

The preceding notice appeared on the front page of *Variety* in December 1941 only weeks after the attack on Pearl Harbor. Sol M. Wurtzel had been the executive producer (and was also occasionally credited as assistant director, "Solly Wurtzel") for many of the Mr. Moto detective pictures produced by Twentieth Century Fox. And although the detective series ended its run two years earlier, the producer's name may have remained linked with the commercially successful films along with its then-heroic Japanese protagonist. The headline transposition of an Oriental movie hero (Moto) to a villain (or "heavy" as the article specifies) not only reflects the dictates of the wartime shift in societal attitudes but also perhaps implicitly exonerates Wurtzel's earlier involvement with the series. Predictably, Japanese American (note the use of the racial epithet "Nipponese") and Chinese actors are also not so subtly equated with the so-called aliens supposedly infiltrating southern California. The reference to the Japanese screen detective Mr. Moto illustrates how the familiarity of an Oriental Hollywood character can provide a convenient classification for an unseen and unknown enemy. At once slanted, manipulated, and altered, a once-singular hero suddenly becomes a symbol for the unequivocal enemy, a massive threat targeted for extinction.

It would be a mistake, however, to minimize the fundamental goal of the Hollywood film industry to provide, first and foremost, popular (and often escapist) entertainment for a mass audience. In spite of the industry's quest for commercial success, Hollywood films have almost always had to formulate their appeal within the context of promoting certain ideals and values while suppressing others. The distinction that can be made during the war years is that the purpose and objective of these values appeared to be simpler and clear-cut as well as strongly essential to the morale and defense of the nation. As a result, many films made during World War II not only provided escapist entertainment but also reflected the national beliefs and expectations of the time, no doubt influenced in part by heightened government involvement. In June 1942 six months after the attack on Pearl Harbor, the government established the Office of War Information (OWI) as the sole contact with the Hollywood film industry. Even though escapist fare was still the order of the day in Hollywood, the studios were also strongly encouraged by government authorities to produce films that explicitly extolled the virtues of democracy and condemned totalitarianism.

A notable feature in Hollywood's attempt to condemn the Japanese attack on Pearl Harbor was the sudden redefinition accorded to heroic cinematic Oriental detective characters such as Mr. Moto. This redefinition invoked the familiarity of these characters but not the esteem and affection they enjoyed prior to the war, as the "Me No Moto" title so clearly illustrates. Mr. Moto (and also to a much lesser degree Charlie Chan) were negatively invoked as symbols of the villainy and treachery of the suddenly homogenous yellow peril wartime enemy. Why would negative invocations of well-known heroic Oriental characters be used as symbols for the Japanese enemy instead of using an unequivocally evil Oriental figure such as Fu Manchu (a professed advocate of Asian world domination)? Rather than reference a known Oriental adversary, the exploitation of amicable Oriental characters by Hollywood perhaps reflects a lingering sense of treachery and betrayal triggered by the nature of the surprise attack on Pearl Harbor as well as the marked ambivalence directed toward these heroic figures in the earlier films discussed in the previous chapter.

An intense quality of animosity was directed toward these Oriental detective characters who seemingly played by Western rules of conduct. Chapter 2 analyzed the complex and often ambivalent nature of the Oriental detective's heroic status that is maintained through a highly codified set of conventions. Indeed, within this archetype a certain measure of explicit role-playing and duplicity coexisted with clearly established Western allegiances. However, during the war the Oriental detective's position as a trusted assimilated figure was suddenly perceived as an unqualified deception. These figures of the popular imagination swiftly became wedded to the political and military interests of Asia—Japan, in particular—as race, previously concealed among a host of idiosyncrasies, revealed itself paramount.

Although these are clearly fictional characters, the depiction of these detectives not only came to represent popular cinematic personalities but also defined the Chinese and Japanese (as well as other) racial groups and cultures for many in Hollywood's mass audience who were not otherwise exposed to these national cultures. If we accept this premise, the scapegoating of well-known fictional Oriental characters during a time of openly hostile feeling toward the Japanese possesses a clearer rationale. This apparent transposition between fictional movie characters and the actual Japanese threat perhaps has its darker and even more disturbing manifestation in the active disregard for distinctions of national allegiance for particular members of the U.S. population.

In general, many portrayals of the Japanese were unequivocally evil. This fact ostensibly troubled the OWI, which officially advocated criticism of "fascism and its ruling cliques, not the German or Japanese people."[6] Of course, other nationalities and ethnic groups have been and continue to be demonized in popular culture depending on whether the United States is at war with their respective countries. However, the case of the Japanese remains unique because of the widespread public acceptance and support for the official internment/ relocation of Japanese Americans for the duration of the war. This racially based collective demonization of the war years manifested itself in films that positioned formerly friendly Oriental screen figures as the enemy from within: a sinister Oriental traitor, a stranger with a different face who lives among us merely pretending to be one of us.

Other virulent depictions of the Japanese included B-level serials such as Republic Pictures' 1942 *G-Men vs. Black Dragons,* which uses racially cosmetized non-Asian actors as part of an Axis spy ring. The story characterizes the Japanese spies as completely irrational, fanatical, and bestial. This depiction reflects a common perception of the Japanese enemy during World War II. Keith Aoki notes the "enduring popularity" in the United States of the "harikiri/kamikaze stereotype, which began circulating during World War II as supposed evidence of the lack of value placed on individual human life by the Japanese— hence, their inhumanity."[7]

The Mr. Moto series ceased production two years before the attack on Pearl Harbor on December 7, 1941. The final Mr. Wong feature was released in January 1941. Only the Charlie Chan series continued to produce features; however, Twentieth Century Fox concluded that series with *Castle in the Desert* (1942). Whether the three series had simply run their course or whether the Pacific War created an inhospitable atmosphere for cinematic Oriental heroes of any nationality, for a brief period between 1942 and 1944 no Oriental detective series was in production. This illustrates a significant shift from the late 1930s, when three series competed for the film audience's attention. By 1944, actor Sidney Toler had acquired the rights to the Charlie Chan character and convinced Monogram to resume the series that year. Strikingly, the first film produced by the studio was a picture titled *Charlie Chan in the Secret Service* (1944). Although the film had little to do with the

Secret Service (the plot revolves around Chan's pursuit of documents from German spies), its title placed the goals of the detective character comfortably in the service of the U.S. government.

Significantly, the OWI closely observed the Charlie Chan series during the war years for material that might be offensive to the U.S. ally China or might prove to reflect undemocratic values to overseas allies. In the case of *Charlie Chan in the Secret Service,* the OWI believed that this film "might damage relations" with China, as "the portrait of the bland and inscrutable oriental who spoke in pidgin English would be taken as an insult by the Chinese."[8]

The agency agreed to pass along the script to the Chinese consul in Los Angeles, T. K. Chang, and contingent on a negative response from him, the OWI threatened to recommend that both this film as well as the entire Chan series cease production. But since Chang did not agree with the OWI about the script, both the film and the series were allowed to continue.[9] The OWI also took issue with the series' subsequent release, *Charlie Chan in the Mystery Mansion* (1944), in which "the local American police were shown as generally incompetent and 'hopelessly stupid' when compared to Chan."[10] The government agency wanted all films to promote the perception of an efficient and just police force operating in a democratic society. Clearly, the OWI saw the Charlie Chan films not as harmless entertainment but rather as contradictory and potentially problematic, depending on its national venue and the particular historic moment.

The Enemy as Cartoon

The cover cartoon for *Collier's* magazine dated December 12, 1942, marking the first anniversary of the attack on Pearl Harbor presents a Japanese military figure about to drop a bomb on the unsuspecting ships. However, this Japanese figure is not rendered in a recognizably human form within an airplane but instead is manifested as a vampire bat. Without a body, this creature possesses a face, wings, and disembodied gloved fingers clutching the bomb. The face has slanted eyes, a broad nose, prominent teeth along with huge fangs, and ears pointed in a demonic fashion. Significantly, this creature is also clothed and armed with recognizable icons from both the German and Japanese military.

The bat wears a Japanese military cap and carries a sword in one hand but also curiously displays a swastika on each wing.

This image represents a site where caricature and propaganda meet to produce an impossible image, a creature of evil, that has almost nothing to do with the reality of a racial type (or human type for that matter) but instead involves the distortion of a number of racial qualities and iconic symbols displayed to induce hatred. Whether inverting the qualities of heroic Oriental film characters or fusing the qualities of both the German and Japanese military, any apparent incongruity of elements appears to be subordinate to the wartime propagandistic task of arousing a visceral reaction in the American people.

The exhibition of exaggerated mannerisms provides a central element within the performances of the Oriental detectives discussed in chapter 2. However, a caricature rendered in pen and ink (e.g., Collier's vampire cover art, editorial cartoons, or war posters of the period) can represent its most extreme manifestations because there is no human body required to mediate the message. Notably, while wartime posters of the Nazi threat also focused on acts of brutality and violence, they did not distort physical or racial elements, as with the Japanese.

The functions of caricature in World War II film animation produced by Hollywood included both portrayals, which sought to identify and vanquish a formidable wartime adversary along with depictions of this same opponent as hopelessly weak and inferior. Cartoon shorts not only provided uniformly antagonistic versions of the Japanese but also utilized humor for comic relief, hence the tendency in this medium to represent the enemy as either buffoon or superman. Of course, it must be noted that even with cartoon animation there are strongly different styles such as the more realistic narrative-heavy *Japoteurs* and the outright burlesque and gag form of the Bugs Bunny franchise, the two examples chosen for discussion in this chapter.

Indeed, an installment of the Superman animated series titled *Japoteurs* (Paramount, 1942) depicts the Japanese enemy—a saboteur based in the fictional Metropolis—as a thoroughly malignant threat to the national security of the United States. However, one of the most striking features of this eight-minute animated short is how this patently antagonistic archvillain is presented as a visual combination of the familiar

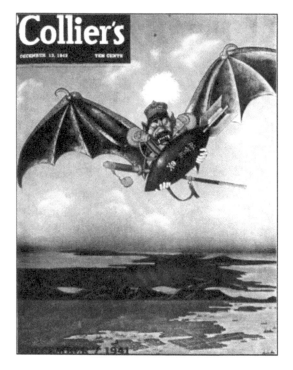

Collier's magazine cover of Japanese vampire bat

Oriental detectives Charlie Chan and Mr. Moto. In this case, key elements of these formerly loyal Oriental cinematic figures are visually inscribed onto this Japanese saboteur figure. The fact that Charlie Chan is a Chinese character or that the Japanese Mr. Moto character in the series at Fox routinely collaborates with exclusively Western interests apparently had little bearing on the appropriation of their immediately identifiable qualities for this villainous character.

The story begins with the image of a newspaper press furiously printing out copies. A headline from the *Daily Planet* newspaper reads "World's Largest Bombing Plane Finally Completed" along with a picture of the plane on the front page. We then cut to an office setting, where a Japanese male figure sneers and uses a cigarette to burn a hole in the front-page newspaper picture of the bomber aircraft.

Next we see an image of a gigantic bomber that dwarfs the regular-sized planes flying into its interior. Enter Lois Lane and Clark Kent, who identify themselves with press passes to a security guard to gain entrance into the bomber. When their official tour is over, Clark proceeds off the plane with other reporters while Lois slips away into a nearby locker. As the plane takes off, Clark realizes that Lois is a stowaway on the aircraft.

Inside the plane, the tip of one bomb unscrews to reveal the Japanese saboteur introduced in the first scene followed by two accomplices. With gun drawn, the lead saboteur ties up the pilot and takes over in the cockpit as he states in stilted English, "Now nothing will interfere with voyage to Tokyo." Clark works his way away from the crowd and states, "This is a job for Superman." While entering the giant bomber, he is greeted by the lead saboteur, who shows Superman that Lois is tied to a bomb shaft that is poised to be dropped. With his hand on the control switch, the saboteur says, "Get off plane immediately or girl will be released." To this Superman responds, "OK little man, you win," and appears to leave.

When the saboteur releases the bomb shaft anyway, Superman rescues Lois and returns her unharmed to the plane. Superman subdues all the Japanese saboteurs, carries Lois to safety, and with only the strength of his body lands the crashing plane safely in Metropolis. A moving marquee flashes "Superman Saves Giant Bomber—Captures Japoteurs."

In *Japoteurs,* released in the autumn of 1942—not yet a year after Pearl Harbor—the sentiment of the enemy as stranger in our midst establishes its prominent theme within the narrative. Initially, the visual identity of the figure reading the front-page newspaper headline remains concealed except for dark hair and clothing, with only the barest indication of dark eyeglasses. We do not see a full face but instead are given only the scant outlines of a human male figure. The surroundings of the office seem standard enough (an American newspaper, a chair, a desk, etc.), and the inclusion of the Statue of Liberty picture on the wall appears to clearly identify the national allegiance of its inhabitant. Also perhaps paradoxically, the Statue of Liberty, so often associated with immigration, could additionally indicate an attitude toward letting Japanese into the country. However, only a moment later this picture is revealed to have a different face on its reverse side: a Japanese flag, an easily recognizable wartime symbol of Japanese nationhood.

This brief yet evocative visual moment expediently introduces elements of duplicity and treachery to the Japanese wartime threat. It effectively promotes that idea of a Japanese enemy emerging from within America's shores who appears to be like us but who is, in fact, poised against us. They possess Western accoutrements. Everything appears to be normal, and yet the reverse is true (as the reverse side of the Statue of Liberty picture revealing the Japanese flag plainly attests), as this film presents the specific nature of the Japanese threat as inherently seditious and subversive, a belief widely held by many U.S. citizens. Indeed, the initial moments in the introduction of the Japanese enemy in *Japoteurs* unfolds in the manner of a warning ruse, a gentle caution for its wartime viewers.

While the series of images that open this cartoon present the specific nature of the Japanese threat through indirect means, the moments immediately following reveal the identity of the figure as Japanese through specific physical traits. As the figure executes the culturally specific gesture of bowing to the picture of the Japanese flag, more of his face becomes visible along with a hint of a mustache and a bow tie. The next shot reveals his entire face sneering in close-up. Finally, we are given physical features and a facial gesture on which to contemplate, and yet this face also accommodates iconic cues. With his dark round glasses clearly visible, the figure's face not only reveals features deemed typically Japanese or generally Oriental (narrow slanted eyes, thin eyebrows, and mustache) but also mirrors those of the familiar Japanese screen detective Mr. Moto.

Invoking the specter of Mr. Moto through his distinctive dark round glasses provides a succinct, visual shorthand that reflects both the complex and often ambivalent nature of the Oriental detective's heroic status as well as establishes this representation of the Japanese enemy as a fundamentally composite construction. At work in the choice of Mr. Moto as wartime enemy is a negotiation between a process of recognition and a strategy that also suggests misrecognition. Embedded in the appearance of this Japanese villain is the vague awareness of familiar screen hero Mr. Moto, who strongly suggests that within a Japanese countenance both friend and enemy coexist. This method of articulation relies equally on an intimacy with and license taken with a familiar character whose semblance simultaneously hastens and heightens this depiction of a wartime adversary.

The subsequent scene inside the bomber aircraft reveals three shadowy figures hiding unnoticed inside individual bombshells. As the first figure emerges from one bomb he is revealed to be the saboteur introduced at the beginning of the film. Even though we have viewed the face of this character closely, in this scene the addition of buck teeth along with a Panama hat with an upturned brim provides important visual traits. It is notable that while the sudden appearance of the buck teeth draws on more generalized Oriental stereotypes, it also specifically rounds out the similarity to the Mr. Moto screen characterizations in which actor Peter Lorre customarily wore a protruding prosthesis over his upper front teeth.

Most notably, the addition of the hat expands the visual repertoire accorded to this villain to include a distinct reference to the character of Charlie Chan. The detective commonly wears Panama hats and light-colored suits throughout the series—an indication of his Hawaiian roots—although he frequently wears dark clothing as well. What persists in both his dark and light dress is his habitual manner of wearing all of his hats with a completely upturned brim. This hat style has easily become the signature piece in Chan's attire and surely would be familiar to wartime film audiences as such. Indeed, after the saboteur knocks on two other bombs, his two accomplices emerge from their individual bombshells wearing identical hats, only in a dark color. With this added level of replication, Chan's hat plainly functions as a potent identifier, an abstract sign, and a symbol for the enemy forces.

A group of Japanese saboteurs makes their way to the cockpit as the pseudo-Japanese musical strain becomes audible again. Significantly, the accretion of details and their suppression illustrate two specific approaches in the construction of a Japanese enemy in this short film. The precise additions of glasses, hat, and buck teeth for the lead villain in this scene contrasts the uniform depiction of his accomplices, whose faces are never fully shown. However, through this apparent divergence a common goal of vilification is nonetheless served in order to create and maintain the Japanese foe as both duplicitous acquaintance and unknown foe.

Predictably, when the lead Japoteur finally speaks, he delivers his proclamation that "nothing will interfere with voyage to Tokyo" in a manner strongly reminiscent of Charlie Chan's distinctive speaking style. There is a hesitant, though determined, quality in his articulation. An accompanying show of politeness displays itself even in this antagonistic context as he bows to the bound pilot before taking his seat to commandeer the plane. Bowing after a declaration of opposition is emblematic of the polite, deferential Oriental detective archetype, although in this instance the villain displays a cursory politeness in the midst of an insurgent act. This scene illustrates how both the addition of dialogue and the repetition of a gesture (bowing) effectively augment the composite structure of this enemy figure.

Of the two lines that the Japanese saboteur speaks, only one is directed at Superman. With his hand on the control switch to drop Lois Lane out of the plane, the saboteur threatens Superman with the words "Get off plane immediately or girl will be released." Superman's response refers to him as "little man," a disparaging remark that ascribes a physical deficiency to an element of racial difference. In this instance, the smaller body of the Japanese villain is targeted to assert a physical superiority and strength on the side of Superman. Notably, this occurs at the moment when Lois is physically threatened with death at the villain's hands. Moments later (after Lois has been safely harbored), Superman swiftly subdues the two accomplices with what clearly appears to be judo throws instead of the more typical roundhouse fisticuffs.

Rendering the Japanese enemy through national symbols and cultural gestures and finally with other Asian characters illustrates how seemingly heterogeneous elements culled from a disparate Oriental repertoire combine to form a homogeneous wartime enemy. The enemy in *Japoteurs* embodies attributes that might appear incompatible in a less agitated historical context or in a less caricatured form. However, within the conventions of Hollywood animation, the incompatible traits that shift from Chinese to Japanese and fictional to factual uniquely blend to create a plausible wartime traitor.

Unlike the diabolical evil displayed by an opponent worthy of a Superman in *Japoteurs,* the Japanese enemy depicted in *Bugs Bunny Nips the Nips* (Warner Bros., 1944) reveals an antagonist played mainly for laughs. However, a series of vigorously exhibited Oriental clichés characterize the wartime threat despite its less sinister nature. Physically focused elements of the Japanese wartime caricature predominate in this cartoon in terms of not only facial features but also the physique.

It should be noted that Bugs Bunny experienced his first bursts of popularity during the wartime period and played a role as a kind of national mascot, according to author Joe Adamson in his book *Bugs Bunny: Fifty Years and Only One Grey Hare*. Both the German enemy (in shorts such as *Herr Meets Hare*) and the Japanese enemy provided sources for Bugs Bunny cartoon plots. Indeed, the Bugs Bunny cartoons during World War II surpassed both Disney and MGM to become the number one short subject by theater owners.

John Dower's award-winning work *War without Mercy: Race & Power in the Pacific War* also chronicles the importance of animation in the war propaganda effort and the place of Bugs Bunny in particular: "In *Know Your Enemy—Japan*, Frank Capra's team enlisted animators from the Walt Disney studio. . . . The bucktoothed Japanese became a standard cartoon figure, prompting comparison to the Looney Tune creation Bugs Bunny; the Warner Brothers studio followed up on this with a short animated cartoon titled *Bugs Bunny Nips the Nips*."[11]

This Merrie Melodie cartoon begins with Bugs singing a song from within a crate. Then he sees an island and quickly swims toward it, landing on the beach. Bugs fervently extols the virtues of the island as he stands on the sandy beach, with palm trees in the background. Suddenly, his poetic words are cut short by rapid gunfire. Bugs runs for cover into a haystack. His head looks out of the top, but a different pair of legs (wrapped in military fatigues) appears at the bottom of the haystack. Then the owner of the arms and feet finally pokes out at the top of the haystack, confronting Bugs nose to nose. The Japanese soldier has buck teeth, a thin mustache, dark eyeglasses, slanted eyebrows, and curly / wavy hair.

The Japanese soldier then pulls out a sword and starts swiping at Bugs, speaking Oriental gibberish or staccato short syllables. Bugs subsequently emerges in the resplendent uniform of a Japanese general. Now wearing black glasses, Bugs stands stiffly at attention as the soldier takes to his knees and begins bowing to him in supplication. However, Bugs eventually reveals his true identity by casually chomping on a carrot.

The soldier takes up his sword again with Oriental gibberish as Bugs takes off in a Japanese plane (identified with an image of the national flag). The soldier then follows Bugs in his own plane. Bugs ties a rope to a tree and fastens it to the soldier's plane. Still speaking gibberish, the soldier jumps out of the plane with a parachute and begins to gently float toward the ground. Bugs Bunny then flies up in his Japanese plane and hands the soldier an anvil with the taunt, "Here's some scrap iron for Japan, Moto!"[12]

Suddenly, Bugs bumps into a Sumo wrestler. He is huge with a large stomach, mustache, goatee, and buck teeth (and a large gap between the front teeth). He wears the one-piece trunk typical of the sport in addition to a Mohawk haircut. The sumo wrestler swiftly ties Bugs's body up in knots. But moments later, Bugs transforms into a geisha girl wearing red lipstick, elaborate wig, and kimono. Bugs speaks lilting Japanese gibberish as he coaxes the wrestler (now struck dumb by attraction) into a near kiss that turns into a fatal blow with a heavy mallet. As the giant falls, Bugs triumphantly yells "Timber!" In a two-page transcription of the cartoon *Bugs Bunny Nips the Nips* by Katharine Lewis, the Japanese soldier is referred to as "JAP" and the sumo wrestler as "JAP NATIVE," and the language (which I characterize as gibberish) of the soldier and sumo wrestler is described as "fake Japanese."[13]

Bugs then suddenly sees several ships flying Japanese flags and floating toward the island. We next see Bugs driving a white truck in a uniform (white coat and cap) in the mold of Good Humor ice cream vendors, except this truck advertises the phrase "Good Rumor" instead. He entices a large crowd of Japanese soldiers with the call "Hurry! Hurry! Get 'em while they're cold." The soldiers speak gibberish and frantically wave money as Bugs calls out to the soldiers while he hastily serves them: "Here, yuh are. Here's yours bowlegs. Here's one for you, monkey face. Now don't shove. Dere's plenty for all. Here yuh are, slant eyes. Everybody gets one."

As soon as the soldiers receive their ice cream they disappear, running away from the truck as fast as they came. Bugs waits a moment before numerous explosions are heard from the direction that the soldiers ran in. His mission is accomplished, and he returns to his introductory reverie. He then spies an American ship and calls to it desperately, shouting for the ship to come and get him. Suddenly another rabbit dressed up as an island beauty in a sarong appears. Bugs, with a loud howl, immediately changes his mind about leaving the island and hops off after her.

Bugs Bunny Nips the Nips demonstrates how caricature in an animated cartoon can facilitate a host of well-worn racial clichés and concepts about the Japanese as well as the Orient as a whole. Set "Somewhere in the Pacific," this eight-minute cartoon begins with Bugs Bunny landing on a supposedly deserted island. Bugs's initial references to the island as a "garden of Eden" and "Shangri-La" clearly recall the otherworldly haven depicted so vividly in the epic feature *Lost Horizon* (1937) as well as in South Sea island films. Yet his intoxicated reverie about the island illustrates both the centrality of this element in Hollywood's construction of the Orient and how the initial perception can be immediately repositioned to create an impression of utter deception and mortal danger, not unlike the widely perceived nature of the attack on Pearl Harbor.

The seductive first impression that successfully lures Bugs unawares into the harsh reality of armed aggression and war again characterizes the wartime Japanese threat as initially (and deceptively) harmless and even pleasant but then just as suddenly as assailing and hazardous. Even in this short where the Japanese soldier is portrayed as a bungling fool, a critical element in the representation of the Japanese / Oriental threat during World War II emerges, one that stresses the peril of being misled as much as the risk of being militarily overpowered.

The first meeting between the Japanese soldier and Bugs Bunny exhibits a more literal manifestation of a composite image. However, what makes the introduction of the Japanese soldier most interesting is that he appears to share the same body with Bugs himself. Divided only by a haystack, Bugs Bunny provides the head that peeks out above while the Japanese soldier furnishes the bowed legs wrapped in military fatigues and the feet (with a large space separating the first toe from the remainder) emerging from below. This combined visual image presents two distinctly separate identities in the guise of a bizarre yet single body, a body that exploits familiar wartime physical distortions attributed to the Japanese race.

In the popular press (particularly in editorial cartoons) race could be reduced to a few distinct attributes that identified and labeled the

Japanese enemy. Michael Renov, in his essay "Warring Images: Stereotype and American Representation of the Japanese, 1941–1991," addresses common World War II physical myths about the Japanese: "The Japanese are distinctively 'othered.' . . . There is a kind of grotesque confusion in the very placement of their facial feature; their eyes slant down to where their noses should be. They have bad teeth, misshapen feet . . . just reward for being a lesser species."[14]

Of course, in this animated cartoon the lower extremities of legs and feet are chosen rather than a face (a similar slow disclosure introducing the villain in *Japoteurs* delays exposure to a face as well). In *Bugs Bunny Nips the Nips* we encounter an enemy even more radically caricatured as a dissected display of physical deformities. Once again, the construction of the Japanese enemy employs an approach that initially denies wholeness to its adversarial subject, presenting its subject through stringently selected parts.

Immediately following, another disembodied image of a hand emerges from the haystack holding a hand mirror. The hand mirror is held up to Bugs's face. His face transforms suddenly into a caricatured image of a Japanese face (extremely slanted eyes and a protruding mouthful of buck teeth). Then finally the face of the Japanese soldier springs out of the haystack, replacing the mirror to face Bugs's nose to nose. The mirror held only by the hand of the soldier provides the catalyst that transforms Bugs's face into a Japanese one. However, the next moment reveals the actual Japanese soldier's face, which confronts Bugs's caricatured interpretation with its own cartoonish impishness. Here, we are presented with one distortion projected as ostensibly more authentic than another (as exhibited in the caricatured playacting in the Charlie Chan films). Only when placed nose to nose with Bugs's Oriental face are the Japanese soldier's features established as more real within the context of the film.

The next sequence introduces two well-known Japanese identities, General Tojo and Mr. Moto. Bugs Bunny's masquerade as a Japanese general wearing a heavily decorated uniform along with black spectacles clearly imitates photographs from the period of the commanding general of the Japanese military. But this visual reference to a historical figure is quickly followed by a spoken reference to the fictional character of Mr. Moto. The wily rabbit gives the soldier an anvil with the taunt "Here's some scrap iron for Japan, Moto!" Once again, a pointed illustration of the inversion of this Oriental hero's status provides a well-acquainted name for the wartime enemy.

Certainly the conventions of the Bugs Bunny cartoon character allow for the protean rabbit to jump in and out of various disguises, including drag. However, in this film the appearance of Oriental clichés such as the moronic sumo wrestler and the coquettish geisha girl (as played by Bugs) reflects the markedly comedic tone in the depiction of the Japanese threat. Through the inclusion of these two relatively harmless civilian character types, the wartime foe is established as both humorous and easily beaten but most importantly through its enactment as a masquerade. Indeed, the concept of masquerade provides a critical feature of the Oriental guise that can be put on and discarded at will.

Bugs Bunny's subsequent full-scale assault on the horde of Japanese soldiers ("Japs! Hundreds of 'em") who come on shore involves a Good Rumor truck (an obvious takeoff on Good Humor ice cream trucks) filled with chocolate-covered ice cream bars embedded with grenades. Bugs greets the hungry soldiers with a host of insults as the soldiers (whose faces are partially obscured) clamor in Oriental gibberish while anxiously handing over money for the ice cream. Even when the Japanese caricature is not available to us visibly (due to the obscured faces and bodies in the crowd of soldiers), Bugs verbalizes its physical elements with remarkable clarity and detail. The racial epithets "bowlegs," "monkey face," and "slant eyes" audibly support the visual clichés rendered in the animation. As Bugs calls out insults, he uses the physically focused elements of the Japanese wartime caricature.

Additionally, the way in which the Japanese soldiers besiege Bugs's ice cream truck imitates a swarm of bees. It is as if the Japanese soldiers (unlike in *Japoteurs*) do not represent a dangerous threat individually but rather simply in terms of their numbers. A mob at once overflowing but easily fooled, in this scene they are rendered less as human figures and more as a scourge in need of extermination.

Both *Japoteurs* and *Bugs Bunny Nips the Nips* share common elements. They include the use of a disjointed, but not incoherent, series of symbols and physical peculiarities to introduce the Japanese wartime adversary. Clear visual and audible references to formerly heroic

Oriental detective characters Charlie Chan and Mr. Moto are reversed to indicate a now duplicitous enemy. They also contain an emphasis on physical difference and peculiarities to propagate a sense of racial inferiority. Finally, the central positioning of deception and treachery (rather than military might) suggests that the preeminent wartime danger of the Japanese targets American psyche. However, the two animated works differ significantly according to their generic conventions in their portrayals of the Japanese threat as malignant infiltrator (as in the action adventure *Japoteurs*) that necessitates a Herculean opposition or as fundamentally buffoonish, easily destroyed or dispensed with (as in the comedic *Bugs Bunny Nips the Nips*).

Of course, the workings of masquerade emerge as a significant feature in the depiction of these figures as well as generally in many Oriental characterizations. Similar in operation to a prosthetic device (notably used on the teeth in so many Oriental depictions), the masquerade is rendered as easily assumed as well as readily removed. The masquerade trope allows the adoption of any number of masks that render the Oriental as essentially a put-on rather than an actual race.

White Chinese and Yellow Japs

The preceding discussion of animated portrayals of the Japanese enemy stresses its fundamentally composite construction. Pitted against the wily Japanese, the Chinese are positioned, with a considerable degree of wholeness, as Asian surrogates for the hopes and fears of most Americans. Significantly, the practice of Caucasian actors portraying Chinese roles, in particular, at this time provides a useful vehicle to consolidate and propagate the wartime political bond between the interests of the United States and its then Chinese allies. A parallel to this practice discussed here occurs notably in Fritz Lang's anti-Nazi *Ministry of Fear* (1944) about Czech opposition to the Nazis in which European actors were cast as the Nazis and the Americans as the Czech.

Hollywood films have generally demonstrated a capricious nature in their depictions of Asian national identity and racial identity (such as the change of Japanese film star Sessue Hayakawa's character in the silent film *The Cheat* [1915] from Japanese to Burmese) based on a perpetually shifting international political climate. Of course, during the war many films also acknowledged, highlighted, or elided these issues but in more consistent and limited patterns. Although films from this period often denied political distinctions among Japanese citizens (mainly between civilians and military personnel) or between Japanese nationals and American citizens of Japanese descent, other movies actively promoted national and cultural differences among Asians, particularly between Chinese nationals and Japanese soldiers.

Despite the recurrent division of Chinese and Japanese, there was more often significantly different treatment of Germans and Japanese in U.S. films during World War II. One of the most common tendencies in this regard suggests a marked discrepancy in the humanity ascribed to either country; in other words, the Germans were to be considered merely inhuman, while the Japanese were regarded as essentially subhuman. This, again, raises the question of whether this level of disparity in mass media images (i.e., poster art, animation, and film) might be responsible in part for why Japanese Americans were interned as a whole community during World War II. This was not the case for German Americans and Italian Americans, who were not touched as a whole community.

Although the term "Jap" did not originate during the war years, its use at this time was indicative of an active drive to isolate the Japanese people from all other national/racial groups in the minds of the American public. The popular press as well as U.S. Army literature espoused the physical differences between the alien Japanese and the suddenly more compatible Chinese. A well-known *Life* magazine article titled "How To Tell Japs from the Chinese," published soon after Pearl Harbor in 1941, closely scrutinizes the faces of General Tojo along with a Chinese man in search of distinguishing features. A wartime pamphlet provides a detailed and telling comparison of the two "Asiatic" groups and states (among other variances) that the eyes of the Chinese "are set like any European's or American's—but have a marked squint"—while the Japanese are said to be afflicted with "eyes slanted toward his nose."[15] Far from proving their case, this article instead exposes a blatant attempt to present the Japanese countenance as somehow defective while manufacturing elements of physical similarity between the Chinese and European, who are implicitly presumed to provide the normative physical standard.

Apart from creating physical distinctions that attempt to ally the Chinese countenance with European physiognomy was the more important exploitation of Sino-Euro (particularly British) political alliances by Hollywood. British actress Merle Oberon's appearance with Chinese troops training in the United States in *Stage Door Canteen* (1943) attests to the effort to depict the Chinese as good Asian defenders of Western democratic ideals. (Ironically, the Anglo-Indian actress born in Bombay hid her own biracial origins by claiming that she was born in Tasmania of British parents.[16]) Notably, this screen appearance does not emphasize the Chinese army's commitment to defend its own borders but rather stresses its able assistance in the British-U.S. war effort.

Like Merle Oberon, Katharine Hepburn appeared in *Stage Door Canteen* as one of the many visible Hollywood figures involved in the war effort. In fact, Hepburn narrated the film *Women in Defense,* written and edited by Eleanor Roosevelt, to encourage women to join the army or to work in defense plants. *Dragon Seed* (1944) attempts to integrate the ideals of a wartime political agenda by utilizing a bifurcation between the good Chinese fighting for democratic ideals and the evil Japanese who torture and humiliate them. Overall, the Chinese characters in the film are portrayed with some degree of complexity, while the Japanese characters are presented primarily as caricatures with no possibility of character development.

Dragon Seed is based on a best-selling novel of the same name by Pearl S. Buck, a former missionary in China and fervent advocate for wartime aid to the Chinese. MGM hoped to draw on the previous commercial and critical success of another Buck adaptation, *The Good Earth* (1937), as well as fulfill the OWI expectations for the film "to make a major contribution to the war effort."[17]

Predictably, the casting of Academy Award winner Katharine Hepburn as the unconventional Jade as well as screen legend Walter Huston as the peasant farmer Ling Tan added a prestigious element to the project from the outset. And yet the overall casting of this film has been erroneously summarized most notably in a review by James Agee in *The Nation* as Caucasian stars (Hepburn, Huston, et al.) solely playing Chinese characters, with Japanese roles portrayed exclusively by Asian actors.[18] In fact, two major supporting Japanese roles were depicted by Caucasian character actors, J. Carroll Naish (as Jap Kitchen Overseer) and Robert Lewis (as Captain Sato).

Clearly, the casting practice of this film follows long-established industrial norms, with Caucasian stars garnering leading as well as substantial supporting roles (both Chinese and Japanese). While Asian actors remain as bit and extra players, it is interesting that the casting of *Dragon Seed* was perceived to split along strict racial lines (Caucasian Chinese and Asian Japanese). This misrecognition suggests a narrative explanation, as the film's scrupulous bifurcation between the good Asian and bad Asian is portrayed not on the basis of character but instead solely in terms of nationality. And although this tendency was not completely unique to *Dragon Seed*, the attempt to create wholly distinct intraracial divisions in this film occurs primarily through the Chinese characters' implicit closeness to American or Western values. This was one approach designed to persuade American audiences that these Chinese were essentially not very different from themselves. Thus, in this film the only acceptable Chinese becomes white Chinese.

"A quaint language"

The construction of white Chinese goes beyond simply casting Caucasian stars that espouse democratic ideals. The creation of distinct similarities and the fabrication of particular differences provide essential components in the performance of the Chinese roles in *Dragon Seed*. As the creative foundation for the film, the screenplay and its evolution can reveal how basic conceptions and ideas were initially negotiated before the start of production. In this regard, the OWI actually had limited influence on script revisions; rather, the Hays Office through its recommended excisions of potentially offensive material appears to have had the most effect on modifications from draft to draft.[19] However, it is documented that the OWI objected to an early draft of the script because of its "backward" depiction of the Chinese characters. A revised script delivered almost a year later pleased the agency, as new dialogue and scenes were added to show how the Chinese characters were willing to make any sacrifice to fight the Japanese invaders.[20]

Since the Hays Office has historically focused its directives to issues of sexuality and violence, its recommendations for *Dragon Seed* were also primarily confined to these areas. However, the Hays Office was also sensitive to the possible censorship from foreign and state

Walter Huston (*far left*) and Katharine Hepburn (*third from left*) in *Dragon Seed*. (MoMA)

authorities. In this vein, the omission of a line of dialogue appearing to sanction female infanticide was strongly suggested because it might prove offensive to the Chinese government. Hays Office head Joseph Breen, in a memo to Louis B. Mayer, underscored the importance of keeping sentiments of the Chinese allies uppermost in mind: "Furthermore, we assume you will get adequate technical advice to make certain that the finished picture contains nothing that would be offensive to our Allies, the Chinese. This is important from the standpoint of getting an export permit from the Los Angeles Board of Review."[21]

The "technical advice" referred to by Breen ordinarily originated from U.S. military sources (during the war) and/or from a national of the country portrayed. Customarily, in film projects boasting a heightened degree of cultural authenticity, a technical consultant was hired to advise on issues ranging from costuming to dialogue.

The Chinese consultant to this film, Wei Hsueh, generated a scrupulously detailed correspondence with MGM. Overall, his comments reveal the highly constructed nature of the Chinese in *Dragon Seed* as well as effectively highlight the major sites of cultural/national contention. A principal issue involved the style of English spoken by the Chinese characters that ironically (if Hsueh's suggestions had been incorporated) would expose some fundamental similarities between Chinese and English speech patterns. However, the film (and the novel on which it was based) reflects an utter rejection of obvious correspondences in favor of a more exploitable fiction. Clearly, even when the explicit goal of the production is to portray wartime Chinese characters as Americanized heroes, the dramatic avenues chosen and rejected reveal a complex negotiation of cultural projection and containment.

Remarkably, Hsueh begins his comments on the screenplay by acknowledging what he considers the "many inaccuracies" originating in the novel (which the script apparently closely follows) as well as making allowances for "dramatic license." He then offers a telling statement characterizing what he terms the overall "phraseology and dialogue" in the screenplay:[22]

> Intellectually and idealistically, there is a great deal in common between our two peoples than most people believe. One of the great contributions this picture could make is to further our mutual understanding by bringing out that similarity.
>
> Hitherto, most Western writers including Pearl Buck handicapped by their lack of the knowledge of the Chinese written and spoken language, have been trying to interpret Chinese thoughts and to inject Chinese flavor in their work by constructing unusual phrases and grammar. As a result, the expressions used are entirely un-Chinese but become literary oddities. Some of the lines in the script do not bear retranslation into Chinese. . . . My point is that we should not make the Chinese speak a quaint language.[23]

One of the hallmarks of Oriental archetypes is an affected or mannered style of English speech, what Hsueh here has characterized as "a quaint language." Notably, his remarks challenge the pretenses of crosscultural accuracy that this production professes to seek. He reveals its basis (the screenplay) to be perpetuating traditionally demeaning and stereotypical traits.

This element of the Oriental guise reveals itself explicitly again and again, particularly in the trade and marketing documents of the Hollywood film industry. For example, the marketing plans for the 1934 MGM film *The Painted Veil* starring Greta Garbo included exploitation of specific elements inspired by the "Chinese background" of the movie. One idea that is recommended to exhibitors is the seemingly curious "Chinese Marriage Proposal Contest" that perpetuates the "quaint language" singled out for criticism ten years later in relation to *Dragon Seed:* "The flowery English and the customary parable parlance of the educated Chinese was perhaps best exemplified in 'The Son Daughter.' In 'The Painted Veil' this manner of speech is employed intermittently. This might be the basis for a Chinese 'Marriage Proposal' contest, whereby the 'proposals' are presented in 'Chinese-English,' limiting same to 25 words."[24]

The examples that Hsueh cites illustrate the highly constructed nature of the Chinese characters even at the level of dialogue. In his translations the lack of sophistication expressed in the script's hackneyed English style of speech becomes quite apparent: "'I have formed a thought' 'I am thinking about a thing' idiomatically translated would be, 'I am thinking of something.' . . . 'put out your price and put in your tongue' change to 'what is your bottom price.' . . . 'I hear them but they are only sounds one after the other' The Chinese would say 'I hear them but they are just like other rumors I hear now and then.' . . . 'I greet you honored cousin' suggest change to read 'Have you been well uncle?'"[25]

Since the finished film is well populated with characters who speak the "quaint" dialogue and not the more familiar and nuanced English translations, one can only assume that Hsueh's recommendations in this area were completely disregarded. It is clear here that Hollywood decided for ideological reasons to present inaccurate portrayals of language, not simply because they didn't know any better. Hsueh's comments ultimately testify to the sovereignty and dominion of Hollywood-created Orientals and yet also disclose one individual's documented attempt to challenge this.

Set in 1937, *Dragon Seed* chronicles the lives of the Ling Tan clan, a peasant family in war-torn China. This simple family of hardworking farmers, we are told in voice-over narration, were "both good and bad, both wise and foolish," and "therefore they were very much like such families in any other land." The story begins peacefully, with the most pressing problem for family patriarch Ling Tan (played by Walter Huston) and Ling's wife (played by Aline MacMahon) involving the halfhearted attempts by Lao Er (played by Turhan Bey) to tame his rebellious new wife Jade (Katharine Hepburn). Bey's Turkish ethnic origins, again, demonstrate Hollywood's tendency to cast exotic foreigner actors who could deliver a distinctly nonnative intonation to American ears rather than necessarily adopt a specifically Asian accent. Their minor familial squabbles soon recede as rumors of war in the north permeate their small village.

Jade attends a village meeting led by students who advocate joining the resistance to the Japanese army invading their northern neighbors. Despite the crowd's general unresponsiveness, Jade fervently expresses her desire to help their cause. While often publicly embarrassed because of her untraditional boldness, privately Lao Er's feelings are deeply stirred by his wife's uncommon passion and strength.

After repeated Japanese airplane bombings from what the villagers term "flying ships," Jade (now pregnant) and Lao Er announce to the family their decision to join a group of freedom fighters on their way to the hills. Although a multitude of refugees fleeing the Japanese pass through the village, Ling Tan and other local farmers refuse to leave their land. When the Japanese army finally arrives in the town, Ling Tan, his scholarly third cousin (played by Henry Travers), and other village elders go to welcome them, hoping that this gesture will initiate a peaceful coexistence with the invaders. They are subsequently stunned by the brutality and cruelty of the Japanese soldiers.

Ling Tan's family tries to flee the cold-blooded military men, but after Ling's elderly mother-in-law and daughter-in-law Orchid are brutally tortured, raped, and killed, his two remaining sons, Lao Ta (played by Robert Bice) and Lao San (played by Hurd Hatfield) join the resistance in the hillside. In the meantime, Wu Lien (played by Akim Tamiroff), Ling Tan's corrupt son-in-law, collaborates with the newly formed government of the Japanese. While Ling Tan and his wife lose their two young grandsons to starvation, Wu Lien and his family live in pampered comfort due to the mercenary largesse of Captain Sato (played by Robert Lewis).

Lao Er and Jade return after the birth of their infant son. Ultimately, Jade and Lao Er lead other farmers to burn their crops and farms in order to deprive the enemy troops of food. Though initially resistant and still clinging to a passivist stance, Ling Tan eventually leaves for the "freelands" to settle with his wife and family as they watch their land burn. The narrator tells us that the future of China will be for Jade's child and children like him, "so truly the seed of the dragon."

Most apparent in the performances of the leading Chinese characters in *Dragon Seed* is the sheer diversity of physical features, makeup, speech, and mannerisms among the actors. First, the contribution of physical features that the actors themselves bring to their roles should not be overlooked. In particular, Katharine Hepburn and Hurd Hatfield (who plays the sensitive and then wayward and bloodthirsty Lao San) possess high cheekbones and a very thin bone structure overall, at times appearing almost skeletal. However, Turhan Bey, the Turkish actor who plays Hepburn's husband, Lao Er, has very full cheeks and lips and a somewhat broader nose than the other actors. His eyes appear naturally more almond-shaped with minimal cosmetic alteration.

Indeed, not only does the degree of cosmetic application vary from actor to actor, it also tends to split along gender lines. Generally, the faces of the male characters in the film remain less made-up than the faces of the female characters. The eyebrows of the male characters do not appear to be arched (only outlined with dark pencil), and the upper eyelids are narrowed only slightly. While actresses Aline MacMahon (Ling's wife) and Agnes Moorehead (as the third cousin's wife) have notably altered eyes and arched eyebrows, Katharine Hepburn appears to possess the most radically altered eyes. She appears simply not to have thinner eyelids, but often in close-up it appears that she has none at all. Interestingly, the star with perhaps the most distinctive visage in the cast reflects the most extreme manifestation of the common focus for Orientalizing facial makeup, the upper eyelids.

Hair as well remains an important part of the physical construction of the Chinese nationals in this piece. Walter Huston, as head of the clan Ling Tan, sports a white mustache grown long at the sides, a long goatee, and a head of white hair combed straight back. His scholarly third cousin wears the same except with the addition of dark round glasses. However, Ling Tan's sons are all clean-shaven, with dark hair combed straight back. All the women pull their hair straight back in small buns at the nape of the neck. Only Hepburn's character, Jade, adds short cropped bangs to her small bun. Significantly, her hairstyle evolves over the course of the film as she becomes more politicized and her untraditional nature is more accepted. She actually wears her hair down in a pageboy style without bangs near the end, a style that renders her facial features even more keen.

Even more conspicuous than the physicality and makeup of the actors is the range in their styles of speech. We have Katharine Hepburn's rather patrician enunciation as contrasted to her screen husband, Turhan Bey, with his Turkish accent as well as the Russian-accented speech of Akim Tamiroff (Wu Lien). Remarkably, Walter Huston and Aline MacMahon (whose American accents in no way resemble Hepburn's or one another) as well as the rest of the cast make no attempt to adopt even pseudo-Chinese accents. So, in this film the spoken expression of their nationality relies almost entirely on the idiosyncratic speech patterns originating in the written dialogue. This, of course, tends to foreground "the quaint language" so criticized by the Chinese consultant on the project. It is this "quaint language" that, regardless of the widely varying accents of the cast, provides a utilitarian (albeit fictitious) common tongue that verbally connects all the actors. In this way, the characters can more plausibly portray members of the same family, village, and nation by speaking a "Chinese" language created not through the consistencies of an accent (which an American actor may or may not be able to master) but rather through idiosyncratic phrasing and syntax.

However, while pragmatic concerns might be considered initially, there is also an aspect of this unusual allowance of so much variation in the performances of the actors that perhaps stems from the wartime ideological thrust of the project. One of the primary goals of the project was to depict American ideology, goals, and ideals using the characters of this Chinese peasant family as mere vessels. Thus, fidelity to the Chinese culture along with fidelity to the customary Hollywood renderings of the Chinese/Orientals seems to have been decidedly less significant to the overall project.

In other words, it might have been preferable to have the cast retain the different American ways of speaking, as one of the aims of this work is to carefully delineate the good Chinese from the bad Japanese through their likeness to Caucasian Americans. What might be interpreted as inferior acting skills in another context at this historical moment could provide a reassuring similarity to wartime audiences. The variation in physicality and speech reveals how certain features are manipulated or omitted altogether to serve the narrative in specific ways. In this case, the Ling Tan clan replicates and embodies the diversity that might be found in an extended American family rather than a Chinese one.

The initial and brief marital conflict in the plot between Jade and her husband serves as a momentary distraction until the central storyline involving the invading Japanese can be introduced. Predictably, Jade becomes the primary channel through which her family learns of the invading threat from the Japanese. Indeed, the scene when Jade first speaks out at a student meeting vividly establishes her role as the single voice of resistance of all the peasants. An important component in her positioning resides in the noticeable reticence of the Chinese villagers (played by Asian extras) whose collective attitude so thoroughly contrasts her individual assertiveness. Interestingly, this depiction of Chinese villagers was also challenged by the Chinese consultant Wei Hsueh: "Description of crowd. As I participated and witnessed many such gatherings, this casual and unconcerned attitude is not typical of the audience reaction to student speakers."[26]

Despite allowances for what Hsueh calls "dramatic licenses," the consultant rejects this apathetic characterization of the Chinese villagers, although it is precisely this approach that permits Jade to initially distinguish herself as a heroine in the narrative.

Throughout the film as well, Jade's character serves as the most explicit mouthpiece of U.S. political ideology. However, this does not imply that Hepburn's performance lacks complexity or tension, particularly as demonstrated by her uneasy attempt to portray an assertive political activist within the guise of a demure Oriental female archetype. Jade stands up in the crowd and verbally responds to the students' call to the villagers to help fight the Japanese in the north by clearly but quietly articulating the words "we are able." Although she speaks in measured tones and with some authority, Jade is initially cast as a rebel strictly within the confines of a traditionally deferential Oriental femininity.

She enacts this utilizing a common set of gestures that have helped personify Asian female archetypes traditionally in Hollywood films (head tilted to one side, eyes looking off and away, soft and rather monotone enunciation). In this scene, Jade appears to be the more traditional woman, with only glimmers of modern and politicized thought nascent within. However, as with the character Lien Wha in *The Son-Daughter,* Jade's manner exhibits gradual but distinct changes over the course of the narrative as she sheds her reticent Oriental guise for a decidedly more familiar and confident American one. Mary Ann Doane's concept of the female masquerade is relevant here in that Jade wears a gendered mask that, in the end, is discarded according to the needs and hardship that she and others endure.

Not only do nuances in the performances of Caucasian actors reveal attempts to construct an Americanized or whitened wartime Chinese character, but the choice of casting Asian actors in key roles can also unwittingly divulge a subtle distrust of all Asian characters. A subsequent scene involving the Chinese students shows them in a somewhat less inspiring light than the initial meeting with the villagers. Lao Er attempts to buy the book *All Men Are Brothers* at his cousin Wu Lien's shop. In the midst of searching for the book, a group of students appears to protest his dealings with Japanese merchants. The students feel that Wu Lien is a traitor to his people as long as he continues to operate this way. Suddenly, a rock is thrown through the front window of the shop, and a mob ransacks the store.

Furthermore, when Wu Lien makes a plea for the sympathies of his fellow merchants (also played by Asian actors), they too are shown turning away from him. In this scene and throughout the narrative, Ling Tan's Caucasian cast family members consistently elicit audience sympathy compared to the supporting characters portrayed by Asian actors, with whom audience sympathy ebbs and flows depending on the ideological undercurrent of specific dramatic moments. Despite the generally explicit narrative bifurcation between the good Chinese and bad Japanese espoused in the narrative, the differentiation in the casting of the Chinese roles evidenced in this scene hardly seems random. Here, the dramatically assumed Chinese national identity of wartime adopted by both Caucasian and Asian actors in this film momentarily gives way to an undeclared and overarching contestation between West and East that plays itself out strictly in racial terms despite any officially professed political alliance.

The Japanese first make their appearance through bomber planes that fly overhead. The Chinese characters respond to the planes by calling them "flying ships." Jade remembers the visual slide presentation at the student meeting where the "magic pictures" showed the same thing. The use of the terms "magic pictures" and "flying ships" again illustrates a reliance on the "quaint language" that the Chinese consultant to the project coined to describe the unnatural (and also perhaps excessively ignorant) style of the written dialogue. Indeed, before the Japanese physically arrive, the Chinese are depicted not only as being completely unaware but also as wholly uncomprehending of the world outside their village. They are described as accepting and understanding of the harsh cycles of nature that threaten their crops, homes, and very lives but not a military attack of war. Once again, consultant Wei Hsueh singles this point out for remark in his script notes: "Because of the propaganda power of the motion picture, the portrayal of the mentality of the Chinese farmers, who account for three fourth of the population, in the way Pearl Buck did in her book would be accepted by millions of movie-goers as being true. Actually the Chinese farmers are better informed than the story has them. This sweeping impression of utter ignorance of three quarters of the Chinese population which this picture would give to the Western world, would be incorrect and injurious to the Chinese national character."[27]

This less than flattering characterization of the Chinese people as guileless innocents is intended to compare favorably in this film with the vicious Japanese soldiers in their destructive "flying ships." And although exalting the Chinese masses seems to be a primary aim of this story, they are also plainly depicted as naive, childlike, and ignorant. The Chinese leading characters receive a far more multifaceted treatment than the Japanese characters who, predictably, inhabit the rather one-dimensional role of invading horde.

When Ling Tan and the village elders assemble to meet the Japanese invaders, they anxiously observe a seemingly endless convoy of trucks and tanks, with no easily discernible human figures. Individual faces and facial expressions, by extension, remain indistinguishable. This unusual vantage point is pronounced enough for one frightened

Chinese elder to comment "but they are machines, how can you talk to machines?" The Japanese are first introduced through the machines of the airplanes and then through the machines of army vehicles.

Finally the lead member of the convoy appears, and although he is not significant in the plot, his appearance and performance style exemplify the uniformity in the depiction of the Japanese enemy at work in this film. He wears a thin mustache, a military cap, and fatigues. As he barks out the words "Where is your inn, farmer," another identical soldier quickly slaps a villager, who attempts to extend a greeting to the troops. This indistinguishable likeness in appearance and demeanor among the Japanese soldiers does not emerge as particularly conspicuous, as all interactions with the Japanese troops by the Chinese characters remain restricted to official contact with the soldiers. And while the basic mandarin costuming for the Chinese characters (dark high-collar jackets with toggle closures and matching wide straight pants) also reflects a visual uniformity among the farmers, individual leading characters over the course of the story wear different outfits depending on changes in social environment and/or status.

While the upper eyelids of the Japanese soldiers reflect the customary cosmetic alteration, their overall uniformity relies primarily on nearly identical costuming and, interestingly, a distinctive delivery of dialogue. Whereas the Chinese characters are accepted as using an array of accents, all the Japanese characters deliver their lines employing an identically flat and piercing intonation. Although Hepburn, in particular, attempts a more monotone and halting delivery, the speech of the Japanese exhibits a mechanized rapidity. This biting yet lifeless speaking style not only adds a robotic element to the soldier figures but also underscores the perception of the invading army as "machines" by the Chinese village elders.

The rape of Orchid, Ling Tan's eldest son's wife, also illustrates how the Japanese enemy is positioned as a collective threat with machinelike as well as bestial qualities. Orchid runs into the woods with her two young children, a toddler and an infant, as a group of Japanese soldiers runs after her. Interestingly, the soldier leading the chase whose face can be most clearly seen is played by a white actor instead of an Asian actor. This scene of sexual violation apparently requires the

156

mediation of a Caucasian actor who directs the actions of the majority of Japanese soldiers played by Asian actors. As the group of men begins to close in on her, Orchid places her children in a relatively safe spot and then runs off in a different direction to create a diversion.

When the soldiers finally trap her, they surround her as a pack of wild animals would their prey. Although Orchid's terrified face fills the frame at this point, the soldiers' upper bodies disappear out of frame. The only identifying images are their uniforms and the guns they carry. On the ground Orchid is surrounded by a circle of rifles that cross and prevent her from escaping. Again, the Japanese are abstracted and depicted as a collective machine. These faceless beasts in the woods surround Orchid in silence. Only after the camera pans to the faces of her children do we hear her screams. Clearly, our sympathies should remain with the Chinese Orchid and her two offspring. The Japanese soldiers are denied any vestige of humanity (even a bad humanity) that a face can elicit.

Not only collectively but also individually, the performance styles of Japanese characters strikingly contrasts those of the Chinese. An illustration of this occurs when Captain Sato enters Wu Lien's shop to recruit the merchant into the newly formed Japanese government (the so-called People's government). Although both actors are Caucasian with similarly rotund physiques, they display very different qualities in their individual performances. Standing stiffly atop the steps leading to the main floor of the shop, Captain Sato sharply delivers his orders to the fearful merchant that he must fully cooperate with the Japanese authorities. Wu Lien bows deferentially as he nervously assures Captain Sato that he does not hate anyone and that he remains a man of peace. Fully uniformed and resolutely focused, the Japanese captain's rigid formality stands in stark contrast to Wu Lien's more emotive and fluid posture.

The Chinese merchant's voice, in particular, noticeably contrasts the Japanese captain's. Heavily accented yet expressive, Wu Lien's vocal timbre possesses a breadth and depth lacking in the unanimated utterances of Captain Sato. Clearly, while we chafe at Wu Lien's traitorous declarations of "peace," our sympathies are elicited through his more enlivened performance that allows us to palpably sense his fear and desperation to survive under the enemy occupation. Although far from heroic as compared to his brethren, the corrupt actions of Wu Lien are rendered merely pathetic when measured against the demonic one-dimensional characterization enacted by Captain Sato and the entire occupying army in this film.

Reviews for *Dragon Seed* were decidedly mixed, although its popularity with the public helped make it one of the top grossing films of the year. Indeed, the film's promotional trailer energetically promises drama presented on a grand scale as well as a heightened degree of historical accuracy:

> Roll-up Title reads—
> Up from the good earth that for centuries has brought life to a freedom loving people . . . rises . . . Pearl S. Buck's best selling novel told with truth and fidelity in the finest motion picture since "the good earth" the valiant spirit of the new china . . . invaded—but never conquered! The mighty story of a mighty nation! Proudly presented by Metro-Goldwyn-Mayer as the picture of the hour.[28]

The shorter revised trailer emphasizes drama and spectacle rather than historical accuracy:

> Pearl S. Buck's best selling novel told with truth and fidelity unrivaled in spectacular grandeur! Unsurpassed in dramatic strength! a nation invaded . . . but never conquered! A cavalcade of courage! Sincerely presented by Metro-Goldwyn-Mayer . . . as one of the most important entertainment events in the annals of motion pictures.[29]

Clearly, MGM appealed to the audience who supported Pearl S. Buck's previous film adaptation of *The Good Earth* but also envisioned promoting this film as an epic historical spectacle. Ironically, the trailer promotes the novel as well as the film as possessing "truth and fidelity," a fact as well as a concern addressed by the Chinese consultant to the film. The language describing the film as "one of the most important entertainment events in the annals of motion pictures" illustrates the prestigious positioning of the film (exactly like *The Good Earth*) to both draw big box office receipts as well as critical accolades.

The *New York Times,* while lauding other aspects of the film's production, negatively remarked on the type of "Orientalizing" makeup and varied accents of the Chinese characters: "There are moments when the audience feels or, at the least, almost feels the real immensity of the theme, that of a big, lumbering nation being stabbed and slashed and humiliated by inexorable and vicious little men. At such times the disk [*sic*] takes a deep and bitter bite. At other times the focus closes down from infinity to a picayunish foreground and shows, simply, a group of muddled people in makeup speaking nonsensically in diverse accents."[30]

Although in this review the entire cast generally received low marks regarding their physical embodiment of a plausible Chineseness, Hepburn's distinctive speech was often singled out for the most severe criticism:

> It seems to be asking too much of an audience to supply the deficiency of Katharine Hepburn's characterization of a Chinese girl. She is brittle and non-resilient throughout, and is constantly betrayed by an accent she has made into her own trademark of sophisticated drama. And speaking of accents, the heavy speech of Akim Tamiroff falls upon the ear as resonantly as the sound of a gefulte [*sic*] fish banged against a temple gong.
>
> These departures are more or less neutralized by the normal performances of Walter Huston, Aline MacMahon and Henry Travers. Nevertheless it is disconcerting to hear one brother of a family talking with a guttural Germanic accent, another in broad Oxonian and still another in something approaching a Midwestern drawl.[31]

Curiously, the Japanese supporting characters, when mentioned, received unqualified approval for their stock interpretations. At once hailed for vividly capturing the grim realism of wartime China while at the same time derided for the performative inconsistencies of its Chinese characterizations, *Dragon Seed* exemplifies the attempt to exploit a wartime narrative as ideological propaganda and commercial entertainment. This film attempts to create sympathetic wartime Chinese characters while negotiating traditional Oriental stereotypes through a conventional Hollywood narrative. However, the obvious narrative conflict between Chinese and Japanese in the plot accommodates more intricate racial/national divisions and alliances.

The narrative pits the good Chinese farmers against the bad Japanese invaders. However, the casting of Caucasians in the leading roles of both nationalities separates the leading Caucasian actors (portraying Chinese or Japanese) from the Asian bit players and extras (cast as Chinese or Japanese). At the level of performance, Japanese and Chinese characters coexist as antithetical configurations.

As wartime boundaries between the so-called yellow and white races initially appears to be reconfigured in favor of our Chinese allies, the good Asians in this film, ultimately the price of this status is to closely resemble and reflect the white values of the West. This sentiment is evidenced in a scene depicting the return of Jade and husband Lao Er to their village with their infant son. Ling's wife refers to the Japanese soldiers as "bandy legs," while Ling Tan further likens them to beasts, lamenting that "the bandy legs are no longer men but beasts" and adding "must we become also as beasts?" The use of the particular racial slur "bandy legs" (or bowlegs) has clear precedents in the American popular press, as discussed earlier in this chapter. In this scene, the reunited Ling Tan clan expresses its solidarity against the Japanese using a reference already very much embedded in the U.S./Western psyche.

Of course, the bifurcated depictions of the Chinese and Japanese extended to contemporaneous government-sponsored wartime propaganda, as exemplified by the celebrated series produced by the noted Hollywood director Frank Capra shortly after the United States entered World War II: "One of the primary objectives of the series was to combat the isolationist sentiments that lingered in the United States, and with this in mind the seven core films that Capra directed were given the collective title *Why We Fight*. President Franklin Roosevelt was so impressed by the first of these documentaries that he urged it to be shown in public theaters as well as to recruits. This was done, and *Prelude to War* went on to win an Academy Award as the best documentary of 1942."[32]

Apart from the broadest overview of the series whereby Japan, Germany, and Italy were hardly to be distinguished (they were the slave world whose leaders were madmen and whose people were a subservient mass), the series did devote one film exclusively to the war in Asia titled *The Battle of China,* completed in 1944.[33] This was an epic attempt to establish the dichotomy of the Chinese people's resistance to Japanese aggression. However, critics of Capra charged that this film was one of his most "exaggerated portrayal[s] of pure good versus pure evil." *The Battle of China* was temporarily withdrawn from circulation due to its complete exclusion of problems between the Chinese themselves. Predictably, the film was re-released and seen by close to four million people before the end of the war.[34]

In the end, the thrust of the cinematic creation/representation of the Japanese enemy often ran the opposite of the inherently decent and noble Chinese. It also ran the course of simplistic stereotyping that may seem at first glance contradictory but ultimately seals the fate in the collective perception of this wartime foe:

> In everyday words, this first kind of stereotyping could be summed up in the statement: you are the opposite of what you say you are and the opposite of us, not peaceful but warlike, not good but bad. . . . In the second form of stereotyping, the formula ran more like this: you are what you say you are, but that itself is reprehensible. . . . Westerners accepted Japanese emphasis on the primacy of the group or collectivity at face value, and used this as prima facie evidence that the Japanese were closer to cattle or robots than to themselves.[35]

Losing Face

The phrase "losing face" derives from a Chinese term and refers to somebody who is humiliated or loses her or his good name, reputation, etc. In the film *First Yank into Tokyo* (1945), released after the end of hostilities in the Pacific, the main character, Major Steve Ross, quite literally loses his face when he chooses to undergo irreversible plastic surgery that would make him appear Japanese to complete an undercover intelligence mission near Tokyo. Depicted as the ultimate patriotic act of heroism and sacrifice within the narrative, nonetheless his character endures experiences ranging from the valiant to the degrading. And although the premise and plot of the film superficially appear to support the status quo and racial hierarchy of power relations, they also allow certain transgressive fantasies of miscegenation while exploring the emotional terrain of dual racial embodiment.

A wartime allegory that explores the issues and consequences arising out of the central theme—the making of a Caucasian into an Oriental—*First Yank into Tokyo* specifically foregrounds (and posits as possible) the physical alteration of a Caucasian into a Japanese in the narrative. Clearly, this proposition of becoming Oriental through physical embodiment that forms the basis for this study informs the analysis of this rich film text. Its seemingly implausible though arguably provocative premise addresses both the dilemma and necessity of establishing strict racial divisions in the world.

Indeed, the common performance practice of Caucasian actors portraying Asian roles effects a specialized (and complex) function in the plot; it is not intended to be perceived as a disguise or a seamless visual element in an actor's interpretation of a role. The racial impersonation by a Caucasian actor becomes, in this vehicle, the racial impersonation of a Caucasian character. Remarkably, through the vantage point of its leading character, Major Ross, the "Japanese" archenemy begins to show the hint of a human face.

This project began before V-E day on May 7, 1945, but was released after the atomic blasts on Hiroshima and Nagasaki in early August of the same year. An initial synopsis of the project (then titled "First Man into Tokyo") provided by the RKO studio publicity department summarizes its unconventional plot:

> Major Steve Ross (Tom Neal), an American ace, is summoned to Washington for a dangerous mission. Somewhere in a Jap prison camp is the American engineer Lewis Jardine (Marc Cramer), inventor of a new tank gun. It is of the utmost importance to our war effort that information about the gun be brought back to Washington. Because he had been brought up in Japan and speaks the language perfectly, Ross is the man for the job. Plastic surgery will give him Oriental features. Intensive training by loyal Japanese-Americans will do the rest. But once his features are changed Ross must retain them for the rest of his life. And because he believes Abby Drake (Barbara Hale)—the nurse he was in love with—has died on Bataan, Ross accepts the assignment.

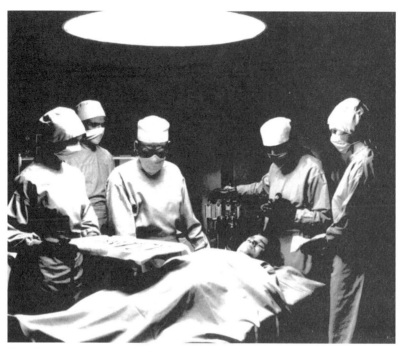

Tom Neal (*on operating table*) in *First Yank into Tokyo*. (MoMA)

Posing as Sergeant Tomo Takashima, Nip war hero sent home to re-
cuperate from shock, he succeeds in becoming an orderly in the prison
hospital where Jardine is a patient [and Abby a nurse]. . . .

Aware that he dare not test Abby's love with the Japanese face
which he must carry forever, he elects to send her and Jardine away
on the sub. . . . Haan Soo (Keye Luke), a Korean operative that as-
sisted Ross in his entry to Japan, chooses to remain with him, while
Abby and Jardine make good their escape, the picture ends with these
two—a brave Korean and the first American to enter Tokyo—laying
down their lives.[36]

This plot summary is of particular interest for what it emphasizes,
excludes, and changes. While this studio outline highlights Ross's alliance with the Korean underground figure, Haan Soo (played by Keye

Luke), the crucial subplot involving the camp commander, Colonel Hideko Okanura (played by Richard Loo), goes undisclosed. Before the war, Colonel Okanura and Ross had been college roommates in the States. Both unusually observant and constantly distracted by the unexplainable familiarity of Ross's Sergeant Takashima, Okanura eventually exposes Ross's ruse through the recognition of a subtle hand gesture. Also, the narrative changes the information about a "new tank gun" to the plans for the atomic bomb. This indicates a dramatic shift surely created to capitalize on public interest in the recent detonations of the new weapon that ended the war with Japan.

"You're as perfect a Jap as we can turn out"

General Stanton, the official who formally requests Ross's participation in the mission, proudly delivers this line after Ross has successfully completed his rigorous training to become a Japanese. This scene announces the U.S. Army's achievement of constructing a Japanese countenance in a Caucasian form, not wholly unlike Dr. Frankenstein's self-satisfaction at having created life through his monster. Like Boris Karloff in the role of Fu Manchu, the element of racial difference interpreted as monstrous emerges as a significant feature in this story as well.

Presented as categorically man-made, Ross's appearance and mastery of Japanese physicality and cultural demeanor initially demonstrate a crowning feat of U.S. ingenuity: a fantasy of racial subjugation through its embodiment. Clearly this element in the film provides an allegorical link to the larger issue of how the casting of Caucasian actors in Asian roles permits a contained and restrained interpretation of Asian roles through the adoption of an Oriental physical guise. However, this collective accomplishment for the U.S. military, although potent, is only temporary, as Ross individually comes to regard himself as a freakish monstrosity who is better off dead.

Yet significantly, surgery completes only part of Ross's racial transformation into a Japanese; the remainder must be acquired through study and practice. General Stanton praises Ross after a time for ultimately passing every test, "in features, actions, mannerisms, dialects." Ross, dressed in a tailored suit, responds by bowing and clicking his heels together and then states facetiously, "Thank you excewancy. It's been a pweasure to study under youw most tawented teachers." To this the delighted general replies, "You're now a full-fledged son of Nippon." This scene explicitly acknowledges culturally specific speech and demeanor as playing a significant role in the construction of the representation of the Japanese soldier.

Understanding the "mental processes" of the Japanese also provides an additional challenge to Ross's potential success on this mission. Despite having claimed an intimate familiarity with Japan due to his upbringing there, Ross, rather than offering a more diverse perspective on the Japanese mind as it were, simply ascribes to the Japanese a "completely reversed approach to things." Nonetheless, he then declares confidently that he understands "every kink in their corkscrew psychology." Ironically, Ross's "tawented teachers" in the ways Japanese are identified as "our Japanese American examining board" by General Stanton.

Curiously, this remark attempts to establish a national solidarity with Japanese Americans, and yet this raises the question of why a Japanese American wasn't simply recruited for this dangerous assignment rather than surgically altering a Caucasian soldier.[37] Perhaps because the military implicitly considered the allegiance of Japanese Americans too tenuous? Most likely the explanation lies not in rational logic but rather in the powerful lure that the fantasy of a Japanized Caucasian provides. As with previously discussed Oriental archetypal characterizations, the Caucasian actor occupies a critical position as figurative conduit to an alternative and socially transgressive ethnic experience while safely containing the experience within an explicitly Western framework.

The film begins when Ross, while on R&R in San Francisco, is summoned to Washington, D.C., without knowing the reason. Still, he doesn't hesitate to answer his country's call. In a meeting with military and government officials in Washington, General Stanton, director of the mission, ominously characterizes the life-altering surgery that Ross elects to have as requiring a "personal courage so far beyond the call of duty." Stanton's words can also be heard in voice-over as medical personnel prepare Ross for surgery: "once your features are changed, they can never be changed back" as well as Ross's simple and dutiful reply,

"I understand, sir." Initially, this film positions the operation squarely in political terms as a heightened expression of patriotism but then immediately shifts Ross's motivation to a darker and more desperate emotional space. Just as Ross lies on a surgical table and a gas mask is placed over his face, his words, in voice-over, can be heard: "I shouldn't have cried. Mom and Dad were dead and Abby, the Japs killed her." As the doctor carefully unwraps his head of bandages, Ross's back faces the camera. Notably, the first display of Ross's new face is withheld from our direct view and instead is witnessed through the grave reactions of his surgeon, a nurse, and General Stanton. Furthermore, the audience's subsequent look at his facial features reflects indirectly in a small mirror as Ross quietly remarks, "I almost believe I'm somebody else." Our own response to Ross's physical transformation, which is mediated through the eyes of others and then framed in a mirror's reflection that incorporates his own gaze, necessitates an integration of the awestruck reactions of the characters. In this way, the burden of the features themselves to astonish is displaced onto other normalized faces (or in the case of Ross, his eyes that reflect a face no longer visible). Clearly, an audience familiar with Caucasian actors made-up to appear Asian in varying contexts requires a precise manipulation of elements to create the desired dramatic impact around the central plot device of the film.

Arriving at the Kamuri prison camp near Tokyo, Ross encounters the commandant Colonel Okanura and his former love, Abby, whom he thought had been killed at Bataan. When Ross recognizes Okanura as a roommate from his college days, Ross panics that he will be discovered. Haan Soo attempts to reassure him, asserting that "not even a brother could recognize you as you are now." Momentarily bolstered regarding Okanura, Ross immediately laments his accompanying estrangement from Abby within his racially altered frame, remarking that "no matter how close people have been to you, they don't see past your face."

At once thrilled and sickened, Ross experiences the social barriers that his constructed physical form presents. He must endure the bullying of a corrupt Major Nogira (played by Leonard Strong), the contemptuous suspicion of Okanura, and the repeated denigration by Abby. Neal's performance as Sergeant Takashima consists primarily of inexpressive poses, standing stiffly while speaking stilted English that is in stark contrast to his spirited interpretation of the (fully) American Major Ross. This is most apparent when contrasted to the performance of Asian actor Keye Luke. Luke's performance as Neal's Korean ally exhibits animated facial expressions, broad smiles, grimaces, and flashing expressive eyes with a voice of varying tones. Of course, much of the lack of vitality in Neal's face could be attributed to his heavy makeup; however, the wartime Japanese guise typically strips the face and voice of much of their facility and vibrancy.

Ross's voiced fear to Haan Soo about Okanura raises important issues involving the multifaceted nature of the Japanese wartime threat. Ross describes Okanura as a "studious, quiet Jap" with "plenty of brains." According to Ross, Okanura had every student on campus "pegged in the right pigeonhole" and, most importantly, knew Ross "backwards, the way I walked, the way I talked." Ross's flashback of Okanura dissolves from the grimacing and thinly mustached colonel sitting behind his desk in the prison camp in uniform, with a Japanese flag hanging on the wall, to Okanura sitting behind a desk in a dormitory room clean-shaven, dressed in a sweater, and smiling. He and Ross banter in this scene as Okanura speaks in detail about his roommate favoring an arm injured during a football game. Ross is pleasantly surprised and amazed at the precise observations of his roommate, and the flashback ends with Okanura generously preparing sukiyaki for himself and Ross, who smiles as he asks, "Do you intend to keep me waiting all day?" We then return to the present-day prison camp as Okanura recites the same line but more ominously.

Although portrayed by the same actor, Richard Loo, Okanura's appearance noticeably changes from his American college days to his tenure as military commandant. Previously clean-shaven with a pleasant demeanor, he now sports a thin mustache and grimaces, barking out his orders. Okanura's previous youthful appearance disguises a distinctly duplicitous personality. Indeed, Ross initially describes the young Okanura's eyes as "hard, like a hunk of steel." Once again, even within a wartime narrative located outside the United States, the threat of infiltration by the Japanese is introduced. Clearly, Okanura was able to reside in (or infiltrate) the United States with his superior (though sinister) mental abilities and quiet (and clearly surreptitious) manner without detection. Of course, his knowledge of Americans gathered at that time proves vital to the success or failure of Ross's mission. In this film, Okanura's experience of and exposure to U.S. culture threatens its very national security through the character of Steve Ross.

Finally, Ross's encounters with Abby provide a complex interweaving of thwarted love through the forbidden specter of miscegenation. Notably, throughout the narrative Ross silently protects Abby from the lustful advances of the Japanese officers. However, Abby repeatedly reacts to Ross as Sergeant Tomo Takashima with a mixture of contempt, stating that she "despises all Japs," and distressed confusion because she feels an "undercurrent" of sympathy for him. After having revealed his identity, mission, and relationship to Abby and to Jardine, Ross needs medical care after being whipped by his superiors (for reversing an unfair charge against the American nurses). Though stoically volunteering to clean his own wounds with antiseptic, Abby offers to tend to his wounds herself.

In a striking display of repressed desire, Abby, trancelike, tenderly dabs at Ross's shirtless frame as his hand (unbeknownst to her) involuntarily moves up to take hers. But he stops himself, thinking better of it, as Jardine stands close by silently and compassionately observing the doomed lovers. After Ross leaves, Abby guiltily confesses to Jardine her unexplained affinity to this soldier: "I don't hate him. What's wrong with me?" Clearly, Abby's confusion exposes the presumption of wartime racial hatred as the norm. Not only does this sentiment acknowledge predominant racial attitudes of the war years, it is precisely this assumption (along with its accompanying epithets) that provides key reference points for repudiation in the films of the postwar era.

Abby's attraction to Ross as Takashima explicitly, though tenuously, introduces the element of miscegenation into the narrative. Is she or isn't she attracted to a Japanese soldier? In this film, the taboo of interracial sexuality is broached and yet operates strictly within socially acceptable norms. Since Ross and Abby have had a previous romantic relationship, the audience can interpret her attraction as rekindled vestiges from that socially sanctioned coupling. However, one of the driving elements in this film addresses the issue of how people can be separated by racial appearance that seldom looks beyond the face.

In this scene, the intimacy enacted between Abby and Ross, in reality two Caucasian American characters, still requires the mediation of an undeniably Caucasian male character, Jardine. Jardine's character serves as a convenient albeit compassionate watchdog viewing the lovers who might be tempted to transgress the established social codes of the prison camp (Abby with humanity, Ross with sexuality). Jardine's supportive nature (he suggests that Ross reveal his true identity to Abby) conceals the larger social function of his presence as tacit preserver of the status quo. This scene clearly illustrates how the threat that interracial sexuality arouses can apparently be assuaged at the level of narrative and yet persist on a broader social level that requires additional dramatic containment.

In the end Ross does reveal his true identity to Abby but only after he has decided on the impossibility of a life together back in the States. She declares her love and willingness to accept him regardless, but he is firm as Jardine leaves with her on a waiting U.S. submarine. Both functioning as a plea for a shared humanity while explicitly espousing a call for U.S. patriotic sacrifice, *First Yank into Tokyo,* traverses the volatile ground of racial difference, miscegenation and, ultimately, racial tolerance.

Unlike *Dragon Seed, First Yank into Tokyo* did not garner a great deal of critical attention or praise. While *First Yank into Tokyo* claimed neither epic nor prestige status, a *Variety* review tended to approach the film strictly in the B movie industrial context: "RKO has a hot exploitation melodrama in 'First Yank Into Tokyo,' which should be able to cash in on its title and fact that it is first picture on subject to be released since surrender of Japan."[38]

The most interesting commentary from *Motion Picture Daily* appears in relation to the plot change of the tank bomb to the atomic bomb, particularly as one of the last images of the film utilizes actual footage from the Hiroshima blast: "This production keeps up with the headlines with newly added references to the atomic bomb. The timeliness in title and theme gives it considerable weight as a promotional picture for the showman."[39]

The performance of Tom Neal (who had previously portrayed wartime Japanese characters) received generally positive notices. Neal played a leading role, Taro—a U.S.-educated but ultimately treasonous

Japanese soldier—in another RKO wartime vehicle, *Behind the Rising Sun* (1943). His enactment of the so-called dual role in *First Yank into Tokyo* drew praise despite its fundamental implausibility. Again, the characterizations of the Asian actors, particularly Keye Luke and Richard Loo, were uniformly praised in the *Hollywood Reporter:* "Producer-director-writer J. Robert Bren has dreamed up the story of an American major who undergoes plastic surgery and comes out a Jap. . . . Tom Neal as the American-gone-Jap turns in a downright performance. . . . Richard Loo, holding himself in check, gives one of his better, more sinister performances. Keye Luke is excellent."[40]

As both a means of racial subjugation as well as an expression of its fluidity, *First Yank into Tokyo* creates an unusual wartime fantasy with decidedly dark elements. Remarkably, the rather implausible premise of *First Yank into Tokyo* occurs, in reverse, in the Monogram release *Black Dragons* (1942), starring Bela Lugosi. Lugosi portrays a Nazi scientist who surgically alters a Japanese spy ring to appear Caucasian, allowing them to infiltrate the United States and impersonate influential American citizens. Even in wartime, both fear and desire of the Oriental enemy coexists and requires close negotiation in its depiction in Hollywood films. Clearly, the idea of racial transformation strongly fascinates, just as race's potential transcendence deeply threatens and thus must ultimately be resolutely denied.

As we have seen in previous chapters, aspects of racist ideology can circulate in film texts through ambiguous images that still survive. This dynamic circulation provides a body of schema of certain images and characterizations that is indicative of the Hollywood cinema's classical consistency, particularly in relation to rules of narrative construction along with a very specific history. This schema also floats around in popular culture. Far from creating inert or fixed stereotypes, different situations, often historically defined, inspire shifting combinations, retooled, redefined, and transformed. Taking off and putting on a racial identity presents a utopian possibility in these films; however, it rarely functions this way outside the cinema. In essence, the Western culture grants an identity, and if a character is not the norm, then that character becomes a caricature. The significance of these images as well as this process is that they have molded and continue to shape preconceptions even to this day.

The industrial practice of casting Caucasian actors/stars in Asian roles continued unabated during the wartime era, albeit under a new rubric: the difficulty of finding willing Asian actors to play Japanese enemy roles as evidenced in the "Me No Moto" *Variety* article cited earlier. In this historical context, even familiar Oriental detective characters were reformulated and villainized to serve the needs of wartime discourse as well as film narratives. Animated shorts such as *Japoteurs* and *Bugs Bunny Nips the Nips* illustrate how the process of fragmentation and reconfiguration of familiar elements created a contemporaneous Japanese enemy. We have seen how formerly heroic Oriental figures can also act as buzzwords or shorthand for the wartime enemy. Also notable in the cartoons are the exaggeration of racial stereotypes that include physical defects, particularly when they lack openly sinister elements.

Dragon Seed exemplifies the effort to individualize Asian identities between Chinese and Japanese; the depictions of the sympathetic Chinese also embody a clearly constructed bias. *First Yank into Tokyo* introduces the concept of racial alteration as both fantasy and threat. Perhaps this representation can also suggest a radical means of comprehending a different race through the destruction of one's own. It is no wonder that during wartime a production of this sort appeared. Physical carnage, injuries, and death predominated in the visual images of this time. Fears of invasion, infiltration, and subjugation fueled many of the wartime narratives; still, continuity exists as prewar elements, and characterizations provided the essential cues with which to identify the enemy.

In this chapter, we have discussed how specific wartime films featuring Caucasian actors as Asians have drawn from a previous body of films. Clearly, the performance practice of Caucasians in Asian roles takes on new meanings and reformulates old ones depending on its historical context. Furthermore, the Oriental performances from this period plainly possess an enduring historical legacy that is influential to the present day. In chapter 4, we will address how these potent wartime characterizations are again reconfigured and adapted to reflect a presumed conciliatory postwar sentiment.

FOUR

Comics and Lovers

Postwar Transitions and Interpretations

"You are like the Chinese dish the Americans invented. What do they call it?"
"Chop Suey."
"That is it. Everything is in it, all mixed up."
—*Flower Drum Song* (1961)

The preceding dialogue occurs during a scene in the film *Flower Drum Song* (1961) that portrays a communal celebration in San Francisco's Chinatown. The guests of honor include both the elder Madam Liang (played by Juanita Hall), granted U.S. citizenship after five years of schooling, and her young nephew Wang Ta (played by James Shigeta) who just graduated college. In this exchange, Madam Liang's brother-in-law Master Wang (played by Benson Fong) expresses a deeply suspicious view of American cultural assimilation when he compares his sister to the U.S.-concocted Chinese dish chop suey. Implicit in his commentary lies a critique of the Western-fabricated Oriental cultural product as well as its rendering as an indiscriminate cultural mix.

Established as somewhat of a curmudgeon, Master Wang's character nevertheless succinctly articulates what becomes the hallmark of the postwar years in Hollywood's depictions of Asian characters. Indeed, during this time the performances and performers of Asian archetypal roles do mix it up in various ways. This chapter will examine how the enactment by non-Asian actors in Oriental roles reworks traditional archetypes and wartime characterizations in its later phase as a predominant Hollywood performance practice.

In both conception and reception, Hollywood's non-Asian Oriental impersonation during this period grew at the same time more inclusive and more exclusive. The range of Oriental comic heroes, musical spectacles, and tragic figures exemplifies a more exclusive demarcation in terms of genre and dramatic treatment but at the same time is more inclusive in terms of the ideological issues addressed. Clearly, these tendencies demonstrate a marked shift away from the stridently virulent depictions of the war years. The critical reception of the films discussed in this chapter also provide evidence of a gradual shift in the discourse toward what appears to be a more conciliatory rhetoric concerning the Oriental figure during the postwar years.

The films discussed in this chapter "belong to a distinct cultural moment in which Americans turned their attention eastward":[1]

> Between 1945 and 1961 American cultural producers churned out a steady stream of stories, fiction and nonfiction, that took Asia and the Pacific as their subject matter. Journalist John Hersey documented the dropping of the atomic bomb on Japan (*Hiroshima*), playwright John Patrick brought U.S.-occupied Okinawa into Broadway theaters (*Teahouse of the August Moon*), novelist James Michener probed the merits of the Korean War (*The Bridges at Toko-Ri*), travel writer Lowell Thomas Jr. explored Tibet (*Out of this World: Across the Himalayas to Forbidden Tibet*), Hollywood director Richard Quine put contemporary Hong Kong onto movie screens (*The World of Suzy Wong*), and photographer Margaret Bourke-White framed views of India (*Halfway to Freedom*).[2]

This obviously raises the question of why Asia and the Pacific held such a fascination for so many Americans during the immediate postwar years. Why did Americans want to produce and devour so many stories about this part of the world? While the intensity of American interest in Asia was certainly not entirely new (as previous chapters attest), part of the reason was that the Cold War made Asia important to the United States in unprecedented ways. U.S. political, military, and economic expansion into the region was massive, with an influence that was unparalleled:

> The great arc stretched from Korea in the north, down through the Chinese mainland and Taiwan, along the offshore island chains of Japan, the Philippines, and Indonesia, out into the Pacific, across the Southeast Asian peninsula, and up into the Indian subcontinent. Hundreds of thousands of Americans flowed into Asia during the 1940s and 1950s as soldiers, diplomats, foreign aid workers, missionaries, technicians, professors, students, businesspeople, and tourists.[3]

Hollywood obviously plays a significant role as a producer of the dominant representations of Asia of the period (explorations of the noncommunist parts of Asia; mainland China, North Korea, and North Vietnam predictably remained largely beyond their chosen boundaries). The films selected for this chapter possess narrative and performative features that epitomize the practice of Oriental impersonation by non-Asian actors as well as anticipate its eventual dissolution. (This closely parallels the narrowing of cultural interest in Asia in the early 1960s as the Vietnam War consumed the attention of the nation to the near exclusion of the rest of the region.)[4] In *The Teahouse of the August Moon* (1956), Marlon Brando's portrayal of an Okinawan interpreter exhibits a mix of caricatured yellowface traits along with performative elements indicating an attempt at greater cultural authenticity. A less ambitious supporting role enacted five years later by Mickey Rooney as Mr. Yunioshi in *Breakfast at Tiffany's* (1961) provides a striking contrast in its rigid adherence to stereotype along with its uniformly critical censure.

Flower Drum Song (1961) offers a non-Caucasian Asian depiction in the figure of African American actress Juanita Hall. Her presence as the Chinese Madam Liang in the film raises the question of how a mixture of physical attributes and cultural differences can affect, embolden, and complicate a racially specific performance. Ricardo Montalban's depiction of Nakamura in *Sayonara* (1957) also presents a multilayered interpretation of an Oriental love interest that exhibits a chameleonlike ethnic and gender identity.

Laurence Harvey's portrayal of a womanizing Eurasian in *A Girl Named Tamiko* (1962) will be discussed as a figure of distress, displacement, and disenfranchisement as well as social change. Interestingly, during the war years Eurasian depictions appeared with less frequency. Perhaps these figures presented an unsettling ambiguity to the prescribed wartime animosity of the Japanese enemy. And finally, in *My Geisha* (1962) Shirley MacLaine enacts the Oriental racial impersonation as a most elaborate ruse. Utilizing one of the most traditional of Oriental archetypes, her characterization exhibits a display of performative and cosmetic features as it comedically deconstructs the entire enterprise.

The Postwar Melting Pot

The communist takeover of China in 1949, the U.S. occupation of Japan from 1945 to 1952, and the Korean War from 1950 to 1953 all affected a reconfiguration of political and ideological relationships with Asia that were established and propagated during World War II. Ironically, the once-valorized Chinese ally suddenly changed into an official enemy of American democratic ideals, while the wartime Japanese foe became an unconditionally conquered people primed for U.S.-decreed democratization. These tumultuous political reversals and events provide a historical and ideological context for the directions taken by Hollywood films depicting the Oriental. Remarkably, it would be nearly ten years after World War II before another major cycle of Caucasian-enacted Oriental characterizations emerged.

The seemingly perennial Charlie Chan series, then produced by the B studio Monogram Pictures, finally drew to a close in the immediate postwar period. With the death of Sidney Toler in 1947, stage actor Roland Winters took over the role of Chan. Winters appeared in seven installments over the next two years before the series was terminated by the studio. Notably, the combat film genre ascended in popularity at the same time. Having gained a high degree of prominence during the war years, combat films of the postwar era such as *Home of the Brave*

(1949), *The Sands of Iwo Jima* (1949), and *An American Guerrilla in the Philippines* (1950) distinguished themselves as vehicles that celebrated the individual heroism of American exploits in the Pacific, China, Korea, and Southeast Asia as well as broached issues of domestic racial and ethnic social tensions.

Often appealing to audiences intimately familiar with documentary war footage, these films boast elaborate battle action sequences. However, instead of focusing on individually antagonistic Japanese characters, the Oriental enemy is relegated to brief screen appearances as extras (if they appear at all), with the Pacific theater acting as simply the setting and backdrop for dramatic action. Invariably these extras were cast along with Asian actors, while the narrative focus remained on the characters drawn from the diverse racial, ethnic, or individual makeup of the American military unit. Significantly, the social problems identified in these narratives rarely included an Asian American perspective. Nevertheless, these narratives propose the social experience of wartime battle as a potentially transformational site at once highly contentious and earnestly conciliatory.

Although often set in exotic international locales far from America's shores, Hollywood's postwar Oriental depictions nonetheless also reflect a heightened awareness of domestic social tensions and concerns exemplified by the social-problem combat films. In fact, issues of racial discrimination (strongly suggestive of the U.S. civil rights activities in the 1950s and 1960s), interracial marriage, and interracial sexuality all are either explicitly or implicitly portrayed (with a single exception) in all the films selected for analysis.

Yellowface

The postwar comedic yellowface variant distinguishes itself through its selection of a few key traits: the makeup almost always includes a set of buck teeth and often black round glasses (whether the actor's eyes have been cosmetically altered or not), although costuming may vary. A high degree of artificiality becomes particularly apparent in this yellowface mode through its rabid displays of caricature and cartoonishness. Ironically, it is precisely this quality that most explicitly exposes the artificiality of Asian racial construction in Hollywood films.

Repeated pratfalls, broad gestures, and facial expressions all contribute to an exaggerated performance style. This more theatrical display of mannerisms attempts to temper its derisive ridicule through the prism of lighthearted amusement. And although this foregrounding of artificiality might invite a semblance of play-acting fun, the result nonetheless produces a clown figure both infantilized and foolish.

The function of the postwar yellowface caricature appears to be a way to mitigate a threat ideally suited to follow the wartime demonization. Utilizing a nonthreatening comedic guise, yellowface provides a venue that expresses many of the same racial anxieties of political domination and sexual potency. This figure maintains its status through mockery and even self-denigration. The yellowface caricature of this era evolves most directly from a propagandistic-laden image of an enemy during the war to a postwar comic figure that nonetheless remains distorted and grotesque.

The yellowface style is much in evidence in Marlon Brando's performance in the 1956 feature *The Teahouse of the August Moon*. Brando, known for a naturalistic method of acting, attempts to modify some clichés but does not abandon the conventions completely. In fact, he relies on them at key moments in the narrative. Brando plays Sakini, an Okinawan interpreter for the U.S. occupation forces on his island. The film is based on the Pulitzer Prize–winning play by John Patrick (who also wrote the screenplay), which in turn was based on a novel by Vern Sneider. The Broadway play was well received, with the role of Sakini, the interpreter, going to the non-Asian actor David Wayne. Wayne and the play received rave reviews in the New York press and went on to an extended run domestically as well as successful runs around the world. Predictably, only non-Asian actors portrayed the role of Sakini in numerous productions staged around the globe (including productions in Australia, Yugoslavia, Western Europe, Israel, and South Africa). This casting preference extended to productions in both Okinawa and Tokyo as well. Remarkably, a woman (Rosina Jimeno) was cast as Sakini in a Mexico City production.[5]

Set in 1946 Okinawa, the plot of *The Teahouse of the August Moon* offers a whimsical rendering of the problems of bringing democracy and productivity to Tobiki, a tiny Okinawan village. Colonel Purdy (played by Paul Ford) takes a blustery approach to his assignment to convert the village into an American-style democracy. Purdy enlists the help of the foundering Captain Fisby (played by Glenn Ford), who in his spotty military career has been asked to transfer from each previously held position. Nonetheless, Purdy puts Fisby in charge, ordering him to enforce a large and detailed set of instructions and goals. The main thing that the village lacks, according to Purdy, is some "get up and go!"

Sakini, as interpreter first to Purdy and then to Fisby, is relied upon ostensibly to translate not only the words but also the profound cultural differences of the U.S. occupation officers to the native villagers. At every turn, however, the prankster Sakini manages through strategically feigned ignorance, confusion, and innocuous tricks to eventually convert Fisby and his men to see the value of doing things the Okinawan way. Lotus Blossom (played by Machiko Kyo), a geisha, aids this endeavor by comically forcing her amorous attentions on the hapless Fisby.

Things turn around in the village once Fisby approves of a plan to help the village become self-supporting, one of his original directives. However, instead of producing small novelty items, the villagers begin producing brandy from their plentiful sweet potato crops. This endeavor proves to be a commercial bonanza, as sales to neighboring U.S. troops soar. News of this economic boom eventually gets back to Purdy, who on discovering the true source of revenue fires Fisby. He then has his men destroy all the stills along with an elegant new teahouse painstakingly constructed by the villagers.

But subsequently in a stunning reversal, Purdy gets a message from Washington stating that a prominent senator approves of the village's unorthodox methods of economic development and will immediately send a congressional group to observe them firsthand. Thinking that the village is a complete shambles because of his actions, Purdy becomes despondent because he believes that his military career is over. Suddenly, Sakini reveals that the villagers, who were "not born yesterday," have saved most of the brandy stills and even more remarkably hidden all the pieces of the supposedly demolished teahouse. The villagers proudly reconstruct the teahouse before the amazed officers' eyes. In a spirit of magnanimity, Purdy reinstates Fisby, while Sakini emerges as a hero who saved the day.

The broad farcical nature of all the performances in the film are evident from the outset. In addition, the underlying theme from which the humor principally emanates—the futile struggle of the conquerors (U.S. occupation forces) to establish cultural dominion over the conquered (Okinawan villagers)—attempts to mitigate the potentially contentious nature of this unequal relationship between countries. Politely addressing the audience in thick pidgin English ("Lovely ladies, kind gentlemen") in the first scene of the film, Sakini blithely voices the successive subjugation of the Okinawan people by "Chinese pirates in the fourteenth century, English missionaries in the sixteenth century, Japanese warlords in the nineteenth century and now American marines." He whimsically positions these situations as learning opportunities rather than oppression and philosophically claims that this is a necessary process for his people: "Okinawans most eager to be educated by conquerors. Not easy to learn, sometimes very painful. But pain make man think. Thought make man wise. And wisdom make life endurable." This seemingly fanciful and playful opening clearly attempts to inspire sympathy for the helpless Okinawans and yet plainly utilizes traditional archetypal features of the Hollywood Oriental, such as politeness in the face of subjugation ("eager to be educated by conquerors") and ready acceptance of humiliation ("sometimes very painful"), couched in the sagacious style of Charlie Chan's pithy aphorisms ("pain make man think," "thought make man wise," "wisdom make life endurable"). *The Teahouse of the August Moon* ostensibly depicts a progressive message of peaceful coexistence through mutual cultural respect and exchange. However, the process of this cultural tug-of-war contains, for all its humor, elements that strongly reinscribe a traditional racial and cultural hierarchy. Marlon Brando's yellowface performance of Sakini provides a central illustration of this dynamic of racial and cultural containment that seems curiously at odds in this evidently reconciliatory tale of cross-cultural understanding.

The first moments of the film depict Sakini roughhousing with a group of rambunctious young village children. He then chuckles with delight as he discovers a stick of tutti-frutti gum in his pocket-sized "ancient dictionary." Of course, the incongruous combination of the ancient Oriental wisdom with an archetypal gift of American GIs—chewing gum—is presented as an amusing cross-cultural combination. However, in addition to introducing a humorous cultural mix, this scene also introduces stock characteristics of the yellowface guise.

Marlon Brando in *The Teahouse of the August Moon*. (MoMA)

Interestingly, Brando's acceptance of this part is ascribed by biographer Bob Thomas to his desire to play less intense film roles.[6]

Before his character has an opportunity to speak, the nature of Sakini's interaction with the children imposes an infantilized cast on his portrayal. His roughhousing with the children as well as his childlike delight in the tutti-frutti gum work to mitigate his more mature philosophical musings about history, oppression, and cross-cultural conflicts expressed subsequently. Also, Brando's black hair wig, eyes Orientally made-up, and wry smile (prominently showcasing his upper teeth) all squarely display the physical features of his yellowface impersonation to the audience as his character speaks directly to the camera. And Sakini's costuming (not unlike the others in the village except for Lotus Blossom) is so severely ripped and ragged that it connotes a vision of a comical beggar.

Although termed a "rascal" throughout the film, Sakini remains essentially a portrayal of comic buffoonery and trickery. Initially, Sakini reports to a blustery Colonel Purdy with whom he punctuates the end of nearly every sentence with "boss." Sakini exhibits a simpleminded nature in an early scene with Colonel Purdy when he enters the colonel's office and startles his boss after firmly nudging him with his finger. The colonel responds angrily with the statement, "Don't put your finger on an officer. If you want to announce your presence, knock." The colonel then retreats again under his desk to retrieve a misplaced magazine. Sakini then knocks on the colonel's backside. Purdy yells, and Sakini reacts, genuinely confused: "Not know, Boss. Do what you ask."

Sakini's obsequious behavior alone does not constitute his caricatured performance when Captain Fisby enters the scene; the interpreter giggles to himself at a statement by one of the officers. When Sakini is finally asked to leave, he does so by stiffly saluting the officers and doing a 360-degree turn, which causes him to almost fall off balance before he leaves. Although Sakini begins as philosophical narrator and guide in the film, soon his role shifts to burlesque and comic relief through his behavior and language.

Brando's style of speech incorporates a full view of his front upper teeth. In this way, even without a prosthesis, a critical feature of the yellowface physical guise emerges. And although Brando does speak a great deal of dialogue in Japanese, his caricatured posing and heavy makeup offset this attempt at cultural authenticity. In fact, during a scene in which Captain Fisby first addresses the people of the village, an Okinawan male villager steps up on the platform to represent the chief of agriculture position. This male villager (played by the Japanese actor Jun Negami) stands next to Brando so that the artifice involved in Brando's performance appears in high relief.

The Japanese actor's eyes are not as small, his front teeth are not as prominent, and his hair is not as slickly styled by comparison. His face possesses a relaxed and natural expression in contrast to Brando's tight (and toothy) smile, wig, and cartoonish gestures. This scene illustrates how the yellowface performance exists in a privileged space where racial difference is portrayed in a familiar distortion. The yellowface performance and the Japanese performance do not simply play side by side. This is a case where the distortion defines and commands center stage.

Still, Sakini's role as interpreter moves this postwar Oriental characterization toward a growing self-consciousness. Clearly, his character plays a central role in the narrative, a go-between managing a series of cross-cultural conflicts and misunderstandings. However, perhaps a compelling rationale behind Brando's enactment of this Oriental role lies in Sakini's explicit status as an interpreter that gives greater license to white actors to inhabit and interpret the part, both literally and figuratively.

Sakini also functions as an asexual figure in the narrative. When he introduces Lotus Blossom, a local geisha girl, to Captain Fisby, Sakini is put in the position of voicing her desire to serve him. Sakini, unlike all the other men in the village, expresses no individual sexual interest in Lotus Blossom. This might have been suggested in script revisions from the Motion Picture Association of America (MPAA). A letter to Dore Schary at MGM from Geoffrey Shurlock on September 19, 1955, states: "We earnestly recommended that some of the reactions of Sakini be examined with the idea of avoiding any impression that Sakini is indulging in duplicity in his attitude toward Lotus Blossom. His dialogue seems innocent enough, but his actions might seem to undo this innocence by being overly sly."[7]

Sakini maintains a secondary position, not as sexual rival but as interpreter and companion, himself, to Captain Fisby. In a scene where the female villagers complain that Lotus Blossom is getting preferential treatment from the male villagers, Sakini is found again playing with some village children outside the captain's office. The interpreter's close identification with children and his exhibition of childlike behavior attempt to counter any sexual threat that he might pose in his central yet ultimately narrowly circumscribed role.

In the end, when faced with Fisby leaving the village in disgrace, Lotus Blossom asks him to take her with him. Sakini interprets and, significantly, inserts his own comments to her while interpreting. He calls it a "silly thing" for her to wish to go to America with the young captain and then dutifully translates Fisby's polite but firm rejection to her. However, subsequently Sakini asks Fisby if he will take him to the United States, a curious request given Fisby's rejection of the idea just moments before. Fisby predictably turns him down, and Sakini returns to the docile childlike companion with no mature needs or desires of his own. In fact, Sakini begins to console Fisby: "Say boss, you not failure."

Interestingly, the happy ending of this film results from a mass deception by the villagers. However, Sakini's simplistic explanation ("we just take away and hide") as well as Purdy and Fisby's delighted reactions position it as a harmless hoax, a stunt of mischievous ingenuity of their childlike charges. Indeed, Sakini receives the highest compliment particularly in the context of postwar politics. Acknowledging the interpreter's wiles, Fisby states conspiratorially, "Sakini, you really are a rascal." But Purdy quickly counters with "No, he's really an American. He's got get up and go."

This site of reconciliation reconfigures (but significantly does not extract) the traditional Oriental duplicity as patently patriotic when operating in the interests of the West. A darker interpretation would suggest that these Okinawans are sneaky, similar to the Pearl Harbor attack on December 7, 1941. Resembling the hidden dark elements in the Chan-Moto-Wong series, is this not the same here, not in a detective guise but concealed much more in the innocuous guise of a comedian? Of course, *The Teahouse of the August Moon* functions partly as a satire on American attitudes as it lampoons the actions of the military brass. Yet the film remains both ironic and ambiguous, particularly as related to the interpretation of Brando's yellowface performance.

Studio promotion and publicity highlighted the film's location shooting and also stressed Brando's studied preparation in his depiction of Sakini. Interestingly, in a television spot on the *Ed Sullivan Show*, the actor's elaborate training for the performance contrasts visuals that convey a magical transformative aspect:

> CU Brando as himself in Western attire.
>
> MARLON BRANDO SPENT TWO MONTHS IN JAPAN BEFORE THE COMPANY ARRIVED,
>
> Brando lowers head and hat hides face.
>
> PERFECTING HIS ACCENT FOR HIS PORTRAYAL OF "SAKINI," THAT ROGUISH OKINAWAN INTERPRETER.
>
> Brando raises hat and we see him in makeup—Sakini.
>
> RECOGNIZE HIM? WELL, HERE HE IS . . . . IN PERSON.[8]

Brando's profile as an actor who takes on challenging roles lends itself to a promotion of the labor (and artifice) involved in undertaking an Oriental role. The text highlights the accent, while the visuals exhibit the cosmetic alteration.

The studio trailer also announces Brando's performance in the role couched in language extolling his range and superior acting ability:

> MARLON BRANDO As "Sakini"
>
> Voice
>
> Marlon Brando, whose talents have ranged from William Shakespeare to Damon Runyon, is "Out of This World" as . . . Sakini
>
> Marlon Brando
>
> Sakini here, boss.
>
> Paul Ford
>
> Don't ever put your finger on an officer.
>
> GLENN FORD
>
> MACHIKO KYO
>
> PAUL FORD [no character names next to these actors, diff from Brando]. . . . ALL THE FUN OF THE GREAT STAGE PLAY IS ON THE SCREEN.[9]

The invocation of Shakespeare juxtaposed with the line "Sakini here, boss" illustrates how Brando's yellowface caricature was intended to be perceived, as merely another in a long line of diverse characterizations that showcase the versatility of this Hollywood star. And yet the same ad explicitly alludes not only to the superior quality of the actor's performance but also implicitly to the Asian racial element specified by the use of the phrase "Out of This World." Surely, this phrase refers to his figurative journey from the West to the other-worldly East.

Still, the choice of Brando as Sakini was greeted with puzzlement by reviewers of the film version of *The Teahouse of the August Moon*. Both Glenn Ford and Brando are cited as unusual choices for the roles they respectively played. Bosley Crowther in his review for the *New York Times* expressed dismay at Brando's "too broad" performance even in the midst of an admittedly broadly satirical fantasy of a narrative.[10] Significantly, Crowther's specific complaints begin with Brando's yellowface guise:

> In the first place, Mr. Brando looks synthetic. A conspicuous make-up of his eyes and a shiny black wig do not imbue him with an oriental cast. And his manner of speaking broken English, as though he had a wad of chewing gum clenched between his teeth, is not only disconcerting but also makes him hard to understand.
>
> More than this, Mr. Brando is too elaborate, too consciously cute. His Sakini is less a charming rascal than a calculated clown.[11]

A *Variety* review also commented on the "offbeat casting" of Brando in the role.[12] *Motion Picture Daily* reviewer Richard Gertner specifically addresses the decidedly mixed critical response to the actor's casting and performance:

> At a preview of the film in New York there was some disagreement noted afterward as to how well he plays the role—some (most of whom had seen David Wayne in the part on the stage) feeling Brando was miscast. But this reviewer sides with those who think otherwise, feeling that the brilliant Brando has pulled off another acting coup. Everything seems astonishingly right—from the realistic Oriental makeup to the

winning air of rascality that he conveys. Whether pro or con Brando will again cause talk.[13]

Interestingly, even the critical dissension around Brando's performance in this film becomes part of the actor's well-known profile as a controversial figure who "will again cause talk."

The film reportedly drew large audiences in Japan, where according to the English-language daily *Mainichi Shimbun* it was welcomed as an alternative to other films taking Japan as their subject: "The center of the applause is Marlon Brando who acts as Sakini, the wily interpreter. . . . Of particular amusement to the Japanese audience is his attempt to speak Nippon-go. . . . Unlike other films which have the themes laid in Japan, the Teahouse of the August Moon is enjoyed for its clean humor and not as something to be laughed at by the people who usually do not like things Japanese being muddled up by Hollywood."[14]

Interestingly, a critical element in the enjoyment of this film for Japanese film viewers lies precisely in Brando's attempt at authenticity (the use of Japanese instead of Oriental gibberish) in his racial impersonation. Paradoxically, the authenticity that Americans would find in this feature (and certainly touted in the U.S. promotion of the picture) would, to the Japanese, be humorous and diverting. Also, this review candidly reveals a long-standing dismissal by the indigenous audience of Hollywood-produced Japanese cinematic portrayals. Even the discourse surrounding Brando's highly caricature performance hints at a growing acknowledgment of how Hollywood's interpretations of Orientals might be lacking. In retrospect, Brando himself characterized the picture as "horrible" in his autobiography, stating that he was miscast in the role of the Okinawan interpreter.[15]

This disapproval becomes more explicit in the early 1960s, particularly evident in the small supporting characterization of a Japanese photographer by Mickey Rooney in *Breakfast at Tiffany's* (1961). The character of Mr. Yunioshi in the film provides an interesting example of how the features of the yellowface performance can both function as comic relief and mitigate and contain key transgressive elements in the narrative as a whole. The main character, Holly Golightly (played by Audrey Hepburn), is a beautiful young woman of questionable repute who eventually falls in love with a handsome writer, Paul Varjak (played by George Peppard). Mr. Yunioshi lives upstairs in her apartment building.

Originally conceived as a Frenchman named Rene in an early script outline, Mickey Rooney's enactment of Yunioshi clearly exhibits the traits of a desperate clown.[16] However, the dialogue remained unchanged. Thus, the basis of this yellowface characterization relies solely on physical cues, delivery, demeanor, and, significantly, decor. Interestingly, Truman Capote's novel originally features a Japanese photographer named Mr. Yunioshi. Notably, scenes where Holly Golightly's profession (as a call girl) begins to emerge with some clarity are routinely truncated by outside distractions. In this 1961 Hollywood film, Rooney's Yunioshi, a Japanese photographer and relatively minor character, often functions as that distraction at key moments in the narrative. This film was produced at a time when the production code had only just begun to lose its influence on motion picture content.

Yunioshi appears only briefly a few times in the film, mainly as a killjoy for Holly Golightly's Bohemian lifestyle. In fact, Holly's primary relationship with Yunioshi involves her routinely buzzing his apartment for entrance into the building because she constantly forgets her own keys. He repeatedly admonishes her in Japanese-inflected fractured English that she "must not disturb him" because he is an artist and therefore "needs his rest." He is primarily characterized as a man who is either resting or working. And yet Yunioshi also displays the features of an outsider who is romantically attracted to Holly. In two instances he calls the police on Holly. Once, he telephones the authorities to break up a loud party in her apartment (which disturbs his attempts to conduct his own tea ceremony). The second time he requests that the police arrest her on alleged criminal conspiracy charges of which she is eventually cleared.

The scene that encapsulates the major components of Yunioshi's characterization, the physical basis for his role as buffoon, his positioning as an outsider (socially and sexually), and the use of the equipment or trappings of his native Japanese culture as the source of comic ridicule occurs immediately after the beginning of the credit sequence. Entering her apartment in the early morning hours, Holly, dressed in a black evening gown, buzzes a doorbell. A white middle-aged man, Mr.

Mickey Rooney on the stairs in *Breakfast at Tiffany's*. (Photofest)

Arbuck, follows her into the entryway. Meanwhile, inside an apartment a Japanese man abruptly wakes up to the buzzing, bumping into a traditional paper lantern hanging overhead.

The disoriented figure is Mickey Rooney in yellowface, that is, wearing Oriental eye makeup, a prosthesis of buck teeth, and thick

189

eyeglasses. On his way to the door, wearing a Japanese kimono, he slips on his futons, bumps into his Japanese-style furniture, and accidentally takes a picture of himself using his elaborate photographic equipment that is set up. Rooney's Yunioshi serves as a kind of ethnic comic relief. In this initial scene, the accoutrements of Yunioshi's home country, Japan, are precisely the props that get in his way.

At the same time Arbuck follows Holly up the stairs trying to convince her to spend some more time with him, a thinly veiled request for sexual favors. Just as she reaches her apartment door, Yunioshi calls down to her: "Miss Gorightry, I protesth!" He further admonishes her for disturbing him. Holly then retreats to her apartment, locking the unwelcome middle-aged suitor out. Yunioshi subsequently directs his protests at the disgruntled would-be suitor, who unceremoniously leaves. Holly immediately reemerges after the man leaves and coquettishly implores Yunioshi to be lenient with her. She then flirtatiously suggests that she might be willing to pose for pictures that Yunioshi suggested previously. The photographer anxiously asks when that might be. Holly evasively replies "sometime," to which Yunioshi longingly responds "anytime."

At first glance, Mr. Yunioshi's character does not seem to depict a real character in any sense, only a bumbling caricature in a Japanese guise, so inept that he stumbles over his own furniture. However, it is precisely the high degree of artificiality in the comic buffoonery of his character that works to mitigate the potentially transgressive implications of Audrey Hepburn's Holly Golightly. Indeed, Yunioshi's first appearance coincides with our introduction to Holly, who must indisputably be depicted in a sympathetic light despite her violation of conventional ladylike conduct (having stayed out all night with a man expecting sexual favors). This, in part, is achieved through Yunioshi's caricatured comic presence that trivializes Holly's questionable conduct by insistently disrupting the argument between her and the middle-aged man who incriminates her.

Certainly, while this assessment does not deny the denigration of the yellowface archetype, it acknowledges how caricatured types are often used as convenient figures to define (and often refine) the leading (and almost always white) characters, as it does in the case of blackface minstrelsy. This applies also to *The Teahouse of the August Moon* in which

Sakini is called upon to comically temper the potentially provocative liaison between Captain Fisby and Lotus Blossom through his role as interpreter. However, Yunioshi's instigation in this scene in *Breakfast at Tiffany's* has an explicitly sexual component as well. When Holly refers to Yunioshi taking pictures of her, her remarks and his response are marked by sexual innuendo that seems vaguely adolescent. And yet a darker element can be ascribed to the role of Yunioshi as well in that under the guise of the ridiculous lurks a type of sex fiend, a voyeur if you will, who can only photograph the desirable Holly Golightly. This interaction that Holly has with Yunioshi contrasts her earlier more adult conflict over sex with Arbuck, a white middle-aged man.

After Holly subtly rejects him with her noncommittal answer "sometime," Yunioshi responds very differently from the earlier middle-aged man, who when put off had protested loudly, yelling and banging on Holly's door. The Japanese man suddenly becomes docile. He simply shrugs and looks longingly. However, when Yunioshi appears even more briefly at later points in the story, it is always as a disgruntled outsider who instigates the forces of order (in the form of the police) onto the disorder of the heroine's life, perhaps the legacy of a resentful and rejected suitor.

Like Brando, Mickey Rooney also later expressed regret and embarrassment in his autobiography for his broad characterization in the film: "I was downright ashamed of my role in Breakfast at Tiffany's . . . and I don't think the director, Blake Edwards, was very proud of it either. I was too cute as, get this, an eccentric Japanese fashion photographer living in a posh New York apartment."[17]

Critical reaction to the actor's performance inspired faint praise ("good for several slapstick laughs") from *Motion Picture Daily* but also attracted criticism ("his caricature of the Japanese is a bit overdone") in the same review.[18] Besides being termed "unnecessary" as well as "incongruous" by *Variety,*[19] the role of the Japanese photographer also drew fire for its caricatural quality from the trade column *Harrison's Reports:* "Mickey Rooney punched away much too hard at his role of the Japanese photographer. It was more Hollywood Sukiyaki than Nipponese Yunioshi."[20] Ultimately, the role was assessed by the *Hollywood Reporter* not only as aesthetically unconvincing but also, significantly, as socially problematic: "Mickey Rooney gives his customary all to the part of a Japanese photographer, but the role is a caricature and will be offensive to many."[21]

Yellowface and its antecedents, especially the virulent anti-Japanese cartoons of the 1930s and 1940s, combine to present the evolution of a racial distortion. Whether for propagandistic or comedic effect, yellowface emerges with the same key elements: weak eyes, protruding teeth, and weak or distorted language skills. What began as an attempt to demonize and vilify the Japanese develops into comedic shtick that also subjugates and distorts. Although we do move from the demonic, the yellowface characterization essentially functions outside of sexuality. A male character may become lustful, but in order to mitigate the potential sexual threat, this figure is rendered ridiculous. However, the differences in critical response to Brando's yellowface performance in the mid-1950s and Rooney's yellowface caricature in the early 1960s suggests a more fundamental change in popular sentiment during the postwar period. Even Hollywood's record on racial representation does not escape the more intense scrutiny, as evidenced in these reviews.

Conflicts between black and white Americans raised during the civil rights movement might provide a historical context for this shift in attitude. This may account in part for the reemergence of the nonsexualized yellowface guise, an obvious adaptation on the blackface model. Furthermore, these narratives can possibly be considered as exotic sites where more incendiary black-white domestic conflicts could be safely played out. In any case, this increasingly controversial performance mode in its later phase becomes decidedly more inclusive, as evidenced in the casting of non-Asian, but not always Caucasian, actors in Oriental roles.

Homegrown Orientals

The films discussed in this chapter thus far reflect Hollywood's postwar bias in depicting America's new allies, the Japanese, rather than America's official enemy, the communist Chinese. However, this does not mean to suggest that China and other Asians remained wholly unrepresented, particularly in relation to this study. John Wayne portrayed Mongol Genghis Khan in *The Conqueror* (1955), while *The Inn of the Sixth Happiness* (1957) featured Robert Donat as a Chinese bureaucrat and Curt Jurgens as a Eurasian rebel soldier. Notably, the films' representations of China harken back to prewar images of the Orient as chaotic, brutal, and dangerous. Even in other films of this period set in Asia, China is generally referred to with a mixture of dread and disdain.

Flower Drum Song (1961), a cheerful adaptation of a successful Rodgers and Hammerstein Broadway musical, provides a rare focus on the indigenous Chinese American community. If the Chinese in mainland China had again become dangerous hordes or pathetic refugees, then the good Chinese Americans in this film exude only boundless energy, particularly evident in their spirit of cultural assimilation. *Flower Drum Song* appears as one of a series of Rodgers and Hammerstein screen adaptations with Asian or Pacific settings, specifically preceded by *The King and I* (1955) and *South Pacific* (1958). This trilogy of works on Asia and the Pacific ultimately linked the American presence in Asia to the story of Asian Americans at home. And most importantly, as could be said about all the film texts included in this study, these narratives were commonly at their core not interested in Asia per se but rather in America and its relationship to Asia.[22]

The popular success of C. Y. Lee's novel, also titled *Flower Drum Song,* on which the play and film were based should be seen within a broader context of Asian American postwar writing. Works by Chinese Americans proved to be the most popular during the 1940s and 1950s. Predictably, the same interest was not extended to those of Japanese Americans: "Americans had far less interest in reading the works of Japanese American writers, who were identified with the wartime enemy and whose traumatic experiences in the internment camps challenged the idea of America as a racially tolerant and inclusive society. John Okada's 1957 novel *No-No Boy,* for instance, which explored the bitter aftereffects of war and internment on a Japanese American family, generated little enthusiasm among white or Asian American readers."[23]

Even in the novel *Flower Drum Song,* Chinese Americans are represented in cultural rather than racial terms. This in turn helps make the case against exclusion from an American society that increasingly defines itself in terms of cultural pluralism.[24] Furthermore, Lee represents (not unlike white ethnic immigrant narratives) the population of Chinatown as fundamentally family-centered rather than conceding their history as bachelor societies during the 1930s and 1940s composed primarily of single males: "U.S. laws prevented Asian immigrants from forming families by restricting the immigration of Asian women, stripping the citizenship of American-born women who married non-citizens, and criminalizing miscegenation. By presenting Chinatown families as somehow representative, when in fact they were a rarity, . . . Lee constructs a similarity between Chinese and European immigrants around one of the issues that most clearly marked the racialization of Asians."[25]

Moreover, Oscar Hammerstein in his libretto excised "Lee's limited, but significant, exploration of the racial discrimination experienced by Chinatown residents": "Amid an otherwise comic framework, . . . Lee's novel forced the reader to confront racism in the labor market, when college-educated Wang Ta could find no job other than as a dishwasher; it illustrated the proletarianization of educated workers, when a character with a Ph.D. in political science could only find work in a grocery store."[26]

This film not only resolutely espouses the delights of American cultural assimilation by Chinese immigrants but also introduces a decidedly unique element in its cultural mix with the casting of African American actress Juanita Hall in the supporting role of Madam Liang. Best known for her role as the Tonkinese Bloody Mary in *South Pacific,* Hall's presence in the otherwise all-Asian (but, significantly, not all Chinese) cast creates the film's own cultural melting pot. Her casting further challenges assumptions of the implausibility of an African American performer impersonating any other race.

Many in the film's cast appeared in the successful 1958 Broadway stage production directed by Gene Kelly. In addition to Hall, Miyoshi Umeki and Jack Soo also performed in the Broadway production. In that production Caucasian, Eurasian, and Asian actors portrayed the male roles, while solely Asian actresses played the female roles with the notable exception of Juanita Hall. Generally, during this period of transition the casting of non-Asian actors for male Oriental roles persisted longer than for female parts. However, by the time the film version was produced in 1961, only Asian actors were cast, with Miss Hall in this instance the sole exception in the entire production. Asian actors at that time had begun to prove their commercial viability in Hollywood films. Indeed, fresh from her successful hit *The World of*

Juanita Hall and Jack Soo in *Flower Drum Song.* (MoMA)

Suzie Wong (1960) the year before, Nancy Kwan received top billing in *Flower Drum Song.*

The argument could be made that both the Broadway adaptation and the film construct Asians, like Europeans, as racially unmarked white as they assimilate into a national American identity. This underlying assumption of a racially blind but culturally tolerant nation even influenced Juanita Hall's comments about her participation in the show given her African American heritage:

> A story about Hall in *Ebony* recounted how C. Y. Lee had once asked Hall . . . if she had much "Chinese blood," because she seemed so Chinese on stage. "There was a time," the reporter wrote, "when she quickly corrected such a mistaken impression by explaining proudly, 'I am a Negro.' Now, a little older, wiser, more tolerant, she smiles, says, 'I'm an American.'" Hall, in keeping with the show's vision of tolerance and integration, rejects the racial label and defines herself in the ostensibly racially unmarked—and increasingly inclusive—terms of nationality instead.[27]

Intergenerational as well as cultural conflicts lay at the heart of the plot in this film. From China, Mei Li (played by Japanese actress Miyoshi Umeki) and her father stowaway by boat to arrive in San Francisco. They head to Chinatown to look for slick nightclub owner Sammy Fong (played by Jack Soo). His mother has arranged for him to marry the "picture bride" Mei Li. Shocked and dismayed, Fong who has had a longtime relationship with club performer Linda Low (played by Nancy Kwan), approaches Madam Liang (played by Juanita Hall) and pitches Mei Li as the perfect bride for her nephew, Wang Ta (played by James Shigeta). Delighted with the young traditional lass, Madam Liang, along with her widowed brother-in-law, Master Wang (played by Benson Fong) take both Mei Li and her father in to live with them. They try to influence Ta to choose Mei Li as his betrothed.

Ta rejects the idea of an old-fashioned arranged marriage as he pursues dating Linda who, dissatisfied with Sammy's lack of commitment, seeks out the young college man as a way to better her social position and to also make Sammy jealous. Neither Ta nor his family know about Linda's job as a singer and dancer at Sammy's nightclub. Complications ensue when Linda announces her engagement to Ta (without his knowledge or consent) at a celebration of Ta's college graduation and Madam Liang's graduation from citizenship school.

Mei Li is devastated, and she and her father decide to return to China. However, Sammy secretly arranges for Ta and his family to see Linda perform a provocative number at the club. Ashamed and hurt, Ta then realizes his appreciation and love for the traditional Mei Li. However, at a family meeting, Madam Liang tries to renegotiate the contract agreed to by Sammy's mother, Madam Fong, so that Mei Li will be free to marry Ta. But Madam Fong insists on honoring the contract, wanting her son Sammy to settle down with a girl from the old country.

The night before the wedding, Mei Li, distraught and desperate, watches a movie on television. The scene depicts a Mexican woman who declares that she cannot marry her love because she entered the country illegally as a "wetback." At the wedding Mei Li saves the day by announcing that "her back is wet," so she cannot marry Sammy. Horrified by the prospect of any impropriety, Madam Fong releases Mei Li from her wedding contract. The ceremony immediately becomes a double wedding, as both Ta and Mei Li as well as Sammy and Linda finally marry.

Cast as the flighty mature Chinese lady Madam Liang, the African American actress Juanita Hall was assumed by even many Chinese to be of Chinese origin. The casting and performance of Hall in the film version of *Flower Drum Song* testifies to Hollywood's ability to surreptitiously present racial hybridity while expressly celebrating the implications of cultural hybridity and assimilation in the text. Hall was cast in both the stage and screen versions of *Flower Drum Song,* and her performance of a Chinese matron illustrates how a judicious selection of racial traits becomes critical in the construction of increasingly more inclusive postwar Oriental characterizations.

How was the African American actress able to physically suggest a Chinese ethnic makeup? Her rather unique physical makeup provides a key. Many African Americans of lighter complexion are referred to as yellow or high yellow in the black vernacular. These blacks not only have lighter skin shades but also possess a slightly yellow cast to their skin and sometimes vaguely Asian features on their faces. In fact, Webster's dictionary officially designates one of the definitions of the term "yellow" as meaning "mulatto," a term used exclusively for those of Anglo-African biracial heritage. This common reference of the term "yellow," used both for Asians and a certain group of African Americans, provides a conceptual link between two racial groups seldom thought of as sharing similar physical qualities.

Hall, whose first major role on Broadway was the mulatto Julie in a 1928 production of *Showboat,* possesses these particular attributes. Probably best known for her role as Bloody Mary in both the stage and screen versions of *South Pacific* (1958), Hall's face and arms are made-up in an even lighter shade in *Flower Drum Song.* Minimal eye makeup helps de-emphasize her eyes, making them appear smaller. Her hairstyle accommodates a delicate wig with short bangs that is both smooth and straight, pulled snugly in a tight bun at the back of her head. Her hefty frame is clothed in Chinese-style dresses in nearly every scene. Also, her speech maintains a clipped and formal sound (if not always identifiably Chinese inflected, it definitely works to sound like a nonnative).

Throughout the narrative, Madam Liang expresses an openness and acceptance of American cultural mores. Most of her scenes involve small disputes with her brother-in-law, Master Wang, who adamantly maintains a strictly traditional stance. The musical number "Chop Suey" epitomizes Madam Liang's fascination with all things American as well as creates a performative site that allows a host of cross-cultural cues to emerge from the cast, particularly in the figure of Hall.

The sequence begins with the announcement of Madam Liang's graduation at the top of her class from U.S. citizenship school. Although both are celebrated, the achievement of Ta's "Auntie" seems to all but overshadow her nephew's admirable but more conventional graduation from college. Costumed in a Chinese-style full-length dress with a high mandarin collar and bright yellow flower design, Madam Liang stands out as traditional in age and in stature among the members of the family and community. And yet she also espouses a desire for assimilation as well as a deep pride in her newly attained American status. In fact, the musical number begins with a chide from her churlish brother-in-law, who opines that "it took you five years to becomes an American, you were Chinese in nine months."

Actor James Shigeta, who plays Madam Liang's nephew Ta, gently leads her around a large garden area where the other characters gather nearby. While Ta shares some of the singing with Madam Liang, the genteel nature of his squiring connotes an old-world respect and tradition. Interestingly, these genteel gestures contrast Hall's brassy voice and exuberant manner. Her performance of this song is truly a combination of perceived Eastern and Western sensibilities and attributes. Accompanied by a chorus of Asian actors, singers, and dancers, the number extols America's virtues by invoking in the song's lyrics figures from contemporaneous popular culture with their seemingly nonsensical cultural combinations ("Hula Hoops and nuclear war, Doctor Salk and Zsa Zsa Gabor"). What is left unspoken is the place of racial mixing, of playing at race, of one race convincingly blending into a different racial landscape.

As Hall moves through the crowd, leading the people in song and dance, her dance moves shift from more delicate minimal movements often associated with Asian body language, such as small shuffling footsteps, to those very untypical of the culture. Of course, the song is meant to showcase the seemingly contradictory elements of the American cultural mix. At one point Hall strikes a provocative flapper pose while aping and singing the lyric "Clara Bow." After the characters at the gathering break into a group square dance, Madam Liang and one of the most Americanized Chinese characters in the film, nightclub owner Sammy Fong, team up to dance the Charleston (a clear indicator of the jazz age). This brief teaming segues into the younger Chinese couples taking the floor in an all-out jazz dance (bumps, grinds, and all).

How does *Flower Drum Song* integrate the talents of the African American actress Juanita Hall into its Chinese cultural mix? This is accomplished in part by bringing her to the fore when the issue of cultural mixing is directly presented in spectacle. In the number "Chop Suey," what is acknowledged is the sensational mix of musical dance styles and cultural icons on the American scene. What is left unacknowledged is the play of race in the performance of Hall, in her Chinese makeup and costuming along with the African American cultural roots of her belting vocal style, body poses, and dance movements. Her African Americanness is not wholly displaced in her Chinese depiction. Elements of her own heritage become artfully incorporated into her unique characterization.

Although described as "uniquely robust" in her role as Madam Liang by the *Hollywood Reporter,* Hall's figure, surrounded by a sea of Asian performers, can truly be said to produce a chameleonlike quality of illusion that quite literally changes color to suit its racial environment.[28] In Hall's case, an authentically Asian cast makes a major contribution in accepting her impersonation as Chinese. And yet despite Hall's overall reception as an "undeniable winner whether singing or acting" in the film, the specter of a growing postwar politicization of race continued to inspire greater scrutiny of Hollywood depictions by the popular press.[29]

Throughout this period the representation of Asians (and other ethnic groups) was often greeted with disdain and suspicion. Accordingly, any analysis of the films from this period requires not only a description of the films but also an indication of their reception. The fundamental premise of *Flower Drum Song* drew criticism from *Variety* for its seemingly adolescent rendering of the Chinese American experience:

> There is something about the main "joke" of this musical that registers disconcertingly as just too precious for words. The humor is derived from the spectacle of observing Orientals "adjusting to" or "adopting"

American customs. It is as if we are being asked to note "how darling" or "how precocious" it is of them to undertake execution of American dances such as the Charleston or the rock 'n' roll, to comprehend the science of baseball, or to grapple with U.S. idioms such as "American plan" or "filter, flavor, flip top box" or "that's bop pop." This is a shopworn device for manufacturing mirth. It comes out hollow, occasionally even distasteful. Chinese-Americans do not figure to be very amused.[30]

In *Flower Drum Song,* issues of reconciliation, cross-cultural hybridity, and assimilation are central to the film. Whether in the form of intergenerational conflict or intra-Asian (immigrant vs. American) differences, this film reconciles these potentially disruptive concerns within the familiar and reassuring generic context of the musical. And yet the Oriental impersonation of Juanita Hall epitomizes a celebration of cross-cultural assimilation in her role as Madam Liang while also incorporating a potentially disconcerting element of African American style in her performance. Unlike Caucasian actors, Hall's performance not only works to contain an Oriental sensibility through her physical embodiment in this role but also integrates and contains distinctly African American performative traits.

Remarkably, the musical number "Chop Suey" allows Hall an opportunity to display a myriad of cultural cues through the diverse references to popular culture in the lyrics. Her performance stands as a testament to the adaptability of the Oriental guise that accommodates ostensibly incongruous elements of African American and Asian physicality. And yet her presence in the film speaks to the historical moment whereby almost all interracial conflict tended to be cast in terms of black and white. The next film, *Sayonara,* will show how this Caucasian–African American paradigm, though implicit (as in *Flower Drum Song*), provides a familiar basis and trajectory for the narrative.

Illicit Lovers

"All you nigger-lovers are goin' home. Soon."

The racial epithet above appears in James A. Michener's novel *Sayonara* on which the 1957 Hollywood feature film was based. It is spoken by

Lieutenant Colonel Calhoun Craford, a character identified as a big-oted Southerner and described as hating "every human being in the world except certain Methodists from his corner of a hill county in Georgia"; his hatred, of course, includes "colored people." Craford's outrage targets the military men in the story who have taken Japanese lovers. Clearly, a phrase usually reserved for transgressive Caucasian–African American social (and often sexual) interactions here includes miscegenation with the Japanese. Although this phrase is not uttered by any character in the film, the issues raised by the film's American–Japanese interracial coupling could certainly be understood and inter-preted through more familiar domestic racial tensions by the audience.

Hollywood films in the 1950s and 1960s increasingly featured Asian actors in leading and substantial supporting roles. Most often, Japanese (and later Eurasian) actresses appeared as dramatic counterparts to es-tablished Hollywood male stars. The film *Sayonara* features an unusual performance by well-known Mexican American actor Ricardo Montal-ban as a Japanese Kabuki performer, Nakamura. Montalban's portrayal uniquely attempts to incorporate familiar elements of the romantic Latin lover type with more traditional Oriental attributes. Further-more, his character as a Kabuki performer displays a host of transgres-sive fantasies of cross-gender masquerade.

Perhaps, the underlying appeal of a well-known actor attempting a racially and ethnically specific film role lies in, as film scholar Don-ald Kirihara suggests, the same pleasure a Japanese audience member experiences watching an *onnagata* (a man who specializes in playing women's parts) in the Kabuki theater. One is never unaware that a man is playing a woman's role; indeed, it is precisely the appreciation of the man's skill and mastery in playing a woman that provides an important component in the pleasure of the spectator.[31]

How significantly this level of appreciation impacts Hollywood's decision-making process remains highly debatable, especially when fac-toring in commercial pressures to cast a well-known cinematic star as opposed to a relatively unknown authentically ethnic actor in a role of a big-budget Hollywood studio picture. The casting of Montalban in the romantic supporting role of Nakamura instead of a lesser-known Japanese actor suggests not only commercial considerations but also perhaps aesthetic ones. In this period, rigidly caricatured yellowface shtick coexisted with the more elastic performance attempted by Montalban. The actor's complex adaptation of an Oriental impersonation in this film expands to accommodate seemingly incongruous elements. Perhaps this complexity accounts for the abrupt nature of Nakamura's departure from the narrative.

The main plot of the film *Sayonara*, set in 1951 during the Korean War, involves an interracial love story between U.S. Air Force major Lloyd Gruver (played by Marlon Brando) and Hana-ogi (played by Miiko Taka), the lead Japanese performer in an all-female dancing troupe. This plotline is paralleled and contrasted by the subplot of another interracial couple, enlisted man Joe Kelly (played by Red Buttons) and his Japanese bride Katsumi (played by Miyoshi Umeki). Both Buttons and Umeki won best supporting Oscars for their roles. Interestingly, the slight romantic subplot between Nakamura and Eileen Webster (played by Patricia Owens) did not originate in the novel but instead was created especially for the film. Whether included to balance or distract from the more central storylines, its resulting brevity in the finished film neither allows their romantic friendship / relationship to develop substantially nor resolve itself conclusively.

After being shipped to Japan for R&R, Lloyd acts as a reluctant best man at Kelly and Katsumi's wedding. Despite military obstacles and official disapproval, the newlyweds attempt to settle into a life together in Japan. In the meantime, Lloyd's fiancée Eileen, daughter of the influential General and Mrs. Webster, surprises him by her unexpected visit to Japan. They attend a spectacular Kabuki performance starring Nakamura in both male and female roles. Eileen is fascinated, while Lloyd remains puzzled. Moreover, Eileen is disappointed by his dutiful attitude and lack of passion toward her. After several heated debates, Eileen and Lloyd decide to part company for a while. Lloyd's colleagues take him to an all-girl revue, where he becomes entranced by the leading performer, Hana-Ogi. He pursues her relentlessly and finally begins a passionate romantic / sexual relationship with her. Their trysts take place at the residence of Kelly and Katsumi.

Sometime later, Nakamura attends a party at a private club and encounters Eileen. She greets him warmly and apologizes for not having attended any Kabuki performances for the last month. He responds

Ricardo Montalban in *Sayonara*. (MoMA)

by stating that "he knows" and that he "has been waiting." Eventually Lloyd's affair with Hana-Ogi is exposed, to the shock and disapproval of the military brass. Eileen moves to protect Lloyd by warning him of the coming attack from the military authorities. However, she is personally devastated when Lloyd ultimately announces that he wishes to marry the Japanese actress. Upset and angry, Eileen runs to Nakamura for consolation.

The pressure builds on Kelly and Katsumi, as the military authorities threaten to ship him back to the States without her. Katsumi, in her desperation to become more acceptable, contemplates quack surgery that promises to alter her eyelids so they will appear more Western. Aghast at this, Kelly reassures her that he loves her just the way she is. The two couples, Kelly and Katsumi, Gruver and Hana-Ogi, attend a Noh play later that evening in which a tragic couple in love decides to commit suicide as a way to be together eternally. Days later Kelly and Katsumi are found dead from gas poisoning, lying in each other's arms.

Gruver pursues Hana-Ogi, determined that she marry him, and after much convincing she accepts.

Although Montalban's Nakamura functions superficially as a platonic love interest for Brando's jilted white American fiancée, Eileen Webster, it is particularly intriguing that his profession as a Kabuki performer allows him to switch seamlessly between male and female parts in the same play. Nakamura's initial appearance in the film occurs fairly early in the story as Eileen and Lloyd observe the Kabuki master perform on stage. This extended sequence shows Nakamura's transformation from a female to a male role by specifically including the process of his being made-up and dressed by assistants backstage during the performance. Indeed, great pains are taken to exhibit Montalban's muscular physique as he is ritualistically dressed and undressed by his assistants.

Shirtless and looking into a mirror, Montalban displays a host of usually contradictory elements. Partially made-up (on the face and neck) in pale white makeup and his hair wrapped in cloth yet displaying a sensual and masculine physique, Nakamura embodies both male and female qualities in his first appearance on screen. As the film cuts between Lloyd and Eileen's conversation in the audience and Nakamura's preparation for his stage role, the process of Nakamura's transformation (through makeup and costuming) exposes the elaborate artifice involved in his profession.

Nakamura emerges in his first incarnation as a woman on stage, where the feminine gestures of small dainty steps and deferential demeanor complete the impersonation. Notably, the elaborate process and construction of Nakamura's gender impersonation backstage becomes as much a spectacle as his official performance on stage. Lloyd reacts uncomfortably to Nakamura's female impersonation, while Eileen expresses great fascination and admiration. Eileen demonstrates a genuine interest in Nakamura's gender-switching training from childhood. The goal of this preparation is to eventually embody both the "grace of a woman and the power of a man" in his Kabuki performances. After his appearance as a geisha, Nakamura assistants are shown peeling away the costume from his nearly naked frame. Clearly, the opportunity to display Montalban's fit body reassures the audience of his undeniable masculinity.

Lloyd and Eileen visit Nakamura backstage in his dressing room after the performance. Montalban's offstage makeup includes altered eyelids, reddened lips, contained gestures, and the halting speech of pidgin English. As Lloyd somewhat rudely expresses a confused wariness of Nakamura's performance practice, the so-named male actress visibly takes offense but replies with traditional Oriental deference.

"I am not necessarily making love to you"

Nakamura's character is introduced as dually gendered (at least on stage) but will shortly transform into a subtle yet persistent love interest for Eileen. Yet the scene where Nakamura explicitly expresses his feelings for Eileen reveals the ways in which the divergent and often contradictory elements of his character are negotiated. While his character functions as a romantic interest in the narrative, he must also evade any transgression of Hollywood's interracial (in this case, white female–Asian male) sexual taboos.

The sequence begins with Eileen entering a Kabuki theater in a formal white evening gown and taking a seat. She is then handed a note by a Japanese male assistant of Nakamura's who tells her that the Kabuki master would like her to join him and some guests for dinner after the performance. Nakamura then enters onto the stage in a distinctly male outfit. Eileen manages to attract his attention, gesturing her acceptance of his invitation.

Eileen is in a balcony seat at the Kabuki theater where Nakamura performs. She enters the well-lit space dressed in white. Here, she is clearly presented as a desirable object of beauty to be admired from a distance by both the film viewer and Nakamura himself. When Nakamura comes out on stage he is heavily made-up as usual, which serves to make him difficult to distinguish from the actual Japanese Kabuki artists doubling for Montalban; the Hollywood actor appears in the stage sequences in the close-up shots.

Eileen's gesture to Nakamura during his performance regarding his dinner invitation may seem to stretch dramatic credibility on one level but adds a strong fictive or unreal context for their relationship on another level. In this instance Eileen, quite literally, responds to a Kabuki performance rather than a flesh-and-blood Japanese man. Granted, this ploy is also utilized as a vehicle for Brando's (Major Gruver's) romantic

Ricardo Montalban (*far left*) and Marlon Brando (*far right*) in *Sayonara*. (MoMA)

involvement with Japanese showgirl Hana-Ogi. However, that couple eventually moves from the world of the stage to the real world, where they confront rigid social conventions and racial prejudice. The tentative coupling of Nakamura and Eileen never substantively moves beyond the theatrical world of make-believe.

The potentially disruptive element of physical intimacy between the two characters is negotiated not only through reaffirmation of a fictitious context but also through the physical separation enforced by the framing of shots and editing. Significantly, the only shots in this sequence where Nakamura and Eileen share the same frame occurs when they are in a public theater separated by stage and balcony and briefly afterward in the restaurant, where they are sitting across from one another among a roomful of other guests.

However, it is during the scene between Nakamura and Eileen when they subsequently retire to the outdoor garden away from the rest of the dinner guests that the mechanisms attempting to mediate a sexually charged scene become most apparent. The couple walks out (in long shot) into the garden area as if on the entryway of a Kabuki stage. Eileen precedes Nakamura, who follows at a discreet distance behind her. They physically maintain this distance throughout the scene, although the content of Nakamura's dialogue grows more intimate.

Once they are in the darkness of the garden outside, Eileen's attention is immediately drawn to a lively party occurring a short distance away. Yet the framing of the people in the distance as well as the inclusion of music originating from that party all work to mimic a stage performance rather than a social gathering based on personal or intimate relationships. The theatricality of this distant gathering obliquely contextualizes Nakamura and Eileen's intimate dialogue as more pose than genuine.

Nakamura and Eileen are shown exclusively in close-up and medium close-up throughout this scene. Nakamura brings up the subject of her fiancé's liaison with Hana-Ogi. He suggests that it will come to nothing because of Gruver's lack of bravery in transgressing social conventions by marrying a Japanese woman. Nakamura also states that the Japanese often look upon marriage to Westerners with disdain and disapproval. But he then states that he does not share in this thinking, as he has had very positive experiences with Americans in the past. Provocatively, he then asserts Eileen's personal influence on his way of thinking, namely that her beauty removes any inhibitions that would prevent him from pursuing a romantic/sexual relationship with her despite racial taboos separating Japanese from white Americans.

Montalban infuses Nakamura's dialogue with an unabashed seductive and romantic quality. Even as he delivers the line "I am not necessarily making love to you," crafted to exemplify an expressly Oriental reserve, it is with the smoldering sensuality of his Latin lover image. Montalban's explicitly sexual Latin inflection of his character is rigorously offset by the editing, which never shows the couple in the same shot. We never know how physically close they are to each other. Furthermore, as Nakamura delivers his romantic dialogue, Eileen's reaction shots and gaze look in the opposite direction of her Japanese suitor. Their eyes never meet, as great efforts are made to neutralize the intimate emotional space created by Montalban's Nakamura.

Indeed, most reviews recognized the role's unrealized potential. *Harrison's Reports* lauded Montalban's characterization for its "charm and refinement,"[32] but *Motion Picture Daily* complained of its underdevelopment: "In the background, there is suggestion, never resolved or defined, that Brando's ex-fiancee, Miss Owens, is being wooed by Ricardo Montalban, who plays a prominent figure in the Japanese theater. Because of the vagueness of their association their romance, if such it is intended to be, lacks significance."[33]

This lack of significance and unrealized potential in Montalban/Nakamura's storyline reveals Hollywood's insistence on maintaining the cultural status quo while appearing to do the opposite. Although *Sayonara* presents postwar thematic issues of social awareness, much has not changed. Why does the film sanction Brando/Gruver's marriage to a Japanese woman in the narrative when the same does not occur for Nakamura and Eileen? Who gets away with the social transgression of interracial marriage and why?

At the forefront of the film's plot is the ultimate suicide of both working-class Joe Kelly and his Japanese bride Katsumi, while Gruver subsequently becomes determined to wed his Japanese love Hana-Ogi. Robert G. Lee, in his book *Orientals: Asian Americans in Popular Culture,* highlights this issue of class in the film as the officer gets his girl while his subordinate is not allowed a similar happy ending: "Class differences, coded as military rank, are underscored by the revelation that Kelly, a forthright but devoted and hardworking soldier, has been promoted and demoted four times for insubordination. . . . Kelly defies the military bureaucracy by writing his congressman to get permission to marry. His class analysis is straightforward and populist: 'There's the generals for the officers and congressmen for the peasants.' This secures Kelly's position as spokesman for the workingman."[34]

However, most appropriate to our discussion here is how Gruver's interracial relationship parallels the Nakamura-Eileen coupling, since the former liaison appears to directly encourage the latter. Gruver possesses not only the privilege of his upper-class status but also that of a member of a conquering nation and occupying force. Why should his desire be denied? In a sense, his desire for marriage to a Japanese national can be rationalized as part of the spoils of military victory.

Surely, Hana-Ogi can be expected to assimilate into his world in the United States. And yet in its closest parallel in the film, the pairing of Nakamura and Eileen does not happen on screen. The resolution for this Japanese male and white American female couple remains open-ended at best and inconclusive at worst.

Although the major plotline of the relationship between Gruver and Hana-Ogi seems to transgress social mores, it does so safely within the dominant power structure that Gruver represents. And yet a marriage in the subplot between Nakamura and Eileen could potentially and significantly challenge social norms. In this case, Eileen would most likely be expected to adapt to Nakamura's Japanese world. *Sayonara* shrinks away from this particular scenario. It does not happen in this film. It cannot happen, so it is omitted. And indeed, a powerful negation is accomplished by omission.

Nakamura's truncated depiction extends the practice of portraying Asian males as feminized figures tending toward asexuality. The casting of Ricardo Montalban, whose previous roles as romantic leads to Lana Turner, Esther Williams, and the like, brings an initial element of sexual titillation to his Japanese character. Still, Nakamura's profession as an *onnagata* places him squarely within an explicitly feminized paradigm. In this way, Marlon Brando's Gruver easily outranks Nakamura's unfamiliar masculinity as an ideal of Western masculine strength in the narrative. So when Eileen looks to Nakamura for some vague comfort (out of her sense of rejection), she is not running to a real man but rather settling for a tentative and stigmatized substitute.

Specifically created for the film, the figure of Nakamura illustrates an attempt to introduce a set of transgressive issues in a seemingly more conciliatory figure. Neither villain nor foe, his character presents an articulate though deferential romantic figure completely dissimilar in temperament to his more macho Western counterpart, Major Gruver. However, this character, who exhibits an accommodating demeanor while also accommodating socially disruptive features, proved too complex for easy reconciliation. All that Nakamura potentially arouses is bluntly checked through select dramatic devices along with his abrupt disappearance from the narrative.

Finally, the use of occupied Japan to dramatize similar themes of U.S. racial tensions plays on familiarity with historically black and white domestic conflicts. The so-called nigger-loving U.S. soldiers as described in the novel who seek to legitimize their romantic and sexual unions with Japanese women are reprimanded using this old Southern-originated label for whites who overstepped acceptable social boundaries with blacks. Gruver's characterization as a Southerner adds an extra layer and resonance of the civil rights conflict occurring mainly in the southern United States during the 1950s. It is not coincidence that Gruver, a Southerner, exists as a most vocal mouthpiece of racism in the beginning of the film (particularly toward Katsumi and Nakamura) and the most visible convert by the end, with his apparently enlightened view that now includes marriage to his female Japanese lover, Hana-Ogi.

Whether packaged in amusing narratives or more melodramatic tales, the range in the performances of Hollywood's Oriental figures in this period come to include portrayals significantly less dependent on cosmetic alteration. Indeed, the racial construction in *A Girl Named Tamiko* of Eurasian Ivan Kalin relies wholly on the adoption of a specific psychological attitude and emotional profile rather than on the introduction of any physical manifestation of racial difference.

Eurasian Angst

The figure of the Eurasian occupied a prominent place on Hollywood screens in the postwar era. From the high-profile portrayals by Caucasian stars, such as Jennifer Jones's performance of Dr. Han Suyin in *Love Is a Many Splendored Thing* (1955), to Eurasian Nancy Kwan's (Anglo-Chinese) ascendance as a Hollywood star in *The World of Suzie Wong* (1960), the Eurasian figure has typically been female with a tragic streak. This figure is not wholly unrelated to the tragic mulatto archetype often discussed in portrayals of African Americans in film and literature, a usually biracial (black and white) female who cannot reconcile the disparity of her divided racial heritage and comes to a ruinous end. However, the concerns most relevant to this study involve how this figure is constructed to explicitly embody the distress of racial inequality. Unlike other Oriental archetypes, the Eurasian figure provides an explicit voice of anguish and resistance even within strictly conventional narratives.

The Eurasian archetype tends to display less (to no) cosmetic alteration than other Oriental types. Enactments by Caucasian performers tend to rely more on costume and the vocalization of misfortune and deprivation. Almost always depicted as a racial pariah, this characterization's inner life drives the narrative forward as much as external events. These depictions remain of interest because their construction is usually based only marginally on physical indications. *A Girl Named Tamiko* provides a lesser-known but nonetheless interesting case whereby physical cues of racial difference become completely nonessential to the story of interracial conflict and strife. British actor Laurence Harvey's performance offers an opportunity to address what kind of elements create an Oriental racial outsider when his race doesn't show.

It is important to place *A Girl Named Tamiko* within the context of postwar Oriental romantic narratives. Numerous internal memos to producer Hal Wallis during the development of this project indicate that the producers and writers of the film were all very much aware of other similar productions:

> This story should make a beautiful film. It has all the exotic color, warmth, and romance of another "Love is A Many Splendored Thing" or "Sayonara" plus many new values all its own. . . . Naturally, it goes without saying that the writing should be most sensitive. Harry Brown, who I understand is to do it, is of course excellent. If, for any reason, he should become unavailable, however, the following might be then considered—John Patrick ("Love Is A Many Splendored Thing," "Teahouse of the August Moon," "Suzy Wong"), Paul Osborn ("Sayonara"), Isabel Lennert ("Sundowners," "Inn of Sixth Happiness"), Robert Anderson ("Tea & Sympathy," "Nun's Story").[35]

Even in conception, this project seemed heavily influenced by the legacy of similar Hollywood narratives.

The plot of the film revolves around the social and professional struggles of Eurasian photographer Ivan Kalin (played by Laurence Harvey), a resident of Tokyo, Japan, who longs to immigrate to the United States. His efforts have been frustrated for twelve years because his biracial parentage (Chinese Russian) classifies him as Chinese, whose quota remains "pitifully small" for entry to the States every year. Finally, after being given only two to three months until his visa approval, Ivan begins the process of saying goodbye. He begins first with his Japanese mistress Eiko (played by Miyoshi Umeki), whom we learn from Ivan is one of the few people in Japan sorry to see him leave.

Rather than embracing his imminent departure for the States, the embittered Eurasian becomes increasingly desperate to develop key professional contacts before he leaves that will determine his professional and social status in the United States. Ivan relentlessly pursues both professionally and romantically Fay Wilson (played by Martha Hyer), an American employee in the consul office with influential ties in the expatriate Japanese community. Eventually they begin an affair in which each, in turn, attempts to exploit the other in the relationship.

In the meantime, Ivan is introduced to a girl named Tamiko Mishima (played by France Nuyen), an upper-class Japanese woman whose own career (as a foreign press club librarian) and lifestyle (frequent contact with the foreign community) scandalizes her conservative brother with whom she lives. Despite the venom that Ivan expresses toward her as Japanese (both his mother and father were killed by Japanese soldiers in China during the war), Tamiko attempts to help him make the contacts he desperately desires. In one instance, she takes him to see a noted Japanese artist, Kimitaka, attacked by the country's traditionalists as betraying his national roots because of his preference for modern art. During the visit the artist, who is always strictly guarding his privacy, expressly refuses to be photographed. Nevertheless Ivan surreptitiously sneaks pictures, unbeknownst to Kimitaka but under the disapproving eye of Tamiko. Ivan claims that he needs this exclusive to make a name for himself with the influential in Japan.

Printed on the front page of the newspaper, the rare photograph garners raves from the influential and even generates a compliment from Kimitaka himself, who claims that the whole episode has taught him to reevaluate his aesthetics and thought. Fay's affair with Ivan spurs her to escape from her own stifling relationship with her influential benefactor, Max Wilson (played by Gary Merrill). She proposes that Ivan leave with her to San Francisco within a week. When Ivan announces this to Tamiko, she becomes distraught and saddened. Both Ivan and Tamiko realize that against all odds they have fallen deeply in love.

France Nuyen, Laurence Harvey, and Martha Hyer in *A Girl Named Tamiko*. (MoMA)

Throwing all thoughts of societal propriety away, Tamiko decides to accompany Ivan to a lake retreat where he is sent on a photo assignment. They spend idyllic days together, but on their way back to their cottage a motorcycle accident injures Tamiko. She disappears after a brief recovery, leaving a note for Ivan that she accepts that their relationship has no future. When summoned to the consul's office to sign

213

his long-awaited visa permit in the presence of Fay and Max, Ivan ultimately decides against it and departs to find Tamiko.

The opening scene of the film finds Ivan in the consul office. He is a familiar figure in a sports jacket, white shirt, and tie, and the Japanese office staff greets him on his way in. Harvey displays no outward signs of Asian racial differences either in makeup, physicality, demeanor, or speech (a vaguely British accent). He follows Fay into her office, where their dialogue alone first identifies Ivan as a racial outcast. He tries unsuccessfully to enlist her aid to help sell his photographs of Japan:

> IVAN: Now, if you could arrange for me to photograph, say Chicago for our rebellious Oriental brethren.
>
> FAY: Your brethren. Looking down on them won't change that.
>
> IVAN: My father was Russian.

This exchange typifies the discourse between Ivan and Fay, a character who constantly reminds him and the audience of his Oriental status. And yet she responds with momentary sympathy to his final statement that his father was Russian.

Great pains are taken in the early scenes of the film to establish Ivan's dual racial heritage as a social stigma that has stood between him and all of his dreams and ambitions. Once in the consul's office, Ivan displays a palpable obsession about the United States. As he longingly views a large wall map of the United States in the consul's office, Ivan asks where the official is from. When he replies that his home was Denver, Ivan relays a list of facts specific to the state of Colorado, such as the state flower and statistics on the population.

The consul responds sympathetically to Ivan's twelve-year predicament and speaks frankly about Ivan's racial classification as Chinese. Ivan again reiterates that "only my mother was Chinese," to which the consul responds, "I know, but unfortunately you were born there." We come to understand the ramifications of Ivan's racial stain or mark through government paperwork and institutional classifications. These define his social interactions (seen with Fay) as well as constrain his physical and personal freedom.

Again, Ivan's interactions with other characters of different races further defines his status as an outsider. When he unnecessarily berates his Japanese photographic assistant Saburo, a British friend named Nigel Costairs (played by Michael Wilding) gently admonishes him. Ivan responds curtly about the rationale behind his abusive behavior: "You are English, Saburo's Japanese. I have no country, I'm nothing." Nigel suggests that these are mere words, to which Ivan answers, "No, they're feelings." Ivan is depicted as psychologically damaged as a result of his interracial parentage. A figure of discontent and resentment, the Eurasian is often allowed to voice the pain of cultural isolation: "Very few people can understand what it feels like to be brought into this world through no fault of your own and find yourself a displaced person. [*bitterly*] A citizen of the world. Without a passport and no place to go. A man needs roots. He has to belong somewhere."

An interesting element in the film is the fact that Ivan's imminent immigration to the United States, rather than healing an old wound, merely intensifies the pain of his distress. Significantly, the narrative begins with the granting of a long-held wish. And yet the plot dramatizes Ivan's desperate attempts to establish himself in Japan's expatriate community. His character appears particularly tormented by the disjuncture between his physical whiteness and his cultural and racial displacement. Indeed, after Ivan encounters Fay at an exclusive restaurant, her benefactor Max thinks that she has offered to help a fellow American. Fay quickly disabuses him of that notion:

FAY: He's Chinese.

MAX: Well, he doesn't look Chinese.

FAY: Well, he is.

He notices her tenseness.

MAX: What's wrong with you?

FAY: I hate climbers.

Attempting to contain her attraction for him through racial denigration, Fay's character becomes critical as she relentlessly reminds us of his inferior racial stock. In fact, her need to ostracize and exoticize Ivan not only feeds her sexual fantasies but also ultimately positions him as a rescuer from her unfulfilled existence with Max.

The nature of Fay's relationship with Ivan reflects the strength that her perceptions have in her attraction and treatment of him as a darkly sexualized figure. His Chinese half attracts her for its exoticism even though no trace of racial difference appears in his looks. Clearly, the idea of Ivan's racial subjugation and deprivation, rather than creating an evident physical difference, creates a compelling exploitative object of dark fantasy for her. This element of deprivation visibly excites her as she inquires whether he has ever "been with a white girl" before. They consummate their relationship after he quietly confesses that he has not.

Ivan's racial identity remains entrenched in the attitudes of and treatment by those around him. In this way, Tamiko also functions to further define and then mirror Ivan's social displacement. Their first conversation occurs in a library, a neutral social setting for the vaguely disreputable Ivan. He is usually seen in bars and his photography studio, the site of numerous sexual conquests. Here, their exchange takes on the features of an intellectual debate as Ivan attributes his stifled professional success principally to Japanese provincialism:

> TAMIKO: Do you think it will be less so in America, particularly for an Oriental or a half-Oriental?
>
> IVAN: I know that in America if you prove that you have talent, you get your chance. No matter what color you are.

Notably, his statement about the United States flies in the face of the racial prejudice he has experienced with the Americans in Japan (particularly as embodied by Fay) while strongly indicting the Japanese. His bias was clearly influenced by the tragic loss of his parents to Japanese soldiers. However, Tamiko tellingly counters that her mother was killed by American soldiers and her father was killed by the Russians, yet she holds no ill will toward the half-Russian Ivan.

In the second half of this narrative, Tamiko and the Japanese become the focus of Ivan's struggle and triumph. This clear shift indicates how the position of the Eurasian (as European and Asian) works to distance the site of racial conflict and interracial sexuality far from America's shores. Remarkably, Ivan's romantic involvement with Tamiko works to gradually whiten Ivan in terms of the tragic interracial narrative. Their relationship evolves primarily in the trip to the countryside of Japan, where a travelogue-type montage depicts the couple in an idyllic and otherworldly setting. Tamiko's abrupt disappearance, after she has risked the social censure of her people along with Ivan's planned departure for the States, resembles a Madame Butterfly/Captain Pinkerton scenario. Suddenly, Ivan becomes the white American leaving his self-sacrificing Butterfly, and yet its postwar incarnation reconfigures his choice that gives the film its happy ending.

In this film, the happy ending became a source of contention between the Production Code authorities and the film's producers. Significantly, many romantic Oriental films of the postwar era such as *A Girl Named Tamiko* provide a body of texts for the production team of *A Girl Named Tamiko* who created their own standards and transgressions: "The situation that the Code people object to, that of a 'sex relationship that culminates in a happy ending,' has been used already in too many films for ours to be singled out. The most flagrant example, of course, is 'SUZIE WONG.' Others include INDISCREET (Cary Grant & Ingrid Bergman), SAYONARA (where Brando and the Japanese girl make love in the room provided by Red Buttons and his Japanese wife in their home)."[36] In crafting the story, producers' memos reflected also some sensitivity to racial slurs typical of the postwar era: "Regarding humor, when Ivan makes it at the expense of Saburo's 'bow-legs' (p. 1) and 'pigeon-toes' (p.14), many people may not think it funny. In fact, jokes at the expense of others' physical defects—particularly throughout the Orient where they are a racial characteristic—may be found offensive. Believe this should be changed."[37] These comments not only indicate a sensitivity to racial slurs but also target those physically focused distortions so vigorously propagated during the war years. In this sense, even an exoticized melodramatic narrative specifically seeks to correct lingering wartime depictions.

It should be noted that less inflammatory though traditionally entrenched Hollywood Oriental archetypes were actively sought out, especially evident in the characterization of Tamiko:

> Tamiko is and should be different. Her whole philosophy is different—because she is Oriental. She knows Ivan's problem. She knows his need, and how much America means to him. . . . So once she decides

to go with Ivan to the mountains, she must, and, as an Oriental, would decide—her eyes open—to accept the situation as it is—not only for its happiness but also for its pain—fatalistically, stoically, and without complaint. This is the measure of her love and sacrifice—and valor.[38]

Here, a specific character profile drawing on traditional Oriental archetypes is clearly delineated in detail. Tamiko, more importantly, is positioned as intrinsically different from Western women, her decision making induced by her particular Oriental sensibility.

An internal memo regarding the promotion of the film relays a very specific strategy that reveals which elements were considered the most marketable:

Wallis called from New York to say that their key line for the ad campaign on TAMIKO is as follows: "Without shame or guilt the ambitious Eurasian used the women of two continents." Hal didn't like that one, so he revised it to read as follows: "He was half Oriental but used the women of two continents without guilt or shame." He feels these can still be improved, and the idea is to show that our hero is part Oriental and uses women.[39]

While promoted as exotic and rapacious, actor Laurence Harvey received decidedly mixed reviews for his role of Ivan. Already known for his "angry young man" screen portrayals, Harvey's complete lack of distinctive cultural mannerisms provided a nearly insurmountable dramatic obstacle in reviews from the *Motion Picture Herald* as well as *Variety,* respectively:

If it is a little difficult to accept Laurence Harvey as half-Chinese half-Russian and of humble birth with China as his native land—without any trace of makeup or mannerisms different from his own usual style—it is also a tribute to his talent that the basic character comes through nevertheless.[40]

Laurence Harvey's character is not one immediately easy to accept and this is one of the flaws. As Ivan Kalin, he's a Chinese-Russian photographer and looks, speaks, and romances like a British matinee idol. Thus there's a certain lack of conviction but this is not too severe a drawback as the story unwinds and the interest mounts.[41]

Whether deemed inappropriate due to his choice not to adopt any Oriental affectation or because of the indelible association with his role in *Room at the Top* (1959), Harvey's performance of Ivan made little critical or commercial impact. However, his portrayal exists as an example whereby racial difference is rendered wholly as a construction of government institutions, hearsay, and the imagination rather than through physical traits. Surely this unusual approach to an overtly racialized characterization can be seen as potentially subversive as well. Harvey re-creates the distressed figure of the Eurasian as an angry young man searching for his place and identity in a hostile world.

Unmasking the Oriental Guise

As demonstrated by Laurence Harvey's interpretation in *A Girl Named Tamiko,* the reconfigured Oriental guise of Hollywood could exist free of any physical affectations. However, at the other end of the spectrum, advances in makeup and technology could also render an Oriental countenance with unprecedented intensity. As an example of the latter, the film *My Geisha* (1962) exhibits the wizardry of technical prowess in the construction of the Oriental while offering a most complex treatment of this fabricated alter ego. And yet despite this technical capability, this film addresses issues of realism and specifically calls into question the use of Caucasian actors in Asian roles.

My Geisha chronicles the antics of movie star Lucy Dell (played by Shirley MacLaine) to convince her director husband, Paul Robaix (played by Yves Montand), that she can play the starring role of a geisha in his film version of the opera *Madame Butterfly.* The story begins with a meeting between Lucy, Paul, and producer Sam Lewis (played by Edward G. Robinson) and actor Bob Moore (played by Bob Cummings) to discuss Paul's latest film venture. He announces his intention to shoot a new version of Puccini's classic opera *Madame Butterfly.* With her longtime leading man Bob cast as Captain Pinkerton, Lucy assumes that she will play the doomed geisha. Paul informs her that she will not and that the part is "outside of her range." He insists on casting a Japanese actress as well as shooting on location in Japan to capture the "reality" missing from other versions of the story.

Paul's casting preference is not only a blow to Lucy's professional ego, but the separation of several months from her husband also distresses her. Nevertheless, she and Sam see Paul off at the airport. Unfortunately, the New York studio office wants to cut back the budget on the project considerably once they find out that the bankable Lucy won't be starring in the film. Hoping to soften the blow, Lucy accompanies Sam to Japan to inform Paul of this development. However, once there, Lucy spies Paul and Bob in a geisha house having the time of their lives.

More than a little jealous, Lucy bets Sam that she can fool her husband by pretending that she's a geisha for the evening. After she successfully fools Paul, Lucy gestures to Sam not to give up the secret. Thinking that she can preserve the "first class" budget on Paul's production through her presence in the cast, Lucy proposes to Sam that she play the role, unbeknownst to Paul, until the shooting ends. In addition to preserving the integrity of her husband's vision, Lucy looks forward to proving that any part is "within her range."

Paul asks Sam to find the "shy" geisha impersonated by none other than Lucy. Sam and Lucy invent the geisha "Yoko Mori" to audition and eventually win the role of Madame Butterfly. As Lucy makes up in the mirror before the audition, she wonders aloud how she will ever get used to the brown contact lenses that she's now required to wear. Sam instead urges her to focus on exuding a "traditional" and "old fashioned" nature in order to convince Paul of her authenticity. After enlisting the services of an esteemed male geisha coach, Lucy commits wholeheartedly to playing the role of her life.

Lucy and her companion Kazumi (played by Japanese actress Yoko Tani) conspire to keep up Lucy's charade. Lucy's Japanese gibberish at a Sumo match impresses Bob and Paul while thoroughly confusing a wrestler introduced to her after the match. Fascinated by Yoko's exoticism, leading man Bob Moore relentlessly pursues Lucy's geisha. Bob, who has been married four times, adamantly decides that he wants to marry Yoko and asks Paul to intercede on his behalf. Although Paul

Shirley MacLaine in *My Geisha*. (MoMA)

thinks this unwise, he accedes. In his conversation with Yoko, Lucy attempts a flirtation to tests Paul's fidelity to her. He passes the test but not before confessing to her his hope that the success of this picture will match the success of his wife so that "I could be the man and she could be the woman."

From an examination of the negative that distorts Yoko's image to resemble Lucy's (her black hair appears red and her brown eyes blue), Paul realizes that he has been duped. Angry and brooding, he goes to Lucy's room and proposes that they make love. Lucy is devastated by his amorous advances toward Yoko. The next day, she enacts the final suicide scene from the film with genuine grief. Paul insists that Sam not reveal to Lucy that he knows her ploy. He wants to "play the game to the finish."

According to plan, Lucy arrives in Japan for the premiere. Paul, thinking that Lucy will reveal her own participation in the film after the screening, anticipates a humiliating event. As Lucy slips away to prepare for her final impersonation of Yoko, her companion Kazumi meaningfully gives Lucy a Japanese fan as a gift. The inscription on it reads: "No one before my husband, not even I." When Lucy appears on the stage, it is as herself. She announces that the role of Madame Butterfly will be Yoko Mori's first and final screen appearance, as the former geisha has entered a Buddhist convent. Deeply moved, Paul joins Lucy on stage and reveals to her that he knew about her ruse. Much relieved about her husband's fidelity, Lucy happily receives the applause not for her own performance but as Paul's doting wife.

This film establishes a self-conscious tone from the outset not only in relation to Lucy / MacLaine's Oriental performance but also in terms of the medium used in its propagation. As Gina Marchetti astutely observes in her book *Romance and the Yellow Peril,* Paul's initial conception of his artistic vision reflects the common predilections involved in postwar Oriental productions. "'Color' and 'realism' are touted in discussions in *My Geisha* of film aesthetics and the Madame Butterfly project. When he first mentions his intention to film Madame Butterfly, for example, Paul exclaims, 'It was made for color film.' He goes on to explain, 'I'm going to use a real Japanese girl. That's the kind of picture it's going to be—real. Not just an opera but real. . . . Lucy in the part of Madame Butterfly would be offensive.'"[42] Of course, in this scene Paul's character expresses the heightened awareness surrounding racial screen images whereby a Caucasian racial impersonation of an Asian could be viewed as potentially offensive.

Lucy's natural style is introduced in our first image of her striking an "unladylike" pose, according to her producer Sam, to shoot pool.

MacLaine is filmed with her backside facing the camera. Once in Japan, her impersonation of a geisha provides a dramatic contrast. Lucy's first role-playing exercise in the geisha house sets the tone for the remainder of her performances in the film. Notably, her impersonation is achieved with the aid of the Japanese geisha. As Lucy begins to put on her white makeup in their dressing room, she and the geisha break up in laughter. This key element creates a type of solidarity between the Japanese geisha and Lucy, a mutual acknowledgment and amusement that sets apart her performance as a put-on, not a put down, of the Japanese people and culture.

Interestingly, the success of her first impression depends a great deal on her surroundings. She enters with two other authentic geishas and silently sits down beside her husband, Paul. Dressed in the geisha trademark wig, hair ornaments, and kimono, Lucy simply mimics the movements of the other women. Her face covered in chalk white makeup, Lucy accomplishes her performance primarily through silence and through giggling, with her hand shyly (and conveniently) covering her mouth. Lighting a cigarette for Paul, Lucy finally dares to speak in a singsong lilt and with a tilt of the head: "You are so funny."

Paul, egged on by Sam, is asked to compare the beauty of the geisha to his wife, Lucy. When he proudly declares that the geisha's bone structure and facial features "absolutely" make her more photogenic than his wife, Lucy achieves her goal. And yet this scene also challenges the audience to view the Caucasian Oriental guise with greater awareness and scrutiny. Unlike the wartime character in *First Yank into Tokyo* whose Oriental masquerade involved permanent disfigurement and personal danger in the name of conquering a Japanese wartime enemy, *My Geisha* reframes the risks and goals of the Oriental impersonation. In this film, the danger does not reside in our Japanese allies but rather shifts to the various masquerades performed among the Westerners themselves, particularly between husband and wife.

As the evening ends, Paul and Bob say goodbye to the group of geisha girls. In the midst of the farewells, Bob invokes the name of the film *Sayonara* after Paul realizes that this is the only word he knows in Japanese. Luckily, he had asked Lucy's geisha what it meant, and she was able to answer. Before they completely disperse, Bob calls out "Marlon Brando" in response to one of the geisha's utterance of the word "sayonara." Once again, a sense of self-awareness (or perhaps self-parody) particularly in terms of this cycle of Oriental postwar films emerges as a familiar cultural point of reference and pleasure. Like the comedic *My Geisha*, *The Teahouse of the August Moon* among other Hollywood films of this era prominently feature the figure of the geisha, the war bride, or the prostitute (as in *The World of Suzie Wong*), indicating a postwar fascination with the sexualized Asian woman.

As Lucy removes her makeup Sam enters, and they jointly decide to continue with the deception for the entire picture. At the moment that they decide, Lucy's face is half made-up. We see her image through her mirror while viewing Sam directly. Strikingly, the Oriental makeup that remains happens to be on the top half of her face (the forehead, eyebrows, eyes, and eyelids), while the bottom half has returned to her normal skin tone. Interestingly, where the makeup remains is where the cosmetic emphasis has historically been in Hollywood impersonations. Visually, Lucy's image at this moment makes a statement that serves to confirm the decision she verbally makes with Sam.

Lucy's second impersonation reveals a more sophisticated cosmetic achievement. Brown contact lenses, eyes slanted upward, eyelids thinned out, and darkened eyebrows physically perfect her disguise from the night before. However, just as Lucy expresses anxiety over adjusting to her brown contact lenses, Sam rushes in to remind her of the crucial nonphysicalized components essential to an Oriental guise. Here, he specifically urges her to stress how "old fashioned" she is to win over Paul.

During the screen test, Lucy fabricates a subtly accented speech along with a suitably poignant story of having been sold into the geisha house at a young age. At each step of the charade the audience becomes aware of the artificiality of Lucy's endeavor but also gains an increased appreciation for the performance practice as an artistic feat. Indeed, during the screen test Lucy is seen principally in a long shot that displays her individual achievement from head to toe.

Initially, most of Lucy's Oriental performances are enacted in the presence of other Japanese actresses who laugh with her, enjoying her prank. This recurrent pattern creates a type of kinship, solidarity, and like-mindedness that appears to supplant any racial or cultural differences between them. Her companion, Kazumi, also gleefully shares in her secret until she becomes wary of Lucy's motives. A crucial scene between Kazumi and Lucy occurs after Kazumi comments on Paul's good looks. Lucy responds in a typically flippant manner. Kazumi states that she could never sustain Lucy's masquerade because of her jealous nature. To that Lucy replies that she is jealous as well, even of her alter ego Yoko.

The split that we are accustomed to perceiving between what we see Lucy playing and who we know she is begins to fuse at this point. In this scene, Lucy's feminine wiles are called into question by Kazumi. It is at this point that Lucy's performance begins to internalize her geisha masquerade. Her appearance begins to affect her sense of values and priorities. Lucy's looks and gestures become less expansive, and she begins to appear more at home in the costume.

This fusion culminates in her performance of the *Madame Butterfly* suicide scene after Paul has pretended to proposition Yoko. Lucy plays out the scene with genuine anguish, her role as Yoko and Butterfly both providing vehicles that express her pain. In this way, the role she inhabits becomes a role she gradually internalizes and adopts. At this point in the narrative, the self-conscious element of Lucy's performance moves away from a mere racial imitation and instead instigates a profound cultural assimilation for her character. This leaves her decision to sacrifice her performance at the end as an anticlimactic event.

Shirley MacLaine received high marks for her performance in *My Geisha* from *Motion Picture Daily,* in part because it "demonstrated her fine talent and versatility" to the fullest but also because it provided a unique twist on the fading Oriental masquerade: letting the audience in on the joke. "Deceptivity as a stellar skein in a plot-pattern is always intriguing if the viewer is let in on it, as you are in this one. . . . Miss MacLaine giving the geisha character such physical and facial believability that it was easy to accept her in the role knowing all the time who she was while Montand was laboring under the belief that he had the real thing."[43]

The notion that tallish, blue-eyed, redheaded Shirley MacLaine could get away with a performance as a Japanese geisha is engagingly amusing, and the fact of the matter is that she succeeds, via a big black wig, brown contact lenses, a carefully prepared mincing walk, and the necessary eye slant and costuming, in offering a highly entertaining impersonation of a geisha.[44]

No stranger to racial impersonations, MacLaine made a strong impression as an Indian princess in the Mike Todd spectacular *Around the World in 80 days* (1956). However, the actress also brought a personal familiarity to her role in *My Geisha,* as she maintained a residence in Japan for many of her most active Hollywood years. This project was conceived as a vehicle for Miss MacLaine, with her husband Steve Parker producing.

Critics embraced *My Geisha's* myriad "impersonations, misunderstandings and double meanings." However, what begins as a spoof of traditional geisha myth ends earnestly as a caution for untraditional women of the West. And yet despite the questionable nature of this culturally coded message, what remains most indelible is the fact that the performance practice of the Oriental masquerade peaked in this film as an artistic endeavor if not as a fantasy of individual transformation.

This film not only takes one of the premiere Western Orientalist texts as the primary dramatic and aesthetic site of contestation but also invokes an essential but often overlooked cohort to the narrative: the more than a century-long legacy of nearly exclusive performances of Cio-Cio San by white actresses:

> Ironically, it was the white women performers that embodied the images and meanings of Asian femininity created by the white male author, playwright, and/or composer. . . . These Orientalist performances by white women took place at the same time that many white women were becoming New Women of the twentieth century, who challenged Victorian gender norms . . . by participating in the women's suffrage movement, demanding birth control, engaging in socialism, expressing themselves in arts and letters, seeking "free love," cutting their hair and smoking cigarettes. The construction of such a new gender identity was closely linked to, and was articulated through, enacting roles and identities other than their own.[45]

The Oriental impersonation not only was part of the emancipation of American women of the early twentieth century but also indicates by the numerous opportunities to perform the roles of Asian heroines the close link to the white women's "material and representation power over real Asian women and men, the power they exercised both on and off stage."[46] *My Geisha* attempts to address a number of historical and aesthetic legacies both in the distant and more recent past with a seemingly innovative spin. Ultimately, however, the film communicates a mixed message. Although the "freedom to cross racial, class, cultural lines—even if it was temporary 'play'—was part of being 'modern' American women," in the past *My Geisha* actually advocates the containment of this autonomy (racist though it may be) in favor of traditional male patriarchal standards.[47]

This later cycle of Oriental impersonation by non-Asian actors offers a divergent mix of styles and approaches. We have seen a process of transition in this chapter as the Oriental guise has moved from demon to clown to lover to finally confronting the issue of realism. Sexuality emerges as an important theme whether contained within a desexualized yellowface caricature or embodied by a mutable yet stigmatized romanticized figure. The yellowface performances of actors as different as Marlon Brando and Mickey Rooney illustrate how this extreme and caricatured racial enactment possesses a life of its own that supersedes individual characters and texts. Ironically, yellowface portrayals remain the primary acceptable form of impersonation to survive. Even when restricted to comedic farce, yellowface performances such as Peter Sellers (as Charlie Chan) in *Murder by Death* (1976) and *The Fiendish Plot of Fu Manchu* (1980) as well as Jerry Lewis in *Hardly Working* (1980) provide a troubling means of ridicule through stock Oriental archetypes.

Whereas the yellowface figures recalls the stock wartime caricatures, the romanticized Oriental figure as exemplified by Ricardo Montalban in *Sayonara* stretches the boundaries established by Oriental characters such as General Yen. While General Yen functions as a malleable projection of Megan's repressed sexual desires, Montalban's Nakamura voices resistance to the societal foundations for interracial sexual taboos. And although his character exhibits elaborate and exotic transgendered displays as a Kabuki actor that might characterize him as a similarly mutable figure, these performances occur solely in the theatrical arena (a space specifically demarcated for highly artificial enactments) rather than emanating from another character's subconscious.

However, Montalban's sexuality and mutability ultimately remain as strictly contained by traditional elements of the Oriental guise as the feminized and asexual Oriental detective.

Ricardo Montalban and Juanita Hall, in particular, as nonwhite Orientals demonstrate the capacity for the inclusion of seemingly contradictory elements into the Oriental masquerade. Their performances strongly suggest the potential to accommodate divergent traits in what might be thought of as highly circumscribed roles. Laurence Harvey's role in *A Girl Named Tamiko* engenders much rancor due to his mixed-race parentage. But despite a lack of distinct visual traits indicating an Asian parent, passing for white is not ever introduced as an option for his character (unlike the character Ursula Georgi, whose murderous rampage expresses her inability to do this). Instead, Ivan voices his distress and frustration while acting out sexually. Overall, the Oriental impersonations of the postwar era shift to present not so much an Other but rather an other race.

Finally, Shirley MacLaine's technically precise enactment in the film *My Geisha* provided the ultimate fantasy that would be difficult to surpass. And yet even within a comedic context the film raises issues of trust, masquerades, and gender relationships. In this film, MacLaine's masquerade becomes the site of both contention and conflict rather than simply an escapist fantasy. Suddenly, the search for realism and authenticity becomes paramount as the Oriental guise operates almost completely as a spectacle of artificiality and theatricality. But it must be remembered that this elaborate geisha ruse works essentially as a vehicle for a Western couple (European or American) to address their marital woes. This example, as comparatively enlightened as it may seem, essentially harkens back to the traditional use of the Oriental guise: to resolve exclusively Western conflicts and concerns.

These postwar interpretations of familiar Oriental archetypes recall traditional archetypes only to reshape them to fit an ostensibly more socially conscious era. The acceptably demonized distortions during the war suddenly became potentially offensive material after the war. For the Japanese in particular, the postwar distortions became embodied figures of both ridicule and romance. And our domestic social ills set the agenda and tone for many screen treatments of race relations.

The once routine, systematic, and automatic practice of Oriental-izing non-Asian actors essentially ended during the mid-1960s. The lessened frequency of this performance mode coincides with the emergence of prominent Asian actors such as James Shigeta, Nancy Kwan, and France Nuyen. Although this ascendance of Asian performers provides a type of denouement to this study's trajectory, it does not necessarily imply a wholly progressive resolution in the depiction of Hollywood's Orientals but rather illustrates a major shift in the still-evolving Oriental guise.

Conclusion

The Fading Oriental Guise?

The lyrics of the song "You've Got to Be Carefully Taught" from the movie musical *South Pacific* (1958) comments on the powerful messages of racial discrimination sent to us as children, often by family members and others close to us. They particularly bring to mind a memory of watching the film for the first time on a local television station in Chicago when I was about eight years old. I instinctively felt even at that young age that the stories of thwarted love and racial prejudice, though set in the exotic South Pacific islands, had little to do with the Tonkinese but rather really enacted the social conflicts of the civil rights movement between African Americans and whites in the United States.

What made the most significant impression upon me in this regard was the portrayal of Bloody Mary by actress Juanita Hall. Her severely styled hair (a tight bun set atop her head) seems designed to cast her facial features in bold relief. Possessing brown skin and a coarse manner and treated with a distinct lack of respect by the common sailors (a far cry from her role as Madame Liang in *Flower Drum Song*), Bloody Mary in an early scene is described as being "nobody," merely Tonkinese, by one of the men. And when she fancies the handsome Lieutenant Cable for her daughter, she offers him a black shrunken head (strategically held beside her own), from which he recoils. So when my mother told me that Juanita Hall was actually a "Negro"—as was my family (it was the 1960s, after all)—I received my first indication (and confirmation) that depictions of racial difference in the movies of Hollywood might not always be what they appear.

Perhaps there is a truth and veracity in the racialized impersonations in Hollywood films, but as stated earlier the film industry has never been interested in depicting truths per se but rather is interested in the creation of fantasies to transport an audience from a relatively mundane existence. In this sense, the veracity of these Hollywood films had less to do with the specific culture being depicted than it does with revealing the desires, fantasies, and ambivalence of the mass audience whom those movies sought to entertain.

This has been a study essentially presented as a narrative with a beginning, middle, and end. Perhaps a different author might have interpreted the films and their contexts another way, resulting in a completely different conclusion. The main purpose of this inquiry was to trace how these culturally constructed characterizations change and modify over time, creating distinctly different meanings depending on the historical framework. From its preeminence as a Hollywood performance practice in the 1930s to its gradual dissolution as a frequent and uniformly accepted form of cinematic enactment in the 1960s, Hollywood's Oriental reflects most often the ambivalence intrinsic in the majority of widely disseminated (mis)representations of Asia and Asians as well as Asian Americans. It has been argued that Fu Manchu and General Yen overlap in their depictions. Clearly, the image of Fu Manchu haunts the dream of Megan in her attempt to process her sexual attraction to the general in *The Bitter Tea of General Yen*. In a broader sense, the dynamic of an Oriental impersonation being injected and reinterpreted within ostensibly divergent film texts occurs with regularity in the films in this study. Surely, the demonization of the Oriental detective character illustrated by the two animated films *Japoteurs* and *Bugs Bunny Nips the Nips* reflects this tendency to recirculate familiar images and invert them according to the historical moment.

Jessica Hagedorn, in her introduction to the anthology *Charlie Chan Is Dead,* describes a litany of Hollywood movie images, with all their contradictory qualities, that she grew up watching in the Philippines:

The slit-eyed, bucktooth Jap thrusting his bayonet, thirsty for blood. The inscrutable, wily Chinese detective with his taped eyelids and wispy moustache. . . . Always giggling. Bowing and scraping. Eager to please, but untrustworthy. The sexless, hairless Asian male. The servile, oversexed Asian female. The Geisha. The sultry, sarong-clad, South Seas maiden. The serpentine, cunning Dragon Lady. Mysterious and evil, eager to please. Effeminate. Untrustworthy. Yellow Peril. Fortune Cookie Psychic. Savage. Dogeater. Invisible. Mute. Faceless peasants breeding too many children. Gooks. Passive Japanese Americans obediently marching off to "relocation camps" during the Second World War.[1]

This ready flip-flopping between insider and outsider, friend and foe, aggressor and weakling, points to the dichotomy also existing within almost every Oriental archetypal figure.

A singularly female trajectory can also be traced between the emotionally wounded but diabolically vengeful Ursula Georgi in *Thirteen Women* and Lien Wha's murderous rage in *The Son-Daughter.* Lien Wha's transformation from a demure innocent to a brave (and politicized) figure parallels that of Jade in *Dragon Seed.* Less obvious parallels can be made between male and female characters as different as Steve Ross of *First Yank into Tokyo* and Lucy Dell in *My Geisha,* who share a desire to explore and/or test the boundaries of racial difference when they self-consciously adopt the identity of an Oriental.

Indeed, the lamentations of Steve Ross from within a surgically irreversible Oriental countenance sounds very much like the melancholy of the Caucasian-looking Eurasian Ivan Kalin in *A Girl Named Tamiko.* Both characters express an unfulfilled desire for acceptance and community that their race denies them. Although made more than fifteen years apart and reflecting very different physical manifestations of racial difference, they still share the angst and distress of an Oriental outsider. In both films the issue of racial identity indicates a shift in the depiction of this distress. While Ross's embodiment of a Japanese soldier is depicted as patriotic and ennobling, the irresolvable conflict between his two identities compels him to sacrifice his own life in the end. However, Ivan's quest for cultural kinship does not involve a pretense within the narrative. His character never considers the issue of racial impersonation in the form of passing as white. Instead, he expresses frustration at the official recognition of only one of his parents (his Chinese mother) as a racial/social category for himself rather than a bi-racial identity. Ross struggles for and hopes that those he loves will see past his constructed racial identity (manifested in the corporeal realm), while Ivan fights a less tangible but just as oppressive process of social categorization.

The postwar yellowface performances of Marlon Brando in *The Teahouse of the August Moon* and Mickey Rooney in *Breakfast at Tiffany's* illustrate live-action variants of the ridiculous and grotesque in the demonization and caricature of the wartime cartoon images from *Japoteurs* and *Bugs Bunny Nips the Nips,* while *Flower Drum Song* and *Sayonara* present a mixture of cultures and genders in the performances of non-Asian though not Caucasian actors Juanita Hall and Ricardo Montalban. Of course, this eclecticism could be said to reflect the myth of *Lost Horizon* that defines the Orient as a place where any transformation (horrible or pleasurable) of identity is possible.

Despite these unexpected parallels, the shift in reception is clearly apparent in reviews of the period. Concerns about offending Asians along with an appreciation and awareness of the Oriental guise as a diverting ploy rather than a vehicle to an Other reality begin to emerge. However, this is not to imply that the lessening frequency of this racially impersonated performance practice ushered in a new era of sensitivity and racial progress. The emergence of Asian actors in prominent roles simply indicated another shift in Hollywood's history rather than providing a happy ending to this narrative. In fact, there is no ending to this narrative. Just as certain Oriental archetypal figures recirculated within the period of this study, they remain central sites of contestation and reconfiguration to this day.

The concentration on Japanese and Chinese portrayals in this study reflects Hollywood's own narrative predilections during the thirty-year time period under consideration. However, after this period a vacuum exists during which Asian characterizations of any sort virtually disappeared from the Hollywood screen. America's involvement in Vietnam may have had some influence on this. It wasn't until the 1980s that Hollywood began to produce a cycle of films about the war. Of course, the martial arts genre (basically produced in Hong

Kong with the exception of *Enter the Dragon* in 1973) gained enormous popularity in the 1970s, with a loyal following particularly among urban youths.

The narrative of Bruce Lee has been chronicled in detail in a number of excellent books, such as *Everybody Was Kung Fu Fighting* by Vijay Prashad and *East Main Street: Asian American Popular Culture,* edited by Shilpa Dave, Leilani Nishime, and Tasha G. Oren. Lee's position as pivotal figure from the yellowface portrayals that trailed off in the mid-1960s (i.e., Henry Silva's undistinguished take on Mr. Moto in 1965 and Shirley Maclaine's depiction of a ditsy Eurasian with Michael Caine in *Gambit* [1966]) to the activist attitude that defined the late 1960s and 1970s remains undisputed. Lee's television career (as Kato in the short-lived Green Hornet series), ultimate rejection from the leading role of Caine in the high-profile series *Kung Fu* in favor of Caucasian actor David Carradine, and subsequent success in Hong Kong martial arts films is the stuff of legend. Although the quantity of Oriental masquerades dramatically dropped off in this period of supposedly more enlightened racial attitudes, the instances where it reared its racist head provoked outrage and resentment that began to cross ethnic and racial lines. The fight of Asians to play their own roles (particularly in the case of Bruce Lee) became linked to the broader yoke of oppression of not only African Americans and Asians but also those of underdeveloped nations around the world (such as India and the African continent). Lee was indeed an international cinematic figure who embodied the volatile culture of his time. When asked about "racial barriers," he told a Hong Kong journalist in 1972 that "I, Bruce Lee, am a man who never follows those fearful formulas. . . . So, no matter if your color is black or white, red or blue, I can still make friends with you without any barrier."[2]

In fact, Lee was one of the first martial arts sifus (masters) to train non-Asians, including people such as Chuck Norris, Roman Polanski, and Kareem Abdul-Jabbar. The antiracism of Lee was not matched by the world in which he lived. "I am a yellow-faced Chinese, I cannot possibly become an idol for Caucasians."[3]

Lee represents one of the last high-profile victims of exclusion from a project in favor of a racialized impersonation by a white actor. The television series *Kung Fu* (1972–75), starring David Carradine, remains one such notorious example. As half Chinese–half white Kwai Chang Caine, Carradine became a household name. As is widely known, Bruce Lee worked on the development of the original network series and was initially set to star as Caine. Ultimately, the producers passed over Lee and gave the part and the stardom to Carradine.

A recent guide to the series, *The Kung Fu Book of Caine* by Herbie Pilato, offers its version of the original casting debate over Bruce Lee and David Carradine. Key production executives describe their reasoning behind the choice of Carradine:

> "In my eyes and in the eyes of Jerry Thorpe (producer/director)," says Harvey Frand, "David Carradine was always our first choice to play Caine. But there was some disagreement because the network was interested in a more muscular actor, and the studio was interested in getting Bruce Lee." Frand says Lee wouldn't have really been appropriate for the series—despite the fact that he went on to considerable success in the marital arts film world. The *Kung Fu* show needed a serene person, and Carradine was more appropriate for the role.[4]

Perhaps Carradine's perceived appropriateness over Lee was his "serene" or decidedly less masculine persona that has historically limited the roles of Asian males. It was also rationalized that since the character was "half-Asian, half-Caucasian, either an Asian or a Caucasian would have been a reasonable choice."[5]

To the dismay of many, Asian Americans in particular, the 1970s *Kung Fu* TV series became a lucrative franchise, spawning a number of made-for-TV movies in the 1980s and even a syndicated updated series in the early 1990s titled *Kung Fu: The Legend Continues.* The irony about the original series is that it became a great vehicle for legendary Asian actors from Hollywood's studio era (e.g., Keye Luke, Victor Sen Yung, Benson Fong, Richard Loo, and Philip Ahn) as well as younger rising talents (e.g., James Hong, Beulah Quo, Soon-Teck Oh, Mako, and Robert Ito), some of whom were regulars on the series while others frequently guest starred. However, this dynamic nevertheless extended the traditional Hollywood casting practice of giving leading roles to white actors while relegating supporting roles to racially authentic Asian actors.

The legacy of Hollywood's Oriental performances still endures to this day and provides an important social and artistic context for resistance, contestation, and reconfiguration, particularly for (but not limited to) Asian and Asian American filmmakers, writers, and performing artists. For instance, two racialized performances by prominent white actors during the 1980s include one by Peter Sellers (his final film role) in *The Fiendish Plot of Dr. Fu Manchu* (1980).

The film includes a depiction of Sellers as Fu Manchu as well as other multiple roles. Although played for laughs, his choice of the title role creates almost a full circle back to some of the earliest villainous Asian images coming out of Hollywood. The same year, Peter Ustinov appeared in the movie *Charlie Chan and the Curse of the Dragon Queen* made up in the full racialized guise.

However, this film production was not without both controversy and protest. A number of high-profile Asian American actors and activists received significant media attention for their protest against yet another resurrection of the Charlie Chan character portrayed by a white actor. Without shutting the production down or preventing its distribution or exhibition, the protesters made a powerful statement about both the offensively retrograde nature of the Charlie Chan franchise and the Oriental guise performance practice.

Apart from these insulting portrayals by two prominent white actors, the problematic in recent years has involved the increased prominence of the Eurasian figure. Whether appearing on television, in films, or on the Broadway stage, the Eurasian as portrayed by white actors continues to draw attention and controversy. The early 1990s introduced a controversy surrounding a Eurasian in the leading stage role in the Broadway show *Miss Saigon*. Clearly, the figure of the Eurasian in recent years has served as an important vehicle for sustaining the acceptability of the Oriental guise. What is particularly troubling about the hotly debated and protested role is the nearly unanimously negative reaction of the mainstream media and the popular sentiment toward Asian American activism against this long-standing performance practice.

The rationale behind the reaction has been termed the "Miss Saigon Syndrome" by author Neil Gotanda. He contends that the unilaterally negative response to the protest reveals "a widespread popular

Peter Sellers in *The Fiendish Plot of Dr. Fu Manchu*. (Photofest)

Peter Ustinov in *Charlie Chan and the Curse of the Dragon Queen*. (Photofest)

belief that racism directed against Asian Americans is insignificant or does not exist."[6] One additional and significant media construct may also contribute to this perception: the model minority myth attributed to Asian Americans beginning in the 1960s. Partly invented as a rebuttal to African Americans who in the 1960s were often advocates of government aid and intervention to reverse systematic racism, the model minority myth, while appearing to compliment the Asian American

Protest during filming of *Charlie Chan and the Curse of the Dragon Queen*. (Photofest)

minority, only invokes another level of racism that denies the effect of racism. Enter the Miss Saigon scenario, which tells us that the Oriental guise can continue through the slippery figure of the Eurasian because it cannot really hurt the Asian American model community. Furthermore, this model minority status is used as a denial of racist portrayals; the Oriental guise is supposed to be flattering, not denigrating.

The influx of actors from Hong Kong (e.g., Jackie Chan, Jet Li, and Michelle Yeoh) along with the release of a number of incendiary films featuring Asian actors exclusively as heartless villains or hapless victims (such as *Year of the Dragon* and *Rising Sun*) in the 1980s and 1990s has received its own share of analytical attention in books as well as the popular press. Standard stereotypical characterizations have been identified and rightfully denounced in films as different as *Sixteen Candles* and *Fargo*. Indeed, the list of media affronts for Asian Americans by Hollywood seems at once predictable and highly variable but has not gone unchallenged. For example, the Media Action Network for Asian Americans, in "A Memo from MANAA to Hollywood: Asian Stereotypes," submitted a list in April 2000 of generalized yet resoundingly familiar racist thematic and character elements in Hollywood films:

> Asian cultures as inherently predatory.
>
> Asian Americans restricted to clichéd occupations.
>
> Asian racial features, names, accents, or mannerisms as inherently comic or sinister.
>
> Asians relegated to supporting roles in projects with Asian or Asian American content.
>
> Asian male sexuality as negative or non-existent.
>
> Unmotivated white-Asian romance.
>
> Asian women as "China dolls."
>
> Asian women as "dragon ladies."[7]

Although this memo was submitted by the media activists in the year 2000, the film titles referenced Hollywood depictions from the 1930s to the 1990s. Notably, the films mentioned do not include any racial impersonations in the list of offensive stereotypes. Indeed, the problem most closely related to this historical study in contemporary terms lies not so much in the relatively less frequent (though outrageous) instances of non-Asian casting in Asian and/or Asian American roles but rather resides much more often in the unrelenting resurrection of long-established stereotypical models that allegedly offer a culturally enlightened version.

In 1999 two versions of the original *Anna and the King of Siam* story were produced. One animated version of *The King and I*, the Rodgers and Hammerstein musical, included a bald Yul Brynner–type king. This is certainly a troubling case in which a non-Asian actor has been allowed to indelibly shape the perception of a major Asian role. The other version was the big-budget live-action film *Anna and the King*, starring Jodie Foster and Hong Kong star Chow Yun Fat. The casting of the Asian star seems at first glance to be a progressive step in terms of Asian representation. The actor's presence reflects the influence and recent popularity of films (and filmmakers) from Asia (i.e., Hong Kong, Taiwan, Mainland China, and Japan) as well as a calculated attempt to inject more ostensible authenticity into a film with prestigious ambitions and appropriateness to a more open-minded era.

But why in the late 1990s did we see a revival of a narrative first introduced to American audiences in the 1940s? Perhaps because it exists as a pretested piece of material that Hollywood tends to favor. Still, what can we make of two versions of essentially the same story in the same year? Does this reveal the strength of the legacy of the Hollywood films that preceded them? Certainly, the animated version is more explicit in its borrowing from the 1950s musical *The King and I*. The live-action *Anna and the King* appears to possess loftier ideals, which poses a more complex example. Still, the source material remains Eurocentric, essentially Orientalist and therefore extremely problematic. While Hollywood was becoming more open to the idea of Asian actors such as Jackie Chan and Jet Li starring in action movies with commercial appeal, dramatic roles remain elusive. Chow Yun Fat reportedly hoped to move beyond his well-established action hero persona from Hong Kong through his performances in Hollywood movies; however, this proved quite difficult:

> After several years, the only acceptable offer for a starring role in a dramatic movie came from the producers of *Anna and the King*. The racial bars in Hollywood were still so strong that the King of Siam was the only sympathetic, dramatic leading character that Hollywood could imagine for an Asian male actor. Nearly a half century after Rodgers and Hammerstein opened the show on Broadway—and despite the protestations of the new film's producers that theirs was not a remake—*The King and I* stood as the only vehicle through which Asia's most glamorous film star could gain a dramatic foothold in America.[8]

Whether associated exclusively with the martial arts genre (a precedent set by Bruce Lee back in the 1970s) or contained within historical Oriental narratives, the challenge remains to break free of conventional narrative paradigms to create new forms and express fresh perspectives. The even more recent case of the film *Memoirs of a Geisha,* for which Caucasian actresses were inexplicably but apparently initially considered for the leading role, is unquestionably disturbing but perhaps not entirely surprising. Many people unfamiliar with the novel on which the film was based were unaware that it was authored by a white male writer. Eventually the film was cast with Asian actresses so that the remnants of the casting controversy focused on the casting of a Chinese actress rather than a Japanese actress in the title role. The key to both of these retrograde examples of highly touted cinematic Asian spectacle is in the initial source material; neither originated from the creative imagination of Asians or Asian Americans. And while prominent Asian American artists such as David Henry Hwang and Amy Tan are sometimes criticized for their attempts to contemporize and rework well-known Orientalist tropes, their work seems to warrant a different sort of critical scrutiny.

One of the goals of this study is to integrate racially specific performances within the classical Hollywood schema rather than construct the racialized cinematic performance as coming closer to or further from a social truth. In this way, we might begin to attribute less truth to such cinematic depictions and instead look at them as simply the fictions that they are. Given this view, images such as Charlie Chan would hold about as much social significance for Asian Americans as Sherlock Holmes does for the British. However, we know that this has not been the case; media's role in identity formation is indisputable. It is also important to distinguish between types of racist images because the differences are revealing, thus allowing more possibilities for change. For example, much of the literature on Asian American representation in Hollywood employs the usage of the term "yellowface" unproblematically, an obvious reference to the practice of blackface for the portrayal of African American characters. However, the racialization of African Americans (heinous though it may be) does not tend to involve a denial of their Americanness, which is a central issue in race media texts and popular culture targeting Asian Americans.[9]

The fight is on. There have been retrospectives on Anna May Wong and Sessue Hayakawa at the esteemed venue of the Museum of Modern Art in 2005 and 2007. Also, in June 2008 Turner Classic Movies presented the film festival "Race and Hollywood: Asian Images in Film" with expert commentary by author and professor Peter X. Feng. Taking control of creative production whether in Hollywood or outside is a goal for all underrepresented (or more accurately misrepresented) racial and ethnic groups. And yet creative artists are more than their racial affiliation. Filmmaker and activist Arthur Dong epitomizes this model of independent Asian American filmmaker. Very rarely included in anthologies of Asian American media makers, he has been prolific in his diverse body of work that includes documentaries on the postwar club scene in Chinatown such as *Forbidden City, U.S.A.* (1989) as well as three films that have "examined the destruction caused by America's war against homosexuality."[10] Yet Dong asserts the following about his most recent film, a documentary titled *Hollywood Chinese*:

> With Hollywood Chinese, I take a lifelong affection for film and combine it with a quest to understand the complexities of cinema. It's my journey into the world of Hollywood moviemaking, to discover how stories and images of the Chinese fit within an entertainment industry that mixes art with commerce, a universal art form that affects the way we see each other and ourselves. I didn't set out to produce a definitive encyclopedic treatment of the topic, but rather, a trip through Hollywood as seen through the lens of eleven accomplished Chinese and Chinese American film artists—as well as some non-Asian who played Chinese in yellowface.[11]

When I asked Arthur about his thoughts regarding the significance of yellowface specifically for contemporary Asian American audiences (and others), his response succinctly articulates the goals for all who hope to transform the culture through the commanding prism of film images: "Personally, I hope that any demeaning caricature, yellowface or not, will cause audiences to have a fuller understanding for three-dimensional characterizations whenever they do occur, however rarely. The historical evidence we see in yellowface performances gives audiences context to understand contemporary concerns regarding their (mis)appropriateness."[12]

Finally, I do wonder where a most troubling depiction of the twenty-first century by the self-acknowledged Eurasian comic Rob Schneider in *I Now Pronounce You Chuck and Larry* (2006) fits into Asian American performance debates in recent years. Schneider's brief though key appearance in an uncredited role as a Japanese minister

Rob Schneider in *I Now Pronounce You Chuck and Larry*

in complete yellowface makeup creates its own set of complex issues. His performance utilizes the traditional Oriental guise: a wig, cosmetically altered eyes, a protruding tooth prosthesis, and large dark glasses. What is there to say when an obviously demeaning caricature comes from within the group, as it were? I think that would be best left to another book.

NOTES

Introduction

1. Robert Young, *White Mythologies: Writing History and the West* (London: Routledge, 1990), 139–40.

2. Edward W. Said, *Orientalism* (New York: Vintage, 1979), 16–17.

3. As often as possible, actors and roles are identified as either specifically Asian or Asian American.

4. David Bordwell, Janet Staiger, and Kristin Thompson, *The Classical Hollywood Cinema: Film Style and Mode of Production to 1960* (New York: Columbia University Press, 1985), xiv. This term is based on the argument in this book that "certain fundamental aspects" of Hollywood filmmaking from 1917 to 1960 achieved a certain level of consistency and standardization that produced "a unified mode of film practice . . . a coherent system whereby aesthetic norms and the mode of film production reinforced one another" (xiv).

5. Gish Jen, "Challenging the Asian Illusion," *New York Times,* August 11, 1991, sec. 2, pp. 1, 12–13.

6. Marina Heung, "The Family Romance of Orientalism: From *Madame Butterfly* to *Indochine,*" in *Visions of the East: Orientalism in Film,* edited by Matthew Bernstein and Gaylyn Studlar (New Brunswick, NJ: Rutgers University Press, 1997), 160.

7. Ibid.

8. Helen Zia, *Asian American Dreams: The Emergence of an American People* (New York: Farrar, Straus and Giroux, 2000), 112.

9. Ibid., 113.

10. Ibid.

11. Min Zhou and James V. Gatewood, eds., *Contemporary Asian America: A Multidisciplinary Reader* (New York: New York University Press, 2000), 637.

12. Ibid., 638.

13. Said, *Orientalism,* 40.

14. Eric Lott, *Love and Theft: Blackface Minstrelsy and the American Working Class* (New York: Oxford University Press, 1993), 6.

15. Mary Ann Doane, *Femme Fatales: Feminism, Film Theory, and Psychoanalysis* (New York: Routledge, 1991), 26.

16. Keith Aoki, "'Foreignness' and Asian American Identities: Yellowface, World War II Propaganda, and Bifurcated Racial Stereotypes," *UCLA Asian Pacific American Law Journal* 4, no. 1 (1996): 22.

17. Krystyn R. Moon, *Yellowface: Creating the Chinese in American Popular Music and Performance, 1850s–1920s* (New Brunswick, NJ: Rutgers University Press, 2005), 56.

18. Ibid.

19. Ibid., 114.

20. Ibid., 116–17.

21. Ibid., 164.

22. Ibid., 130.

23. Ibid., 133.

24. Works such as Donald Bogle, *Toms, Coons, Mulattoes, Mammies and Bucks* (New York: Bantam, 1973); Jim Pines, *Blacks in Films* (London: Studio Vista, 1975); Daniel Leab, *From Sambo to Superspade* (Boston: Houghton Mifflin, 1976); Lester Friedman, *Hollywood's Image of the Jew* (New York: Frederick Ungar, 1982); and Patricia Erens, *The Jew in American Cinema* (Bloomington: Indiana University Press, 1984).

25. Works such as Richard Dyer, *The Matter of Images* (New York: Routledge, 1993), and Lester Friedman, ed., *Unspeakable Images: Ethnicity and the American Cinema* (Urbana: University of Illinois Press, 1991), respectively.

26. Works such as Ward Churchill, *Fantasies of the Master Race: Literature, Cinema and the Colonization of American Indians* (Monroe, ME: Common Courage, 1992); Chon Noriega, ed., *Chicanos and Film* (Minneapolis: University of Minnesota Press, 1992); Manthia Diawara, ed., *Black American Cinema* (New York: Routledge, 1993); Ed Guerrero, *Framing Blackness* (Philadelphia: Temple University Press, 1993); Mark Reid, *Redefining Black Film* (Berkeley: University of California Press, 1993); Rosa Linda Fregoso, *The Bronze Screen: Chicana and Chicano Film Practices* (Minneapolis: University of Minnesota Press, 1993); James Snead, *White Screens/Black Images* (New York: Routledge, 1994); and bell hooks, *Reel to Real: Race, Sex and Class at the Movies* (New York: Routledge, 1996).

27. Darrell Y. Hamamoto, *Monitored Peril: Asian Americans and the Politics of TV Representation* (Minneapolis: University of Minnesota Press, 1994).

28. Matthew Bernstein and Gaylyn Studlar, eds., *Visions of the East: Orientalism in Film* (New Brunswick, NJ: Rutgers University Press, 1997), 1.

29. Ibid., back cover.

30. Gina Marchetti, *Romance and the Yellow Peril: Race, Sex and Discursive Strategies in Hollywood Fiction* (Berkeley: University of California Press, 1993), 2.

31. Eugene Franklin Wong, "On Visual Media Racism: Asians in the American Motion Pictures" (PhD diss., University of Denver, 1977), 40.

32. Ibid.

33. Ibid.

34. Michael Rogin, *Blackface, White Noise: Jewish Immigrants in the Hollywood Melting Pot* (Berkeley: University of California Press, 1996), 12.

35. Ibid.

36. Charles Affron's *Star Acting: Gish, Garbo and Davis* (New York: Dutton, 1977) is a more specialized but also very useful work.

37. Richard Schechner, *Performance Theory,* rev. and expanded ed. (New York: Routledge, 1988), 251.

38. Marvin Carlson, *Performance: A Critical Introduction* (London: Routledge, 1996), 53, 54.

39. Ibid., 54.

40. Coco Fusco, *The Bodies That Were Not Ours and Other Writings* (London: Routledge, 2001), 9–10.

41. Josephine Lee, *Performing Asian America: Race and Ethnicity on the Contemporary Stage* (Philadelphia: Temple University Press, 1997), 12.

42. Jessica Hagedorn, ed., *Charlie Chan Is Dead: An Anthology of Contemporary Asian American Fiction* (New York: Penguin, 1993), xxi.

43. Charles Musser, "Ethnicity, Role-playing, and American Film Comedy: From Chinese Laundry Scene to Whoopee (1894–1930)," in *Unspeakable Images: Ethnicity and the American Cinema,* edited by Lester D. Friedman (Urbana: University of Illinois Press, 1991), 43.

44. Charles Musser, *The Emergence of Cinema: The American Screen to 1907* (Berkeley: University of California Press, 1990), 287.

45. Ibid., 306.

46. Nick Browne, "American Film Theory in the Silent Period: Orientalism as an Ideological Form," *Wide Angle* 11, no. 4 (1989): 26.

47. Ibid.

48. Donald Kirihara, "The Accepted Idea Displaced: Stereotype and Sessue Hayakawa," in *The Birth of Whiteness: Race and the Emergence of U.S. Cinema,* edited by Daniel Bernardi (New Brunswick, NJ: Rutgers University Press, 1996), 92.

49. Daisuke Miyao, *Sessue Hayakawa: Silent Cinema and Transnational Stardom* (Durham, NC: Duke University Press, 2007), 6.

50. Kirihara, "The Accepted Idea Displaced," 96.

51. Miyao, *Sessue Hayakawa,* 7.

52. Ibid., 158.

53. Ibid., 219.

54. Ibid., 216.

55. Hayakawa is mentioned along with other silent stars under the subheading "Silent Stars Who Failed the Test" in Donald Crafton, *The Talkies: American Cinema's Transition to Sound, 1926–1931* (Berkeley: University of California Press, 1997), 500.

56. Review of *Daughter of the Dragon* in *Variety*, August 25, 1931.

57. Sonia Shah, ed., *Dragon Ladies: Asian American Feminists Breathe Fire* (Boston: South End Press, 1997), xiv.

58. Darrell Y. Hamamoto and Sandra Liu, eds., *Countervisions: Asian American Film Criticism* (Philadelphia: Temple University Press, 2000), 28.

59. Anthony B. Chan, "Yellowface: The Racial Branding of the Chinese in American Theatre and Media," *Asian Profile* 29, no. 2 (2001): 159.

60. Graham Russell Gao Hodges, *From Laundryman's Daughter to Hollywood Legend: Anna May Wong* (New York: Palgrave Macmillan, 2004), 151.

61. Ibid., 152–53.

62. Karen J. Leong, *The China Mystique: Pearl S. Buck, Anna May Wong, Mayling Soong, and the Transformation of American Orientalism* (Berkeley: University of California Press, 2005), 71.

63. Hodges, *From Laundryman's Daughter to Hollywood Legend*, 153.

64. Ibid., 128.

65. Ibid.

66. Anthony B. Chan, *Perpetually Cool: The Many Lives of Anna May Wong (1905–1961)* (Lanham, MD: Scarecrow, 2003), 117.

67. Cheng-Sim Lim, "Program Notes for *Daughter of the Dragon*," UCLA Film and Television Archive Tenth Festival Presentation, July 28–August 26, 2000, Catalogue.

68. Homi K. Bhabha, *The Location of Culture* (London: Routledge, 1994), 2.

69. "Loretta Goes Oriental," *Photoplay*, March 1932. A subsequent article titled "So Hollywood Goes Oriental" featuring the performances of Helen Hayes in *The Son-Daughter* and Sylvia Sidney in *Madame Butterfly* appeared in *Photoplay* the next year. "So Hollywood Goes Oriental," *Photoplay*, January 1933, 73.

70. Ibid.

Chapter 1

1. Robert Young, *White Mythologies: Writing History and the West* (London: Routledge, 1990), 40.

2. Allen L. Woll and Randall M. Miller, eds., *Ethnic and Racial Images in American Film and Television: Historical Essays and Bibliography* (New York: Garland, 1987), 35.

3. Thomas Doherty, *Pre-Code Hollywood: Sex, Immorality, and*

Insurrection in American Cinema, 1930–1934 (New York: Columbia University Press, 1999), 269.

4. Review of *The Bitter Tea of General Yen* in *Variety,* January 17, 1933, 14.

5. William F. Wu, *The Yellow Peril: Chinese Americans in American Fiction, 1850–1940* (Hamden, CT: Archon, 1982), 165.

6. Frank Capra, "Bitter Times and Bitter Tea," in *The Name above the Title: An Autobiography* (New York: Macmillan, 1971), 140.

7. Ibid.

8. Ibid., 141.

9. Ibid.

10. Review of *The Bitter Tea of General Yen* in *Variety,* January 17, 1933, 14.

11. Edward Lowry and Richard de Cordova, "Enunciation and the Production of Horror in White Zombie," in *Planks of Reason: Essays on the Horror Film,* edited by Barry Keith Grant and Christopher Sharrett (Lanham, MD: Scarecrow, 2004), 175.

12. Doherty, *Pre-Code Hollywood,* 269.

13. Lowry and de Cordova, "Enunciation and the Production of Horror in White Zombie," 182.

14. Ibid., 175.

15. Robin Wood, "Returning the Look: Eyes of a Stranger," in *American Horrors: Essays on the Modern American Horror Film,* edited by Gregory A. Waller (Urbana: University of Illinois Press, 1987), 82.

16. Krystyn R. Moon, *Yellowface: Creating the Chinese in American Popular Music and Performance, 1850s–1920s* (New Brunswick, NJ: Rutgers University Press, 2005), 129.

17. Doherty, *Pre-Code Hollywood,* 268.

18. Moon, *Yellowface,* 129–30.

19. Mary Ann Doane, *Femme Fatales: Feminism, Film Theory, and Psychoanalysis* (New York: Routledge, 1991), 25.

20. Ibid., 26.

21. Leland Poague, *Another Frank Capra* (Cambridge: Cambridge University Press, 1994), 34.

Chapter 2

1. Earl Derr Biggers, "Creating Charlie Chan," *New York Times,* March 22, 1931, 12.

2. Review of *Think Fast, Mr. Moto* in *New York Times,* August 16, 1937, 15.

3. John P. Marquand, *Your Turn, Mr. Moto* (Boston: Little Brown, 1935), 20.

4. Earl Derr Biggers, "Creating Charlie Chan," *New York Times,* March 22, 1931.

5. Earl Derr Biggers, "The House without a Key," in *Celebrated Cases of Charlie Chan* (Indianapolis: Bobbs-Merrill, 1925), 76–77.

6. Biggers, *Celebrated Cases of Charlie Chan,* 78, 79.

7. Review of *Charlie Chan at the Circus* in *Newsweek,* March 28, 1936.

8. Review of *Charlie Chan's Secret* in *Variety,* January 22, 1936, 15.

9. Review of *Charlie Chan's Greatest Case* in *New York Times,* October 7, 1933, 18.

10. Brian Taves, "The B Film: Hollywood's Other Half," in *Grand Design,* edited by Tino Balio (New York: Scribner, 1993), 314, 317. The author defines the term "programmer" as a particular category of film that has the "flexibility to play any part of the program" (315), in other words to play either the top or bottom half of a double bill of entertainment.

11. Review of *Charlie Chan Carries On* in *Variety,* March 25 1931, 24.

12. Review of *Charlie Chan in London* in *Variety,* September 18, 1934, 14.

13. Review of *Charlie Chan's Chance* in *New York Times,* January 23, 1932, 18.

14. Review of *Charlie Chan's Secret* in *New York Times,* January 18, 1936, 19.

15. Review of *Charlie Chan's Secret* in *Variety,* January 22, 1936, 15.

16. Marquand, *Your Turn, Mr. Moto,* 20.

17. Ibid., 5, 6.

18. Ibid., 7, 8.

19. Ibid., 71.

20. Review of *Mr. Moto's Gamble* in *Time,* March 28, 1938, 38.

21. Review of *Think Fast, Mr. Moto* in *New York Times,* August 16, 1937, 15.

22. Review of *Think Fast, Mr. Moto* in *Variety,* August 18, 1937, 27.

23. Ted Sennett, *Masters of Menace: Greenstreet and Lorre* (New York: Dutton, 1979), 38.

24. Review of *Mr. Moto's Last Warning* in *Variety,* January 25, 1939, 11.

25. Review of *Mr. Moto in Danger Island* in *Variety,* March 22, 1939, 20.

26. Review of *Mysterious Mr. Moto of Devil's Island* in *New York Times,* September 19, 1938, 16.

27. Ibid.

28. Brian Taves, "The B Film: Hollywood's Other Half," in *Grand Design,* edited by Tino Balio (New York: Scribner, 1993), 336.

29. William K. Everson, *The Detective in Film* (Secaucus, NJ: Citadel Press, 1972), 22.

30. Review of *Mr. Wong, Detective,* in *New York Times,* November 21, 1938, 14.

31. Review of *Mr. Wong, Detective,* in *Variety,* November 23, 1938, 14.

32. Review of *Mr. Wong in Chinatown* in *New York Times,* July 31, 1939, 9.

33. Frederick C. Othman, "Keye Luke Sleuths on His Own," *Hollywood Citizen News,* October 4, 1940, 10–11.

34. Eugene Franklin Wong, "On Visual Media Racism: Asians in the American Motion Pictures" (PhD diss., University of Denver, 1977), 113–14.

35. Ibid.

36. Gary Y. Okihiro, *Margins and Mainstreams: Asians in American History and Culture* (Seattle: University of Washington Press, 1994), 140.

37. Ibid., 142.

38. Ibid., 145.

39. Review of *Mr. Wong in Chinatown* in *New York Times,* July 31, 1939, 9.

Chapter 3

1. Edward W. Said, *Orientalism* (New York: Vintage, 1979), 16, 17.

2. Sheng-Mei Ma, *The Deathly Embrace: Orientalism and Asian American Identity* (Minneapolis: University of Minnesota Press, 2000), 109–10.

3. "Inside Stuff—Pictures," *Variety,* October 25, 1944, 22.

4. Ibid.

5. "Me No Moto," *Variety,* December 31, 1941, 1.

6. Keith Aoki, "'Foreignness' and Asian American Identities: Yellowface, World War II Propaganda and Bifurcated Racial Stereotypes," *UCLA Asian Pacific American Law Journal* 4, no. 1 (1996): 38.

7. Ibid.

8. Ibid.

9. Clayton R. Koppes and Gregory D. Black, *Hollywood Goes to War: How Politics, Profits and Propaganda Shaped World War II Movies* (Berkeley: University of California Press, 1987), 239.

10. Ibid.

11. John W. Dower, *War without Mercy: Race and Power in the Pacific War* (New York: Pantheon, 1986), 84.

12. Warner Bros. files, Wisconsin State Historical Society, Madison, Wisconsin. I have viewed the cartoon numerous times, and it is clear that Bugs Bunny does say "Moto." However, in the Warner Bros. transcription the sentence appears as "Here's some scrap iron for Japan, Mato!" (an obvious typographical error).

13. Warner Bros. files, Wisconsin State Historical Society, Madison, Wisconsin.

14. Michael Renov, "Warring Images: Stereotype and American Representations of the Japanese, 1941–1991," in *The Japan/America Film Wars: World*

War II Propaganda and Its Cultural Contexts, edited by Abe Mark Nornes and Fukushima Yukio (Switzerland: Harwood Academic, 1994), 108.

15. "How to Tell Japs from the Chinese," *Life,* December 22, 1941, 81.

16. Charles Higham and Roy Moseley, *Princess Merle: The Romantic Life of Merle Oberon* (New York: Coward-McCann, 1983), 10.

17. Ibid.

18. Review in *The Nation,* August 5, 1944, 165.

19. The Hays Office, established in 1922 and headed by Will Hays and later administrated by Joseph Breen, was a self-monitoring office for Hollywood's motion picture industry to remove potentially offensive material from motion picture scripts and finished films.

20. Koppes and Black, *Hollywood Goes to War,* 241.

21. Joseph Breen to Louis B. Mayer, June 16, 1943, Production Code Administration Records, Margaret Herrick Library, Academy of Motion Picture Arts and Sciences, Beverly Hills, California (hereafter PCA Files, Academy Library).

22. "Notes and Comments No. 27," Wei Hsueh to MGM, July 28, 1943, 1, Script Collection, Academy Library.

23. Ibid.

24. Lon Kurashige and Alice Yang Murray, *Major Problems in Asian American History* (Boston: Houghton Mifflin, 2003), 193.

25. Ibid., 5, 6, 7.

26. Ibid., 8.

27. Ibid., 3.

28. *Dragon Seed* trailer dialogue cutting continuity, 8/17/44, Script Collection, Academy Library.

29. *Dragon Seed* revised trailer dialogue cutting continuity, 8/17/44, Script Collection, Academy Library.

30. Review of *Dragon Seed* in *New York Times,* July 21, 1944.

31. Ibid.

32. Dower, *War without Mercy,* 15.

33. Ibid., 17.

34. Ibid., 17–18.

35. Ibid., 30.

36. From RKO Radio Studio Handbook of Publicity Data for "First Man into Tokyo" issued March 6, 1945, by Perry Lieber Studio Publicity Director RKO Radio Pictures, Inc., Hollywood California, PCA, MPAA Files, Academy Library.

37. Also pointed out by Thomas Doherty, *Projections of War: Hollywood, American Culture, and World War II* (New York: Columbia University Press, 1993), 138.

38. Review of *First Yank into Tokyo* in *Daily Variety* (Trade Showing), August 31, 1945.

39. Review of *First Yank into Tokyo* in *Motion Picture Daily,* September 10, 1945.

40. Review of *First Yank into Tokyo* in *Hollywood Reporter,* August 31, 1945.

Chapter 4

1. Christina Klein, *Cold War Orientalism: Asia in the Middlebrow Imagination, 1945–1961* (Berkeley: University of California Press, 2003), 2.

2. Ibid., 2–3.

3. Ibid., 5.

4. Ibid., 5–6.

5. Script Collection, Margaret Herrick Library, Academy of Motion Picture Arts and Sciences, Beverly Hills, California.

6. Bob Thomas, *Marlon: Portrait of the Rebel as an Artist* (New York: Random House, 1973), 105.

7. Production Code Administration Records, Margaret Herrick Library, Academy of Motion Picture Arts and Sciences, Beverly Hills, California.

8. Subject for the *Ed Sullivan Show* dated November 7, 1956, Script Collection, Academy Library.

9. Alternate trailer dialogue, cutting continuity and trailer footage, December 13, 1956, Script Collection, Academy Library.

10. Bosely Crowther, review of *The Teahouse of the August Moon* in *New York Times,* November 30, 1956, 19.

11. Ibid.

12. Ibid.

13. Richard Gertner, review of *The Teahouse of the August Moon* in *Motion Picture Daily,* October 17, 1956.

14. Review of *The Teahouse of the August Moon* in *Mainichi Shimbun,* January 13, 1957, Daniel Mann files, Academy Library.

15. Marlon Brando and Robert Lindsey, *Brando: Songs My Mother Taught Me* (New York: Random House, 1994), 37.

16. Truman Capote's *Breakfast at Tiffany's* Dramatic Outline by Sumner Locke Elliot, April 16, 1959, Script Collection, Academy Library.

17. Mickey Rooney, *Life Is Too Short* (New York: Ballantine Books, 1991), 236.

18. Review of *Breakfast at Tiffany's* in *Motion Picture Daily,* October 5, 1961.

19. Review of *Breakfast at Tiffany's* in *Harrison's Reports,* September 30, 1961.

20. Ibid.

21. Review of *Breakfast at Tiffany's* in *Hollywood Reporter,* October 6, 1961.

22. Klein, *Cold War Orientalism,* 8, 10.

23. Ibid., 227.

24. Ibid., 228–29.

25. Ibid., 229.

26. Ibid., 230.

27. Ibid., 236.

28. Review of *Flower Drum Song* in *Hollywood Reporter,* November 8, 1961.

29. Review of *Flower Drum Song* in *Film Daily,* November 10, 1961.

30. Review of *Flower Drum Song* in *Variety,* November 8, 1961.

31. Author interview with Donald Kirihara, spring of 1994.

32. Review of *Sayonara* in *Harrison's Reports,* November 16, 1957.

33. Sherwin Kane, review of *Sayonara* in *Motion Picture Daily,* November 13, 1957.

34. Robert G. Lee, *Orientals: Asian Americans in Popular Culture* (Philadelphia: Temple University Press, 1999), 164.

35. Memo to Hal Wallis from Dick Sokolove, "Tamiko by Ronald Kirkbride," November 9, 1960, Script Collection, Academy Library.

36. Memo to Hal Wallis from Dick Sokolove, "4/12/61 Screenplay by Ed Anhalt," April 29, 1961, Script Collection, Academy Library.

37. Memo to Hal Wallis from Dick Sokolove, "Screenplay 12/2/60 by Harry Brown," December 5, 1960, Script Collection, Academy Library.

38. Memo to Hal Wallis from Dick Sokolove, "4/12/61 Screenplay by Ed Anhalt," April 13, 1961, Script Collection, Academy Library.

39. Letter to Herb Steinberg and Edward Anhalt at Paramount Studios from Paul Nathan, September 27, 1962, Script Collection, Academy Library.

40. Review of *A Girl Named Tamiko* in *Motion Picture Herald,* December 12, 1962.

41. Review of *A Girl Named Tamiko* in *Variety,* December 5, 1962.

42. Gina Marchetti, *Romance and the "Yellow Peril": Race, Sex, and Discursive Strategies in Hollywood Fiction* (Berkeley: University of California Press, 1993), 181.

43. Review of *My Geisha* in *Film Daily,* April 7, 1962.

44. Review of *My Geisha* in *Motion Picture Daily,* March 19, 1962.

45. Mari Yoshihara, *Embracing the East: White Women and American Orientalism* (Oxford: Oxford University Press, 2003), 78.

46. Ibid., 79.

47. Ibid., 100.

Conclusion

1. Jessica Hagedorn, ed., *Charlie Chan Is Dead: An Anthology of Asian American Fiction* (New York: Penguin, 1993), xxii.

2. Vijay Prashad, *Everybody Was Kung Fu Fighting: Afro-Asia Connections and the Myth of Cultural Purity* (Boston: Beacon, 2001), 127.

3. Vijay Prashad, *Everybody Was Kung Fu Fighting: Afro-Asia Connections and the Myth of Cultural Purity* (Boston: Beacon Press, 2001), 127.

4. Herbie J. Pilato, *The Kung Fu Book of Caine: The Complete Guide to TV's First Mystical Eastern Western* (Boston: Charles E. Tuttle, 1993), 32.

5. Herbie J. Pilato, *The Kung Fu Book of Caine: The Complete Guid to TV's First Mystical Eastern Western* (Boston: Charles E. Tuttle, 1993), 32.

6. Neil Gotanda, "Asian American Rights and the 'Miss Saigon Syndrome,'" in *Asian Americans and the Supreme Court: A Documentary History*, edited by Hyung-Chan Kim (New York: Greenwood, 1992), 1087–88.

7. Lon Kurashige and Alice Yang Murray, eds., *Major Problems in Asian American History* (Boston: Houghton Mifflin, 2003), 470–71.

8. Christina Klein, *Cold War Orientalism: Asia in the Middlebrow Imagination, 1945–1961* (Berkeley: University of California Press, 2003), 271–73.

9. Ibid., 235.

10. Arthur Dong, press release for *Hollywood Chinese,* produced, directed, written, and edited by Arthur Dong, 2007.

11. Ibid.

12. Author interview with Arthur Dong, June 2008.

BIBLIOGRAPHY

Adamson, Joe. *Bugs Bunny: Fifty Years and Only One Grey Hare.* New York: Henry Holt, 1990.

Affron, Charles. *Star Acting: Gish, Garbo and Davis.* New York: Dutton, 1977.

Altman, Charles F. "Towards a Theory of Genre Film." In *Film Historical/ Theoretical Speculations, 1977 Purdue Film Studies Annual: Pt. 2.* Pleasantville, NY: Redgrave, 1977.

Aoki, Keith. "'Foreignness' and Asian American Identities: Yellowface, World War II Propaganda and Bifurcated Racial Stereotypes." *UCLA Asian Pacific American Law Journal* 4, no. 1 (1996).

Balio, Tino. *Grand Design: Hollywood as a Modern Business Enterprise, 1930–1939.* New York: Scribner, 1993.

Belton, John. *Widescreen Cinema.* Cambridge: Harvard University Press, 1992.

Bernstein, Matthew, and Gaylyn Studlar, eds. *Visions of the East: Orientalism in Film.* New Brunswick, NJ: Rutgers University Press, 1997.

Biggers, Earl Derr. *Celebrated Cases of Charlie Chan.* Indianapolis: Bobbs-Merrill, 1925, 1926, 1928, 1929, 1930.

———. "Creating Charlie Chan." *New York Times,* March 22, 1931.

Birmingham, Stephen. *The Late John Marquand: A Biography.* Philadelphia: Lippincott, 1972.

Bogle, Donald. *Toms, Coons, Mulattoes, Mammies and Bucks: An Interpretive History of Blacks in American Film.* New York: Bantam, 1973.

Bordwell, David, Janet Staiger, and Kristin Thompson. *The Classical Hollywood Cinema: Film Style and Mode of Production to 1960.* New York: Columbia University Press, 1985.

Brando, Marlon, and Robert Lindsey. *Brando: Songs My Mother Taught Me.* New York: Random House, 1994.

Browne, Nick. "American Film Theory in the Silent Period: Orientalism as an Ideological Form." *Wide Angle* 11, no. 4 (1989): 23–31.

Cabarga, Leslie. *The Fleischer Story in the Golden Age of Animation.* New York: Nostalgia Press, 1976.

Capra, Frank. *The Name above the Title: An Autobiography.* New York: Macmillan, 1971.

Carlson, Marvin. *Performance: A Critical Introduction.* London and New York: Routledge, 1996.

Chan, Anthony B. "Yellowface: The Racial Branding of the Chinese in American Theatre and Media." *Asian Profile* 29, no. 2 (2001): 159–77.

Chang, Williamson B. C. "M. Butterfly: Passivity, Deviousness, and the Invisibility of the Asian-American Male." In *Bearing Dreams, Shaping Visions: Asian Pacific American Perspectives,* edited by Linda A. Revilla, Gail M. Nomura, Shawn Wong, and Shirley Hune. Pullman: Washington State Press, 1993.

Choy, Philip P., Lorraine Dong, and Marlon K. Hom, eds. *Coming Man: 19th Century American Perceptions of the Chinese.* Seattle: University of Washington Press, 1994.

Churchill, Douglas W. "Hollywood Calls the Shadow and His Pals." *New York Times,* May 23, 1937.

Churchill, Ward. *Fantasies of the Master Race: Literature, Cinema and the Colonization of American Indians.* Monroe, ME: Common Courage, 1992.

Clover, Carol. "Dancin' in the Rain." *Critical Inquiry,* 21 (Summer 1995): 722–47.

Crafton, Donald. *The Talkies: American Cinema's Transition to Sound, 1926–1931.* Berkeley: University of California Press, 1997.

Crowther, Bosely. "How Doth the Busy Little 'B.'" *New York Times,* January 2, 1938.

———. Review of *The Teahouse of the August Moon. New York Times,* November 30, 1956, 19.

Curry, Ramona. *Too Much of a Good Thing: Mae West as Cultural Icon.* Minneapolis: University of Minnesota Press, 1996.

Diawara, Manthia, ed. *Black American Cinema.* New York: Routledge, 1993.

Dick, Bernard F. *The Star Spangled Screen: The American World War II Film.* Lexington: University Press of Kentucky, 1985.

Doane, Mary Ann. *Femme Fatales: Feminism, Film Theory, Psychoanalysis.* New York: Routledge, 1991.

Doherty, Thomas. *Projections of War: Hollywood, American Culture, and World War II.* New York: Columbia University Press, 1993.

Dower, John. *War without Mercy: Race and Power in the Pacific War.* New York: Pantheon, 1986.

Dyer, Richard. *The Matter of Images: Essays on Representations.* New York: Routledge, 1993.

Erens, Patricia. *The Jew in American Cinema.* Bloomington: Indiana University Press, 1984.

Everson, William K. *The Detective in Film.* Secaucus, NJ: Citadel Press, 1972.

Fregoso, Rosa Linda. *The Bronze Screen: Chicana and Chicano Film Practices*. Minneapolis: University of Minnesota Press, 1993.

Friedman, Lester. *Hollywood's Image of the Jew*. New York: Frederick Ungar, 1982.

———, ed. *Unspeakable Images: Ethnicity and the American Cinema*. Urbana: University of Illinois Press, 1991.

Fusco, Coco. *The Bodies That Were Not Ours and Other Writings*. London: Routledge, 2001.

Gertner, Richard. Review of *The Teahouse of the August Moon*. *Motion Picture Daily*, October 17, 1956.

Gotanda, Neil. "Asian American Rights and the 'Miss Saigon Syndrome.'" In *Asian Americans and the Supreme Court: A Documentary History*, edited by Hyung-Chan Kim. New York: Greenwood, 1992.

Gotanda, Philip Kan. *Yankee Dawg You Die*. New York: Dramatists Play Service, 1991.

Grant, Barry Keith, and Christopher Sharrett, eds. *Planks of Reason: Essays on the Horror Film*. Lanham, MD, Toronto, and Oxford: Scarecrow, 2004.

Guerrero, Ed. *Framing Blackness: The African American Image in Film*. Philadelphia: Temple University Press, 1993.

Hagedorn, Jessica, ed. *Charlie Chan Is Dead: An Anthology of Contemporary Asian American Fiction*. New York: Penguin, 1993.

Halliwell, Leslie. *Halliwell's Filmgoer's and Video Viewers Companion*. New York: Harper and Row, 1988.

Hamamoto, Darrell Y. *Monitored Peril: Asian Americans and the Politics of TV Representation*. Minneapolis: University of Minnesota Press, 1994.

Harris, Neil. *Cultural Excursions: Marketing Appetites and Cultural Tastes in Modern America*. Chicago: University of Chicago Press, 1990.

Henderson, Brian. "The Searchers: An American Dilemma." *Film Quarterly* 34 (1980–81): 9–23.

Higashi, Sumiko. "Ethnicity, Class, and Gender in Film: DeMille's *The Cheat*." In *Unspeakable Images: Ethnicity and the American Cinema*, edited by Lester Friedman. Urbana: University of Illinois Press, 1991.

Higham, Charles, and Roy Moseley. *Princess Merle: The Romantic Life of Merle Oberon*. New York: Coward-McCann, 1983.

Hine, Darlene Clark, ed. *Black Women in America: An Historical Encyclopedia*. Brooklyn, NY: Carlson, 1993.

Hirano, Kyoko. *Mr. Smith Goes to Tokyo: Japanese Cinema under the American Occupation, 1945–1952*. Washington: Smithsonian Institution Press, 1992.

hooks, bell. *Reel to Real: Race, Sex and Class at the Movies*. New York: Routledge, 1996.

"How to Tell Japs from the Chinese." *Life*, December 22, 1941, 81.

"Inside Stuff—Pictures." *Variety*, October 25, 1944, 22.

"Japanese Offended by Bugs 'Toon." *Fort Collins Coloradoan,* February 5, 1995, C1.

Jen, Gish. "Challenging the Asian Illusion." *New York Times,* August 11, 1991, sec. 2, pp. 1, 12–13.

Kane, Sherwin. Review of *Sayonara. Motion Picture Daily,* November 13, 1957.

Kirihara, Donald. "The Accepted Idea Displaced: Stereotype and Sessue Hayakawa." In *The Birth of Whiteness: Race and the Emergence of U.S. Cinema,* edited by Daniel Bernardi. Rutgers, NJ: Rutgers University Press, 1996.

Koppes, Clayton R., and Gregory D. Black. *Hollywood Goes to War: How Politics, Profits and Propaganda Shaped World War II Movies.* Berkeley: University of California Press, 1987.

Kracauer, Siegfried. "National Types as Hollywood Presents Them." *Public Opinion Quarterly* 13, no. 1 (1949): 53–72.

Leab, Daniel. *From Sambo to Superspade: The Black Experience in Motion Pictures.* Boston: Houghton Mifflin, 1976.

Lee, Robert G. *Orientals: Asian Americans in Popular Culture.* Philadelphia: Temple University Press, 1999.

Leong, Charles. "Mandarins in Hollywood." In *Moving the Image: Independent Asian Pacific American Media Arts,* edited by Russell Leong. Los Angeles: UCLA Asian American Studies Center and Visual Communications, Southern California Asian American Studies Central, 1991.

Lim, Cheng-Sim. Program Notes for *Daughter of the Dragon.* UCLA Film and Television Archive Tenth Festival Presentation, July 28–August 26, 2000. Catalogue.

"Loretta Goes Oriental." *Photoplay,* March 1932.

Lott, Eric. *Love and Theft: Blackface Minstrelsy and the American Working Class.* New York, 1993.

MacLaine, Shirley. *Don't Fall Off the Mountain.* New York: Bantam, 1985.

Maltby, Richard. "The Production Code and the Hays Office." In *Grand Design: Hollywood as a Modern Business Enterprise 1930–1939,* edited by Tino Balio. New York: Scribner, 1993.

Maltin, Leonard, ed. *Leonard Maltin's 1996 Movie and Video Guide.* New York: Penguin, 1995.

Marchetti, Gina. *Romance and the "Yellow Peril": Race, Sex, and Discursive Strategies in Hollywood Fiction.* Berkeley: University of California Press, 1993.

Marquand, John P. *Thank You, Mr. Moto.* Boston: Little, Brown, 1936.

———. *Your Turn, Mr. Moto.* Boston: Little, Brown, 1935.

"Me No Moto." *Variety,* December 31, 1941, 1.

Michener, James A. *Sayonara.* New York: Random House, 1953, 1954.

Morella, Joe, Edward Z. Epstein, and John Griggs. *The Films of World War II.* Secaucus, NJ: Citadel Press, 1973.

Musser, Charles. *The Emergence of Cinema: The American Screen to 1907.* Berkeley: University of California Press, 1990.

———. "Ethnicity, Role-playing, and American Film Comedy: From Chinese Laundry Scene to Whoopee (1894–1930)." In *Unspeakable Images: Ethnicity and the American Cinema,* edited by Lester D. Friedman. Urbana: University of Illinois Press, 1991.

Naremore, James. *Acting in the Cinema.* Berkeley: University of California Press, 1988.

Noreiga, Chon, ed. *Chicanos and Film: Representation and Resistance.* Minneapolis: University of Minnesota Press, 1992.

North, Jeanne. "No More Chinese, Myrna?" *Photoplay,* April 1933, 53.

Nugent, Frank S. "Charlie Chan in Honolulu." *New York Times,* December 31, 1938, 7.

O'Sullivan, John. "From the Editor--Interesting Times." *National Review,* March 24, 1997, 4.

Othman, Frederick C. "Keye Luke Sleuths on His Own." *Hollywood Citizen News,* October 4, 1940, 10–11.

Parish, James Robert, ed. *The Great Movie Series.* South Brunswick, NJ: A. S. Barnes, 1971.

Pearson, Roberta E. *Eloquent Gestures: The Transformation of Performance Style in the Griffith Biograph Films.* Berkeley: University of California Press, 1992.

Pilato, Herbie J. *The Kung Fu Book of Caine: The Complete Guide to TV's First Mystical Eastern Western.* Boston, MA, and Rutland, VT: Charles E. Tuttle, 1993.

Pines, Jim. *Blacks in Film.* London: Studio Vista, 1975.

Poague, Leland. *Another Frank Capra.* Cambridge: Cambridge University Press, 1994.

Ragaza, Angelo. "A Different Drummer." *American Movie Classics Magazine,* May 1997.

Reid, Mark. *Redefining Black Film.* Berkeley: University of California Press, 1993.

Renov, Michael. "Warring Images: Stereotype and American Representations of the Japanese, 1941–1991." In *The Japan/America Film Wars: World War II Propaganda and Its Cultural Contexts,* edited by Abe Mark Nornes and Fukushima Yukio. Switzerland: Harwood Academic, 1994.

Review of *The Bitter Tea of General Yen. Variety,* January 17, 1933.

Review of *Breakfast at Tiffany's. Harrison's Reports,* September 30, 1961.

Review of *Breakfast at Tiffany's. Hollywood Reporter,* October 6, 1961.

Review of *Breakfast at Tiffany's. Motion Picture Daily,* October 5, 1961.

Review of *Breakfast at Tiffany's. Variety,* September 20, 1961.

Review of *Charlie Chan at the Circus. Newsweek,* March 28, 1936.

Review of *Charlie Chan Carries On. Variety,* March 25, 1931, 24.

Review of *Charlie Chan in London. Variety,* September 18, 1934, 11.

Review of *Charlie Chan's Chance. New York Times,* January 23, 1932, 18.

Review of *Charlie Chan's Greatest Case. New York Times,* October 7, 1933, 18.

Review of *Charlie Chan's Secret. New York Times,* January 18, 1936, 19.

Review of *Charlie Chan's Secret. Variety,* January 22, 1936, 15.

Review of *Daughter of the Dragon. Variety,* August 25, 1931.

Review of *Dragon Seed. Daily Variety,* July 17, 1944.

Review of *Dragon Seed. Hollywood Reporter,* July 17, 1944.

Review of *Dragon Seed. The Nation,* August 5, 1944, 165.

Review of *Dragon Seed. New York Times,* July 21, 1944.

Review of *Dragon Seed. Variety,* July 19, 1944.

Review of *The Fatal Hour. New York Times,* January 13, 1940, 11.

Review of *First Yank into Tokyo. Daily Variety* (Trade Showing), August 31, 1945.

Review of *First Yank into Tokyo. Herald-Tribune,* October 25, 1945.

Review of *First Yank into Tokyo. Hollywood Reporter,* August 31, 1945.

Review of *First Yank into Tokyo. Motion Picture Daily,* September 10, 1945.

Review of *First Yank into Tokyo. Variety,* September 5, 1945.

Review of *Flower Drum Song. Film Daily,* November 10, 1961.

Review of *Flower Drum Song. Hollywood Reporter,* November 8, 1961.

Review of *Flower Drum Song,* music by Richard Rodgers, lyrics by Oscar Hammerstein II, St James Theater, New York. *New York Mirror,* December 2, 1958.

Review of *Flower Drum Song. Variety,* November 8, 1961.

Review of *A Girl Named Tamiko. Motion Picture Herald,* December 12, 1962.

Review of *A Girl Named Tamiko. Variety,* December 5, 1962.

Review of *Mr. Moto in Danger Island. New York Times,* March 20, 1939, 13.

Review of *Mr. Moto in Danger Island. Variety,* March 22, 1939, 20.

Review of *Mr. Moto's Gamble. Time,* March 28, 1938, 38.

Review of *Mr. Moto's Last Warning. Variety,* January 25, 1939, 11.

Review of *Mr. Wong, Detective. New York Times,* November 21, 1938, 14.

Review of *Mr. Wong, Detective. Variety,* November 23, 1938, 14.

Review of *Mr. Wong in Chinatown. New York Times,* July 31, 1939, 9.

Review of *My Geisha. Film Daily,* April 7, 1962.

Review of *My Geisha. Motion Picture Daily,* March 19, 1962.

Review of *Mysterious Mr. Moto. Variety,* June 1, 1938, 12.

Review of *Mysterious Mr. Moto of Devil's Island. New York Times,* September 19, 1938, 16.

Review of *Sayonara. Harrison's Reports,* 16 November 1957.

Review of *The Teahouse of the August Moon. Mainichi Shimbun,* January 13, 1957.

Review of *The Teahouse of the August Moon. Variety,* October 17, 1956.

Review of *Thank You, Mr. Moto. Variety,* January 12, 1938, 15.

Review of *Think Fast, Mr. Moto. New York Times,* August 16, 1937, 15.

Review of *Think Fast, Mr. Moto. Variety,* August 18, 1937, 27.

Review of *Thirteen Women. Variety,* October 18, 1932.

Rogin, Michael. *Blackface, White Noise: Jewish Immigrants in the Hollywood Melting Pot.* Berkeley: University of California Press, 1996.

Rooney, Mickey. *Life Is Too Short.* New York: Ballantine, 1991.

Said, Edward W. *Orientalism.* New York: Vintage, 1979.

Schatz, Thomas. *Boom and Bust: American Cinema in the 1940s.* Berkeley: University of California Press, 1997.

Schechner, Richard. *Performance Theory.* New York: Routledge, 1988.

Sennett, Ted. *Masters of Menace: Greenstreet and Lorre.* New York: E. P. Dutton, 1979.

Snead, James. *White Screens/Black Images: Hollywood from the Dark Side.* Edited by Colin MacCabe and Cornel West. New York: Routledge, 1994.

"So Hollywood Goes Oriental." *Photoplay,* January 1933, 73.

Stauer, Joseph. "New Charlie Chan Will Try to Get It Right with Wong." *Hollywood Reporter,* June 14–16, 1996.

Taves, Brian. "The B Film: Hollywood's Other Half." In *Grand Design: Hollywood as a Modern Business Enterprise 1930–1939,* edited by Tino Balio. New York: Scribner, 1993.

Thomas, Bob. *Marlon: Portrait of the Rebel as an Artist.* New York: Random House, 1973.

Toll, Robert C. *Blacking Up: The Minstrel Show in Nineteenth-Century America.* New York: Oxford University Press, 1974.

von Sternberg, Josef. *Fun in a Chinese Laundry.* San Francisco: Mercury House, 1965.

Waller, Gregory, ed. *American Horrors: Essays on the Modern American Horror Film.* Urbana: University of Illinois Press, 1987.

Watkins, Mel. *On the Real Side: Laughing, Lying, and Signifying—The Underground Tradition of African-American Humor That Transformed American Culture, from Slavery to Richard Pryor.* New York: Simon & Schuster, 1994.

Wolfe, Charles. *Frank Capra: A Guide to References and Resources.* Boston: G. K. Hall, 1987.

Woll, Allen L., and Randall M. Miller, eds. *Ethnic and Racial Images in American Film and Television: Historical Essays and Bibliography.* New York: Garland, 1987.

Wong, Eugene Franklin. "On Visual Media Racism: Asians in the American Motion Pictures." Unpublished PhD dissertation, University of Denver, 1977.

Wu, William F. *The Yellow Peril: Chinese Americans in American Fiction, 1850–1940.* Hamden, CT: Archon, 1982.

Xing, Jun. *Asian America through the Lens: History, Representation, and Identity.* Walnut Creek, CA: AltaMira, 1998.

Young, Robert. *White Mythologies: Writing History and the West.* London: Routledge, 1990.

SELECT FILMOGRAPHY

The Bitter Tea of General Yen (1932)
Studio: Columbia
Director: Frank Capra
Producer: Walter Wanger
Screenplay by Edward Paramore, story by Grace Zaring Stone
Music: W. Franke Harling
Photographed by Joseph Walker
Cast: Barbara Stanwyck (Megan), Nils Asther (General Yen), Toshia Mori (Mah-Li), Walter Connolly (Jones), Gavin Gordon (Bob), Richard Loo (Captain Li)

Breakfast at Tiffany's (1961)
Studio: Paramount
Director: Blake Edwards
Producer: Martin Jurow, Richard Shepherd
Screenplay by George Axelrod, novel by Truman Capote
Music: Henry Mancini
Photographed by Franz Planer
Technicolor
Cast: Audrey Hepburn (Holly Golightly), George Peppard (Paul Varjak), Buddy Ebsen (Doc), Martin Balsam (O. J. Berman), Mickey Rooney (Mr. Yunioshi), John McGiver (Tiffany salesman)

Bugs Bunny Nips the Nips (1944)
Studio: Warner Bros.
Director/Supervisor: I. Freleng
Producer: Leon Schlesinger
Animation: Gerry Chiniquy
Story: Tedd Pierce
Voice Characterization: Mel Blanc

Musical Direction: Carl W. Stalling
Technicolor

Charlie Chan at the Opera (1936)
Studio: Twentieth Century Fox
Director: H. Bruce Humberstone
Associate Producer: John Stone
Screenplay by Scott Darling and Charles S. Belden from a story by Bess Mere-
dyth based on the character "Charlie Chan" created by Earl Derr Biggers
Music: Samuel Kaylin, opera "Carnivale" written by Oscar Levant
Cast: Warner Oland (Charlie Chan), Boris Karloff (Gravelle), Charlotte Henry
(Mlle. Kitty), Thomas Beck (Phil Childers), Margaret Irving (Mme. Lilli Ro-
chelle), Keye Luke (Lee Chan), William Demarest (Sergeant Kelly)

Charlie Chan in Paris (1935)
Studio: Twentieth Century Fox
Director: Lewis Seiler
Producer: Sol M. Wurtzel
Screenplay by Edward T. Lowe and Stuart Anthony, story by Philip MacDon-
ald based on the character "Charlie Chan" created by Earl Derr Biggers
Photographed by Ernest Palmer
Cast: Warner Oland (Charlie Chan), Mary Brian (Yvette Lamartine), Thomas
Beck (Victor), Erik Rhodes (Max Corday), Keye Luke (Lee Chan)

Charlie Chan's Secret (1936)
Studio: Twentieth Century Fox
Director: Gordon Wiles
Associate Producer: John Stone
Screenplay by Robert Ellis and Helen Logan, original story by Robert Ellis and
Helen Logan in collaboration with Joseph Hoffman based on the character
"Charlie Chan" created by Earl Derr Biggers
Photographed by Rudolph Mate
Cast: Warner Oland (Charlie Chan), Rosina Lawrence (Alice Lowell), Charles
Quigley (Dick Williams), Edward Trevor (Fred Gaige), Astrid Allwyn (Janice
Gaige)

Dragon Seed (1944)
Studio: Metro-Goldwyn-Mayer
Director: Jack Conway, Harold S. Bucquet
Producer: Pandro S. Berman
Screenplay by Marguerite Roberts and Jane Murfin, novel by Pearl S. Buck

Photographed by Sidney Wagner

Music: Herbert Stothart

Cast: Katharine Hepburn (Jade), Walter Huston (Ling Tan), Aline MacMahon (Ling's Wife), Akim Tamiroff (Wu Lien), Turhan Bey (Lao Er), Hurd Hatfield (Lao San), J. Carrol Naish (Jap Kitchen Overseer), Agnes Moorehead (Third Cousin's Wife), Henry Travers (Third Cousin), Robert Bice (Lao Ta), Robert Lewis (Captain Sato), Frances Rafferty (Orchid), Jacqueline de Wit (Wife of Wu Lien)

First Yank into Tokyo (1945)

Studio: RKO

Director: Gordon Douglas

Screenplay by J. Robert Bren

Cast: Tom Neal (Major Ross), Barbara Hale (Abby Drake), Marc Cramer (Jardine), Richard Loo (Colonel Okanura), Keye Luke (Haan-Soo), Leonard Strong (Major Nogira), Benson Fong (Captain Tanabe), Clarence Lung (Major Ichibo), Keye Chang (Captain Sato), Michael St. Angel (Captain Andrew Kent)

Flower Drum Song (1961)

Studio: Universal

Director: Henry Koster

Producer: Ross Hunter (in association with Joseph Fields)

Screenplay by Joseph Fields, based on the novel by C. Y. Lee and the Broadway musical book by Fields

Music: Richard Rodgers

Photographed by Russell Metty

Panavision, Technicolor

Cast: Nancy Kwan (Linda Low), James Shigeta (Wang Ta), Juanita Hall (Auntie [Madame Liang]), Jack Soo (Sammy Fong), Miyoshi Umeki (Mei Li), Benson Fong (Wang Chi-Yang), Reiko Sato (Helen Chao), Patrick Adiarte (Wang San), Kam Tong (Dr. Li), Victor Sen Yung (Frankie Wing), Soo Yung (Madam Fong)

A Girl Named Tamiko (1962)

Studio: Paramount

Director: John Sturges

Producer: Hal B. Wallis

Screenplay by Edward Anhalt, novel by Ronald Kirkbride

Music: Elmer Bernstein

Photographed by Charles Lang Jr.

Panavision, Technicolor

Cast: Laurence Harvey (Ivan Kalin), France Nuyen (Tamiko), Martha Hyer (Fay Wilson), Gary Merrill (Max Wilson), Michael Wilding (Nigel Costairs), Miyoshi Umeki (Eiko), Steve Brodie (James Hatten), Lee Patrick (Mary Hatten), John Mamo (Minya), Bob Okazaki (Kimitaka), Richard Loo (Otani), Philip Ahn (Akiba)

Japoteurs (1942)
Studio: Paramount
Director: I. Sparber
Animation: Myron Waldman and Graham Place
Story: Jay Morton, Superman comic strip created by Jerome Siegel and Joe Shuster
Musical Arrangement: Sammy Timberg
Technicolor

Lost Horizon (1937)
Studio: Columbia
Director: Frank Capra
Producer: Frank Capra
Screenplay by Robert Riskin, novel James Hilton
Music: Dmitri Tiomkin
Photographed by Joseph Walker
Cast: Ronald Colman (Robert Conway), H. B. Warner (Chang), Thomas Mitchell (Barnard), Edward Everett Horton (Lovett), Sam Jaffe (High Lama), Isabel Jewell (Gloria), Jane Wyatt (Sondra), Margo (Maria), John Howard (George Conway)

The Mask of Fu Manchu (1932)
Studio: Metro-Goldwyn-Mayer
Director: Charles Brabin, Charles Vidor
Screenplay by John Willard, Edgar Woolf, and Irene Kuhn, based on stories by Sax Rohmer
Photographed by Tony Gaudio
Cast: Boris Karloff (Fu Manchu), Myrna Loy (Sah Lo Fee), Lewis Stone (Dr. Smith), Karen Morley (Sheila), Charles Starett (Shan Greville), Jean Hersholt (Dr. Berg), Lawrence Grant (Sir Lionel Barton)

Mr. Moto's Last Warning (1939)
Studio: Twentieth Century Fox
Director: Norman Foster
Executive Producer: Sol Wurtzel

Screenplay by Philip MacDonald and Norman Foster, based on a novel by J. P. Marquand

Photographed by Virgil Miller

Cast: Peter Lorre (Mr. Moto), Ricardo Cortez (Fabian), Virginia Field (Connie), John Carradine (Danforth), George Sanders (Eric Norvel), Robert Coote (Rollo), Margaret Irving (Madame Delacour), John Davidson (Hakim), Teru Shimada (Fake Mr. Moto)

Mr. Wong in Chinatown (1939)
Studio: Monogram
Director: William Nigh
Associate Producer: William Lackey
Screenplay by Scott Darling based on the James Lee Wong series in *Collier's* magazine written by Hugh Wiley
Photographed by Harry Neumann
Cast: Boris Karloff (Mr. Wong), Grant Withers (Inspector Street), Marjorie Reynolds (Bobbie Logan), Lotus Long (Princess Lin Wha)

My Geisha (1962)
Studio: Paramount
Director: Jack Cardiff
Producer: Steve Parker
Screenplay by Norman Krasna
Music: Franz Waxman
Photographed by Shunichuro Nakao
Technirama, Technicolor
Cast: Shirley MacLaine (Lucy Dell), Yves Montand (Paul Robaix), Robert Cummings (Bob Moore), Edward G. Robinson (Sam Lewis), Yoko Tani (Kazumi)

The Phantom of Chinatown (1940)
Studio: Monogram
Director: Phil Rosen
Producer: Paul Malvern
Screenplay by Joseph West, story Ralph Bettinson based on the James Lee Wong series in *Collier's* magazine written by Hugh Wiley
Photographed by Fred Jackman Jr.
Cast: Keye Luke (Jimmy Wong), Lotus Long (Win Len), Grant Withers (Street), Paul McVey (Grady), Charles Miller (Dr. Benton), Virginia Carpenter (Louise Benton), John Dilson (Charles Fraser), John Holland (Mason), Dick Terry (Toreno), Huntley Gordon (Wilkes), Rob Kellard (Tommy Dean), William Castello (Jonas), Victor Wong (Charley One)

Sayonara (1957)
Studio: Goetz Pictures Inc.–Pennebaker Productions–Warner Bros.
Director: Joshua Logan
Producer: William Goetz
Screenplay by Paul Osborn, from the novel by James A. Michener
Music: Franz Waxman
Photographed by Ellsworth Fredericks
Technirama, Technicolor
Cast: Marlon Brando (Major Lloyd Gruver), Miiko Taka (Hana-ogi), Red
    Buttons (Airman Joe Kelly), Patricia Owens (Eileen Webster), Ricardo
    Montalban (Nakamura), Miyoshi Umeki (Katsumi), Kent Smith (General
    Webster), Martha Scott (Mrs. Webster), James Garner (Captain Bailey),
    Doug Watson (Colonel Calhoun)

The Son-Daughter (1932)
Studio: Metro-Goldwyn-Mayer
Director: Clarence Brown
Screenplay by Claudine West, Leon Gordon, and John Goodrich, play David
    Belasco and George Scarborough
Cast: Helen Hayes (Lien Wha/Star Blossom), Ramon Navarro (Tom Lee),
    Lewis Stone (Dr. Dong Tong), Warner Oland (Fen Sha), Ralph Morgan
    (Fung Fou Hy), Louise Closser Hale (Toy Yah), H. B. Warner (Sin Kai)

The Teahouse of the August Moon (1956)
Studio: Metro-Goldwyn-Mayer
Director: Daniel Mann
Producer: Jack Cummings
Screenplay by John Patrick, based on his play, adapted from the novel by Vern
    Sneider
Music: Saul Chaplin
Photographed by John Alton
CinemaScope, Metrocolor
Cast: Marlon Brando (Sakini), Glenn Ford (Captain Fisby), Machiko Kyo (Lotus
    Blossom), Eddie Albert (Captain McLean), Paul Ford (Colonel Purdy), Jun
    Negami (Mr. Seiko), Nijiko Kiyokawa (Miss Higa Jiga)

Think Fast, Mr. Moto (1937)
Studio: Twentieth Century Fox
Director: Norman Foster
Executive Producer: Sol Wurtzel
Screenplay by Howard Ellis Smith and Norman Foster, based on the novel by
    J. P. Marquand

Photographed by Harry Jackson

Cast: Peter Lorre (Mr. Moto), Virginia Field (Gloria Danton), Thomas Beck (Bob Hitchings), Sig Rumann (Nicholas Marloff), Murray Kinnell (Mr. Wilkie), Lotus Long (Lela), J. Carrol Naish (Adram)

Thirteen Women (1932)

Studio: RKO

Director: George Archainbaud

Executive Producer: David O. Selznick

Screenplay by Bartlett Cormack and Samuel Ornitz, novel by Tiffany Thayer

Music: Max Steiner

Cast: Ricardo Cortez (Sergeant Clive), Irene Dunne (Laura Stanhope), Myrna Loy (Ursula Georgi), Jill Esmond (Jo Turner), Florence Eldridge (Miss Gersten), C. Henry Gordon (Swami Yogadachi)

EXTENDED SELECT FILMOGRAPHY

The following list is of notable films, from the silent era to the present day, that prominently feature non-Asian actors in Oriental roles. Costars' names are placed in parentheses.

1910s

Madame Butterfly (1915). Cast: Mary Pickford.
Broken Blossoms (1919). Cast: Richard Barthelmess (Lillian Gish).

1920s

Shadows (1922). Cast: Lon Chaney.

1930s

Daughter of the Dragon (1930). Cast: Warner Oland (Anna May Wong, Sessue Hayakawa).
Charlie Chan series (1931–48). Cast: Warner Oland.
The Mask of Fu Manchu (1932). Cast: Boris Karloff, Myrna Loy.
The Bitter Tea of General Yen (1932). Cast: Nils Asther (Barbara Stanwyck).
Thirteen Women (1932). Cast: Myrna Loy (Irene Dunne).
The Son-Daughter (1932). Cast: Ramon Navarro, Helen Hayes.
Madame Butterfly (1932). Cast: Sylvia Sidney (Cary Grant).
The Hatchet Man (1932). Cast: Loretta Young, Edward G. Robinson.
Shanghai Express (1932). Cast: Warner Oland (Marlene Dietrich, Anna May Wong).
Mr. Moto series (1937–39). Cast: Peter Lorre.
Lost Horizon (1937). Cast: H. B. Warner (Ronald Colman).
The Good Earth (1937). Cast: Paul Muni, Luise Rainer.
Mr. Wong series (1938–40). Cast: Boris Karloff.

1940s

The Shanghai Gesture (1941). Cast: Gene Tierney, Ona Munson.
Behind the Rising Sun (1943). Cast: Tom Neal, J. Carrol Naish.

Dragon Seed (1944). Cast: Katharine Hepburn, Walter Huston, Turhan Bey.

First Yank into Tokyo (1945). Cast: Tom Neal (Barbara Hale).

China Sky (1945). Cast: Anthony Quinn (Randolph Scott).

Blood on the Sun (1945). Cast: Sylvia Sidney (James Cagney).

Anna and the King of Siam (1946). Cast: Rex Harrison, Lee J. Cobb (Irene Dunne).

1950s

Love Is a Many Splendored Thing (1955). Cast: Jennifer Jones (William Holden).

The Conqueror (1955). Cast: John Wayne (Susan Hayward).

Teahouse of the August Moon (1956). Cast: Marlon Brando (Glenn Ford).

The King and I (1956). Cast: Yul Brynner, Rita Moreno (Deborah Kerr).

Sayonara (1957). Cast: Ricardo Montalban (Marlon Brando).

The Inn of the Sixth Happiness (1958). Cast: Curt Jurgens, Robert Donat (Ingrid Bergman).

1960s

Breakfast at Tiffany's (1961). Cast: Mickey Rooney (Audrey Hepburn, George Peppard).

Flower Drum Song (1961). Cast: Juanita Hall (Nancy Kwan, James Shigeta, Miyoshi Umeki).

A Majority of One (1961). Cast: Alec Guinness (Rosalind Russell).

A Girl Named Tamiko (1962). Cast: Laurence Harvey (France Nuyen, Martha Hyer).

My Geisha (1962). Cast: Shirley MacLaine (Yves Montand, Robert Cummings).

Dr. No (1962). Cast: Joseph Wiseman (Sean Connery, Ursula Andress).

Gambit (1966). Cast: Shirley MacLaine (Michael Caine).

The Brides of Fu Manchu (1966). Cast: Christopher Lee.

You Only Live Twice (1967). Cast: Sean Connery.

1970s

Murder by Death (1976). Cast: Peter Sellers (David Niven, Peter Falk).

1980s

The Fiendish Plot of Dr. Fu Manchu (1980). Cast: Peter Sellers (Helen Mirren).

Charlie Chan and the Curse of the Dragon Queen (1981). Cast: Peter Ustinov.

The Year of Living Dangerously (1983). Cast: Linda Hunt (Mel Gibson, Sigourney Weaver).

Remo Williams: The Adventure Begins (1985). Cast: Joel Grey (Fred Ward).

INDEX

Page numbers in italics refer to illustrations